Conflict, Negotiation and European Union Enlargement

Each wave of expansion of the European Union has led to political tensions and conflict. Existing members fear their membership privileges will diminish and candidates are loath to concede the expected benefits of membership. Despite these conflicts, enlargement has always succeeded – so why does the EU continue to admit new states even though current members might lose from their accession? Combining political economy logic with statistical and case study analyses, Christina J. Schneider argues that the dominant theories of EU enlargement ignore how EU members and applicant states negotiate the distribution of enlargement benefits and costs. She explains that EU enlargement happens despite distributional conflicts if the overall gains of enlargement are redistributed from the relative winners among existing members and applicants to the relative losers. If the overall gains from enlargement are sufficiently great, a redistribution of these gains will compensate losers, making enlargement attractive for all states.

CHRISTINA J. SCHNEIDER is a Fellow at the Niehaus Center of Globalization and Governance at Princeton University and an External Researcher at the Max Planck Institute of Economics.

Conflict, Negotiation and European Union Enlargement

CHRISTINA J. SCHNEIDER

CAMBRIDGE
UNIVERSITY PRESS

University Printing House, Cambridge CB2 8BS, United Kingdom

Cambridge University Press is part of the University of Cambridge.

It furthers the University's mission by disseminating knowledge in the pursuit of education, learning and research at the highest international levels of excellence.

www.cambridge.org
Information on this title: www.cambridge.org/9780521514811

© Christina J. Schneider 2009

This publication is in copyright. Subject to statutory exception and to the provisions of relevant collective licensing agreements, no reproduction of any part may take place without the written permission of Cambridge University Press.

First published 2009
First paperback edition 2011

A catalogue record for this publication is available from the British Library

Library of Congress Cataloguing in Publication data
Schneider, Christina J.
The politics of EU enlargement : accession negotiations, distributional conflicts, and discriminatory membership / Christina J. Schneider.
   p. cm.
Includes bibliographical references and index.
ISBN 978-0-521-51481-1
1. European Union–Membership.   I. Title.   II. Title: Politics of European Union enlargement.
JN30.S356   2008
341.242′2–dc22
2008041169

ISBN 978-0-521-51481-1 Hardback
ISBN 978-1-107-40442-7 Paperback

Cambridge University Press has no responsibility for the persistence or accuracy of URLs for external or third-party internet websites referred to in this publication, and does not guarantee that any content on such websites is, or will remain, accurate or appropriate.

To my parents

Contents

List of Illustrations	*page* x
List of Tables	xi
List of Acronyms	xiii
Acknowledgements	xv

1	**Introduction**	**1**
	1.1 The politics of EU enlargement	5
	1.2 Organization of the book	8
2	**EU enlargements and transitional periods**	**12**
	2.1 Timeline of European Union enlargement	13
	2.2 The formal EU enlargement process	16
	2.3 Accession negotiations and enlargement outcomes	19
	2.3.1 Implementation of the acquis communautaire	20
	2.3.2 The formulation of a common EU position	24
	2.4 Conclusion	30
	2.5 Appendix	31
3	**A rationalist puzzle of EU enlargement?**	**33**
	3.1 Widening and deepening: two pillars of EU integration	34
	3.1.1 Functionalism and neo-functionalism	35
	3.1.2 Intergovernmentalism	36
	3.1.3 New institutionalism	37
	3.2 Integration theories and the calculus of EU enlargement	38
	3.2.1 The gains of EU enlargement	41
	3.2.2 The costs of EU enlargement	44
	3.3 The puzzle of EU expansion	47

	3.4	Alternative explanations of EU enlargement	49
	3.5	Conclusion	52
4	A theory of discriminatory membership		55
	4.1	Basic assumptions of the theoretical model	56
	4.2	The calculus of EU enlargement	57
		4.2.1 The emergence of distributional conflicts	61
		4.2.2 The resolution of distributional conflicts	65
		4.2.3 The transitional nature of discrimination	69
	4.3	Hypotheses on expansion and differentiated membership	73
	4.4	Conclusion	76
5	EU enlargement, distributional conflicts, and the demand for compensation		77
	5.1	Research design	79
		5.1.1 Dependent variables	81
		5.1.2 Model specification	83
	5.2	Free movement of workers	85
		5.2.1 Variables and data sources	86
		5.2.2 Estimation results	91
		5.2.3 Predicted probabilities	94
		5.2.4 Conclusion	103
	5.3	Common Agricultural Policies	104
		5.3.1 Variables and data sources	108
		5.3.2 Estimation results	110
		5.3.3 Predicted probabilities	113
		5.3.4 Conclusion	120
	5.4	Common Structural Policies	120
		5.4.1 Variables and data sources	121
		5.4.2 Estimation results	122
		5.4.3 Predicted probabilities	126
		5.4.4 Conclusion	131
	5.5	The demand for compensation: conclusion	132
	5.6	Appendix	134
6	The discriminatory of membership		138
	6.1	Research design	139
		6.1.1 Dependent variable	140
		6.1.2 Explanatory variables	140
		6.1.3 Model specification	143

6.2	Estimation results	144
6.3	Predicted probabilities	151
6.4	Conclusion	155
6.5	Appendix	157

7 **Discriminatory membership and intra-union redistribution**   158

7.1	The puzzle	160
7.2	ERDF/ESF and the second Mediterranean enlargement	162
7.3	ERDF/ESF and EU Eastern enlargement	165
7.4	Comparison of the two cases	172
7.5	Conclusion: structural transfers and discriminatory membership	177

8 **Conclusion**   182

Bibliography   189

Index   205

List of Illustrations

2.1	EU enlargement: formal accession process	page 17
4.1	The impact of enlargement on EU member states	63
5.1	Free movement of workers: effect of EU member share of foreigners	98
5.2	Free movement of workers: effect of industry employment	99
5.3	Free movement of workers: effect of candidate GDP and unemployment rate	101
5.4	Common Agricultural Policies: effect of agriculture GVA	116
5.5	Common Agricultural Policies: effect of expected size of the EU	117
5.6	Common Agricultural Policies: effect of EU member budget contributions	118
5.7	Common Structural Policies: effect of EU member ERDF/ESF amount	128
5.8	Common Structural Policies: effect of candidate GDP	129
5.9	Common Structural Policies: effect of EU member budget contributions	130
6.1	Discriminatory EU membership: effect of EU member council power	147
6.2	Discriminatory EU membership: effect of budget ceiling	149
6.3	Discriminatory EU membership: effect of (predicted) demand for discrimination	154
7.1	Average structural funds per capita	159
7.2	Structural funds, euros/ECU per capita	174
7.3	Development of the common EU budget and ERDF/ESF	176

List of Tables

2.1	Application and accession of countries to the European Union	*page* 15
5.1	Free movement of workers: probit model	92
5.2	Free Movement of Workers: model fit	93
5.3	Free movement of workers: predicted probabilities	97
5.4	Free movement of workers: joint effect	102
5.5	Common Agricultural Policies: actual and estimated EAGGF subsidies	106
5.6	Common Agricultural Policies: probit model	111
5.7	Common Agricultural Policies: model fit	111
5.8	Common Agricultural Policies: predicted probabilities	115
5.9	Common Agricultural Policies: joint effect	119
5.10	Common Structural Policies: probit model	123
5.11	Common Structural Policies: model fit	124
5.12	Common Structural Policies: predicted probabilities	127
5.13	Common Structural Policies: joint effect	131
A-1	Distributional conflicts: multivariate probit model	134
A-2	Free Movement of Workers: descriptive statistics	136
A-3	Common Agricultural Policies: descriptive statistics	137
A-4	Common Structural Policies: descriptive statistics	137
6.1	Discriminatory EU membership: area models	144
6.2	Discriminatory EU membership: model fit	145
6.3	Discriminatory EU membership: predicted probabilities	152
A-5	Discriminatory EU membership: descriptive statistics	157

List of Acronyms

CAP	Common Agricultural Policies
CSP	Common Structural Policies
CEE	Central and Eastern European
CFP	Common Fisheries Policies
COAM	Common Organization of Agricultural Markets
COREPER	Committee of Permanent Representatives
DGB	Deutscher Gewerkschaftsbund
EAGGF	European Agricultural Guidance and Guarantee Funds
EC	European Community
ECSC	European Coal and Steel Community
ECU	European Currency Unit
EDC	European Defense Community
EEA	European Economic Area
EFTA	European Free Trade Association
ERDF	European Reconstruction and Development Funds
ESF	European Social Funds
EU	European Union
FMW	Free Movement of Workers
FYRM	Former Yugoslav Republic of Macedonia
GDP	Gross Domestic Product
GNP	Gross National Product
GVA	Gross Value Added
IGC	Intergovernmental Conferences
IMF	International Monetary Fund
IMP	Integrated Mediterranean Programs
JHA	Justice and Home Affairs
NATO	North Atlantic Treaty Organization
OLS	Ordinary Least Squares
PPS	Purchasing Power Standards

SURE	Seemingly Unrelated Regression
TEU	Treaty on European Union
UK	United Kingdom
UN	United Nations
VAT	Value-Added Tax
WEU	Western European Union

Acknowledgements

Unfortunately, truthful gratitude cannot be expressed with words (Goethe)

This book would not exist without generous help and support from various directions. I would like to thank, first of all, my family and friends, for their enduring patience, encouragement and good suggestions.

I owe a great debt of gratitude to Thomas Plümper for his intellectual guidance, many stimulating debates, and sound advice throughout the whole project. As my dissertation advisor he has constantly supported me in my research and has generously given his time to read and thoughtfully comment on my various chapter drafts. This book is based on my dissertation which I wrote at the Department of Politics and Management, University of Konstanz, Germany. My work was generously funded by the German Research Foundation with the project "Integration Gains and Distributional Conflicts: The Logic of Discriminatory and Conditional Membership in International Institutions."

The work has also gained from the fruitful discussions with colleagues and friends from the University of Konstanz, the Max Planck Institute of Economics, and the University of Oxford. At the University of Konstanz, I first of all would like to thank my colleague Christian Kraft. Our countless discussions and his supporting presence have immensely contributed to the success of the project. I also would like to thank Christoph Knill, Thomas König, Gerald Schneider, and the participants of the doctoral seminar for their valuable comments at the early stages of the project. I am deeply indebted to David Audretsch and my colleagues at the Max Planck Institute of Economics, Jena, for generous financial support and the intellectually stimulating environment which helped me finishing the first draft of the book manuscript. At the University of Oxford, where I started to teach in January 2007, I received helpful comments from Dave Armstrong, Jorge Bravo, Sara Binzer Hobolt, Indriđi Indriđason, Mark Pickup, David Rueda, David Soskice, Jen Tobin, Piero Tortola, the participants of the Political Economy seminar, and the participants of the International Relations Faculty seminar. Additionally, I thank Patrick Brandt, Anne Etienne, Céline Laukemann, Lisa Martin, Susanne Michalik, Frank Schimmelfennig, Alex Schmotz, Laura Seelkopf, and Vera Troeger for their thoughtful comments on various aspects of this project and for reading the (too) many different drafts of this book. Special thanks go to Branislav Slantchev who perused the entire manuscript and proof-read the final draft of this book, and also to Manuela Lopez who helped me to translate the main idea of the book – the existing conflict between the gains of EU enlargement and the emergence of distributional conflicts – into a basic design of the book cover.

At Cambridge University Press, I would like to thank John Haslam as the commissioning editor of Social Sciences as well as Carrie Cheek as the assistant editor for their expert handling of my manuscript. I also owe an immense debt of gratitude to the anonymous reviewers for their excellent comments on the manuscript.

Unfortunately, I cannot thank everyone who has directly or indirectly contributed to the success of this work. My special thanks therefore go to everyone who I did not mention and who inspired, motivated, and encouraged me in various stages of my project.

1 Introduction

> *"We are here to undertake a common task – not to negotiate for our own national advantage, but to seek it to the advantage of all"*
> (Jean Monnet)[1]

The enlargement of the European Community (EC) and later the European Union (EU) was never particularly popular.[2] Indeed, the first attempt at widening the EU culminated in the Community's "first real crisis" when Charles de Gaulle, then-President of France, rejected the British accession in a dramatic press conference at the Élysée Palace (Nicholson and East 1987, 39). He claimed that Britain's conditions for joining the Union were unacceptable to France. In addition to fearing that a rise in Atlanticism would undermine French dominance in Europe, de Gaulle was particularly concerned about the impact British membership would have on the Common Agricultural Policies (CAP). Political tensions arose from opposite interests of French farmers and the British government that sought to protect the interests of European Free Trade Association (EFTA) members, British farmers, and the Commonwealth. Moreover, it seemed impossible to compromise on granting the Commonwealth access to the common market without hurting the French interest in protecting European farmers from non-European producers. To make matters worse, the expansion of the common market to the Commonwealth would decrease France's benefits from preferential agreements with its former colonies (Ludlow 1997, 159).

In the course of the accession negotiations, de Gaulle argued that the United Kingdom was too different politically and economically from the six founding members to be included in the Community without threatening the structure and cohesion of the current

---

[1] Monnet (1976, 323).
[2] In this book, I use the term EU when I refer to either the EC or the EU.

1

system. He therefore opposed any further steps that would lead to the accession of the UK to the EC:[3]

In short, the nature, the structure, the economic situation, that characterize England, differ profoundly from the Continent. How then could England, as she lives, as she produces, as she trades, be incorporated into the Common Market as it was conceived and as it works?

(Charles de Gaulle, January 1963)

The French persisted in their objections despite strong criticism from all other member states and the British government. This eventually caused the collapse of the accession process, which delayed British entry into the EU for ten years.

Serious tensions arose again thirty-five years later with another EU enlargement – the accession of Central and Eastern European (CEE) countries from the former Soviet bloc. Domestic concerns spilled into conflict among EU member states when negotiations with the CEE countries (about labor markets liberalization for example) revealed considerable divergence in national preferences. Whereas most member states favored granting CEE countries access to the labor market upon accession, German and Austrian workers expected the mass influx of cheap unskilled labor from the East to cause major market disruptions. The German government, which faced elections at that time, responded to these fears and insisted that the migration problem would have to be solved before accession negotiations could proceed. Echoing domestic public debates and the opinion of major labor organizations, the government claimed that the EU could not cope with immigration any more. Consequently, the acceding states would have to be excluded from labor market integration until there was structural and economic evidence of declining migration pressure. The debate about the free movement of labor noticeably delayed the accession of the CEE candidates.

Even though nearly every round of enlargement was accompanied by distributional conflict, the EU has grown to 27 member countries with more states likely to join in the future. The widening of the Union seems unstoppable despite mounting public resentment within the existing member states. The Former Yugoslav Republic

---

[3] This speech was given during a press conference at the Élysée Palace in January 1963.

Introduction

of Macedonia (FYRM) formally applied for membership in 2004. Croatia and Turkey have started accession negotiations. The EU itself has indicated that Albania, Bosnia and Herzegovina, Montenegro, and Serbia (including Kosovo under United Nations (UN) Security Council Resolution 1244) could become members if they fulfill the EU accession criteria.[4]

Without doubt, political conflicts triggered by the fear of enlargement complicate the continuing expansion of the EU. Whereas each enlargement clearly increased the aggregate gains of EU membership both for old and new members, it remains quite puzzling that the Southern (to Greece in 1981, and to Spain and Portugal in 1986) and Eastern expansions succeeded despite the misgivings of member states that expected conflicts with distributional consequences.

The puzzle of continuing enlargement of the EU despite these distributional conflicts has received much attention in the literature.[5] The answers can be grouped into two major categories depending on whether one approaches the puzzle from a rationalist or a sociocultural perspective. According to most economists and some political scientists, the market and geopolitical benefits from integration can outweigh the costs from diminished political autonomy under certain conditions.[6] If integrating more states into the European legal framework increases the political and economic stability of new members, then the political stability and the economic prosperity of the entire region would increase as well. Current members then stand to benefit from expansion, and this should induce them to support it.

According to scholars with a sociological and cultural perspective, European integration is a quasi-natural process driven by joint values and socialization.[7] The willingness to expand is determined less so by economic cost-benefit calculations than by the cultural affinity of candidates and current members and the degree to which they

---

[4] The European Commission even "reaffirmed at the highest level its commitment for eventual EU membership of the Western Balkan countries" on its web page for enlargement (http://ec.europa.eu/enlargement). See Chapter 2 for a detailed description of the formal accession process and the criteria for EU membership.
[5] See for example Baldwin et al. (1997), Brenton (2002), Breuss (2002), Böri and Brücker (2000), Schimmelfennig (2001, 2003), Friis and Murphy (1999), and Torreblanca (2001).
[6] See for example Baldwin et al. (1997) and Moravcsik and Vachudova (2003).
[7] See for example Fierke and Wiener (1999), Sedelmeier (1998, 2002), and Schimmelfennig (2001, 2003).

share common norms and values. Schimmelfennig (2001, 2003), for example, argues that the "drivers of enlargement" within the EU referred to a historically developed pan-European vision and rhetorically entrapped the "brakemen of enlargement" into accepting the applicant countries regardless of costs.

I propose a new way of thinking about the seemingly smooth process of EU enlargement. First, I analyze the EU enlargement rounds focusing on the formal structure and the actual process of the multilateral negotiations about the conditions under which enlargement takes place. It may be obvious that an understanding of EU enlargement should require an examination of the accession negotiations. However, recent approaches tend to treat the enlargement process as a black box. Instead of looking at the accession negotiations and the deals agreed upon during these talks, these analyses tend to examine the consequences of enlargement to determine whether it was desirable or not. In contrast, I analyze the negotiations between the heads of governments to show the conditions they demanded and the side-payments they extracted before supporting the widening of the Union in the formal enlargement talks.

Second, I do not treat the EU as a homogenous bloc that negotiates with an (equally homogeneous) group of applicant countries. Like Schimmelfennig, I contend that enlargement affects current members in fairly diverse ways. It is not just outsiders and insiders that engage in distributional conflict, but also relative winners and losers within the Union itself. Indeed, the intra-Union conflict may dominate the enlargement process. Understanding this type of conflict is crucial for gaining insight into the multilateral character of accession negotiations and the outcomes of the enlargement process.

Third, I argue that EU expansion is not a simple process with a dichotomous outcome in which countries are either accepted or rejected. Instead, outcomes vary substantially in their terms – like the transitional limitation of membership rights – and this variation can be explained as a result of bargaining over the allocation of enlargement gains across states. That is, the terms of enlargement are *endogenous* to the accession negotiations.

Fourth, I take into account the institutional context – the formal procedures and requirements for enlargement. For instance, enlargement requires the unanimous approval of EU members. A single "nay" vote by even the smallest one among them would derail the enlargement process. But if enlargement causes distributional conflict, then this requirement implies that one can no longer attribute successful enlargement to positive overall gains. Instead, one must show why no member state chose to wield its veto to stop it.

Finally, I approach the puzzle of EU enlargement from an historic perspective. By analyzing all accession negotiations and outcomes from the early 1970s to 2004, I can draw a more complete picture of the political economy of differentiated membership and widening of the EU.

1.1 The politics of EU enlargement

My main argument is that the various EU enlargement rounds "succeeded" *despite* distributional conflicts because governments managed to redistribute EU enlargement gains (a) among the applicant countries and EU member states, and (b) from the relative winners to the relative losers among EU members.

EU enlargement increases the aggregate gains of membership for all current members and at the same time triggers distributional conflict between current and future members. Every enlargement round has fostered political stability and economic growth in Europe. For example, the Eastern enlargement contributed tremendously to the economic development of the accession countries whose economies grew by approximately 3.8% per year between 1997 and 2005 (EU Commission 2006a). However, each of these rounds also saw serious frictions, especially when new members were expected to receive large shares of the European Agricultural Guidance and Guarantee Funds (EAGGF) and European Reconstruction and Development Funds (ERDF). The integration of labor markets further aggravated these frictions because the applicant countries' per capita income and wages were significantly lower than those of the member states. Although these expectations were partly exaggerated, there is no doubt that enlargement affects EU members unequally. Enlargement does not necessarily divide countries into *absolute* winners and losers, but it does cause tensions between *relative* winners and losers.

Distributional conflict poses a threat to the successful conclusion of accession negotiations because the enlargement of the EU has to be approved unanimously. This specific institutional environment gives the relative losers of enlargement an opportunity to engage in delaying tactics in order to obtain a redistribution of enlargement costs and benefits that is more favorable to them. Because they can, at least in theory, delay indefinitely a compromise on the policy being negotiated, the relative losers can credibly threaten the supporters of enlargement to withhold agreement until sufficiently attractive re-distributional measures are accepted. The relative winners of enlargement, on the other hand, have no incentives to demand compensation at the expense of the applicant states.

A good example of the relationship between distributional conflict and the demand for compensation is provided by the debates on the Common Fisheries Policies (CFP) of the Community in the second Mediterranean enlargement round. Some EU member states – France and Ireland in particular – were wary of integrating Spain into the CFP immediately after accession. The cause of this reluctance was the enormous size of the Spanish fishing fleet whose 17,000 boats exceeded numerically the combined fleet of all other member states, and reached almost 70% of the combined tonnage. France and Ireland feared that their domestic fishing sectors would suffer grievously from such a drastic increase in competition, and requested catching quotas for Spain for a transitional period of at least ten years. Tensions arising from the integration of the acceding states into the CFP escalated over the course of negotiations. French and Irish Navy patrol boats repeatedly fired on Spanish fishing trawlers that were operating illegally in French and Irish waters. In response, Spanish fishermen burned foreign lorries. As a result of these conflicts, the French and the Irish governments made it very clear that they would delay accession until the distributive problems were adequately solved.

When a distributive conflict arises between a group of member states and some applicants, then the relative winners and losers of enlargement within the EU and the candidate states have to negotiate during the accession talks the conditions under which the applicants may accede to the Union.[8] The resolution of this conflict in the form of redistribution of enlargement gains in favor of enlargement skeptics clears the way for the admission of applicant states.

EU members use two principal strategies to tilt the balance of costs and benefits in favor of enlargement. Differentiated (or

---

[8] See Chapter 2 for a description of the formal EU enlargement process.

discriminatory) membership serves as one instrument of redistribution.[9] The enlargement gains can be reallocated in favor of adversely affected members at the expense of candidates by granting newcomers temporarily restricted membership rights. This compensation secures the votes of the potential losers while maintaining Pareto-efficiency in the longer run because its transitional nature ensures that new members are not permanently worse off.[10]

During the second Mediterranean enlargement round, France's and Ireland's refusal to approve the provisional closure of the *acquis* chapter "Common Fisheries Policies" threatened the entire accession process.[11] This induced the relative winners to search for a solution to the conflict. Although the Spanish government rejected a proposal with transitional limitations in 1984, it eventually agreed on a compromise to avoid further delay. Under the terms of the compromise, Spain would not be fully integrated into the CFP for seven to ten years. By (temporarily) surrendering some of its membership benefits – and thereby partially defraying the expected costs for France and Ireland over the transition period – Spain increased the likelihood that these two countries would approve its accession.

Whether the candidates are forced to accept some temporary exclusions from the *acquis communautaire* also depends on their bargaining power and the importance of enlargement for the relative winners within the Union. This suggests an alternative instrument to cope with opposition arising from distributional conflict: supporters of enlargement among current EU members can pay some of the costs themselves to compensate the losers. For example, they can offer to increase their contributions to the common EU budget.

---

[9] Throughout the book, I will use the terms "differentiated membership" and "discriminatory membership" interchangeably. See Chapter 2 for an in-depth definition of discriminatory membership.

[10] During the accession negotiations, EU members form expectations about the costs and benefits of enlargement. Because they tend to discount the future relative to the present, member states will be more concerned about what happens in the short term than far in the future. Differentiated membership puts off paying the costs of enlargement while allowing the benefits to accrue immediately. Because of discounting, this ensures that the present net gain from enlargement is much higher. See Section 4.2.3 in Chapter 4 for the rationale of transitional periods.

[11] The *acquis communautaire* is the body of common rules and laws in the EU. For the enlargement talks, it is divided into chapters representing the different common policies of the Union. See Chapter 2 for a more detailed description of the common *acquis* and a description of the formal enlargement process.

The accession of Spain and Portugal triggered conflict not only with France and Ireland over the CFP, but also with Greece over the distribution of structural aid. Having recently achieved membership status, Greece was particularly concerned that the accession of two relatively poor countries would cause an unfavorable shift of structural transfers. Consequently, the Greek government declined to approve the accession of the two candidates until the current members offered a deal that largely secured Greece's benefits from the ERDF. The German government, which expected political and economic gains from the second Mediterranean enlargement, agreed to raise its contributions to the common budget thereby preparing the ground for the Integrated Mediterranean Programs (IMP).[12] The IMP provided for additional transfers to the Mediterranean countries in the Union, and these transfers asymmetrically benefitted Greece because of the fixed distributional rules. Through the IMP the relative winners of enlargement inside the Union defrayed some of the enlargement costs to compensate the relative losers.

According to this perspective, EU widening can succeed even when some members expect serious losses in one or more policy areas. This can be accomplished when relative winners (members and candidates alike) transfer some of their enlargement gains to compensate the relative losers who fear the distributional consequences of enlargement.

1.2 Organization of the book

In this book I analyze the politics of EU enlargement by combining political economy reasoning with multi-method empirical tests. Both elements are equally important. I build on a framework that integrates intergovernmentalist and institutionalist theories with basic political

---

[12] Germany expected to gain from the Mediterranean enlargement because of the accession of Spain and Portugal for several reasons. First, their accession to the Union promised an increase in political stability and a strengthening of the Atlantic Alliance. Furthermore, the economic gains from market integration were tremendous because Germany was already the largest exporter to both countries and a net importer of Mediterranean agricultural products. Enlargement reduced the risks for German investments and did not adversely affect the economy because Germany did not have to worry about competition from low-priced, labor-intensive goods from the applicants (Tsoukalis 1981, 146f.). See Chapter 7 for a detailed analysis of the second Mediterranean enlargement and the debates around the establishment of the IMP.

Organization of the book

economy assumptions to provide a general theoretical explanation of the relationships among distributional conflict, differentiated membership, and EU enlargement. I then study quantitative and qualitative evidence to triangulate the theoretical expectations and elucidate the links among the preferences of EU member states towards expansion, the course of accession negotiations, and the likelihood of differentiated membership.

Chapter 2 provides a description of the formal process of EU enlargement and some facts about the EU accession negotiations and outcomes. The detailed description of the sequence of steps that lead to enlargement highlights the important role the formal accession process and multilateral negotiations play in EU's enlargement decisions. The historical data show how the accession process allows current members to suspend temporarily the implementation of the common *acquis*. I then examine the accession talks on the chapter "Free Movement of Workers" during the Eastern enlargement. The analysis demonstrates how national politics can influence how member states formulate a common position on the terms of accession. This provides a strong rationale for opening the black box of accession negotiations.

Chapter 3 motivates the main argument with a review of the existing literature. I provide an overview of the major approaches to EU enlargement and discuss why the Southern and Eastern enlargement rounds appear puzzling. While I draw on insights from previous work to provide an explanation of all five EU enlargement rounds, my political economy approach offers a more integrative theory of EU enlargement. Most importantly, whereas I agree with Schimmelfennig that distributional conflicts typically arise in accession negotiations, I show that enlargement can be explained from a rationalist perspective if one accounts for the fact that members and candidates can negotiate the distribution of its costs and benefits.

Chapter 4 develops the theoretical argument. The theory combines intergovernmentalist and institutionalist approaches with political economy logic and focuses on the emergence and resolution of distributive conflicts between EU members and candidates during enlargement negotiations. I argue that distributional conflict is a stumbling block to enlargement because relative losers will condition their support for expansion on receiving adequate compensation. When such distributional conflict arises, enlargement cannot proceed unconditionally. In this case, either the relative winners within the Union or the applicant must bear a disproportionate burden of enlargement costs to induce the relative losers to cooperate. From this theory, I derive several testable hypotheses about the conditions that make enlargement more likely to succeed.

In the main empirical part of the book, I test the implications of my theory and examine empirically the relationship between distributional conflicts in the enlargement process, the course of accession negotiations, differentiated membership, and the probability of enlargement. The study relies on a unique data set comprising all five EU enlargement rounds and three policy fields – the Free Movement of Workers (FMW), the Common Agricultural Policies (CAP), and the Common Structural or Cohesion Policies (CSP). I begin with an analysis of the origins of distributional conflict between insiders and outsiders and its effect on the course of accession negotiations. I then study how this conflict affects enlargement outcomes, and then examine the relationship between discriminatory membership and the distribution of enlargement gains across EU member states.

Chapter 5 clarifies the conditions under which distributional conflicts arise in the accession process and how these conflicts affect EU members' interests and the strategies they pursue during the negotiations. In general, EU members tend to demand restriction of membership rights for newcomers when they anticipate being disadvantaged after the expansion. For example, the major beneficiaries of EU structural transfers will oppose the unconditional accession of a candidate that is likely to shift these transfers away from them. Analogously, EU members with serious labor market problems will demand continued protection of labor markets.

Chapter 6 uses these results to analyze whether the emergence of distributional conflict influences the outcomes of enlargement talks. The empirical examination shows that candidates are less likely to be admitted unconditionally if distributional conflict arises. Under these circumstances, the likelihood that applicants receive limited membership rights increases sharply. At the same time, the analysis demonstrates that discrimination is not merely an instrument for the deliberate maximization of enlargement gains for current EU members. Even though the applicant states are typically in a weak bargaining position in the accession process, they only have to accept transitional limitations of their membership rights when distributional conflict emerges. This chapter also provides the first account of alternatives to differentiated membership: If current EU members are willing to internalize some of the enlargement costs, then the likelihood of discrimination diminishes.

Organization of the book

Chapter 7 offers a detailed comparative study of the Mediterranean and the Eastern expansions. The accession of Portugal and Spain to the CSP caused intense debates among member states about the distribution of structural transfers after the enlargement. However, despite this conflict neither Spain nor Portugal were forced to accept limited access to these funds. Comparing the two enlargement waves explains why this was the likely outcome, and highlights the trade-off between discriminatory membership and intra-union redistribution. In the 1980s, Greece threatened to veto unconditional enlargement because the accession of Spain and Portugal would have diminished its gains from structural aid. Whereas Germany and other net contributors to the budget offered to redistribute their enlargement gains – thereby increasing the funds available to Greece – in that case, they refused to pursue such a course during the Eastern enlargement. The study shows that the choice of enlargement strategies depends on existing institutional constraints and the proposals initially brought forward by the relative losers of enlargement. Like Greece during the second Mediterranean expansion, the net recipients demanded an increase in structural transfers during the Eastern expansion. In both cases, the intergovernmental debates within the EU concentrated on these transfers. In the second Mediterranean enlargement, the main contributors to the budget agreed to set up the IMP and the possibility to phase-in membership rights for Spain and Portugal was only touched upon. In the Eastern enlargement, the negotiated outcome was quite different because *Agenda 2000* prohibited any further expansion of the ERDF. As a result, EU member states looked for other solutions and eventually coordinated on the qualification of membership rights for the applicant countries of Central and Eastern Europe.

Chapter 8 summarizes the findings of this book and discusses their theoretical and political implications for future enlargement rounds like the possible accession of Turkey to the EU. I provide an overview of recent developments in the EU and current debates within the EU member countries, and demonstrate the increasing importance of discrimination for further integration in the EU. I also recapitulate the main findings on the redistribution of enlargement gains within the EU and examine alternative approaches that might help to achieve further expansion. Differentiated integration, for example, may serve as an instrument to overcome potential deadlocks in general. I then conclude with a discussion of the normative implications of discriminatory membership in the EU.

2 | EU enlargements and transitional periods

Accession negotiations play a key role in the relationship between distributional conflicts, differentiated membership, and the outcomes of the enlargement process. This chapter lays the foundation of the main argument by providing an overview of the formal accession process, the policy instruments used to reconcile conflicts of interest between existing members and applicant countries, and the influence of national politics on the formulation of a common European Union (EU) position by member states. Even this brief overview amply demonstrates the potential for frictions during the enlargement process. It also shows what strategies governments can use to resolve these conflicts to obtain the unanimous approval of member states to admit the applicant countries.

I begin with a short history of the five EU expansions and a description of the formal accession process, which show why accession negotiations should not be treated as a black box. The relative winners of enlargement, the relative losers, and the candidate states bargain over the terms under which accession will take place. The implementation of the *acquis communautaire* is at the center of these negotiations because it gives the participants an opportunity to redistribute the costs and benefits from accession by agreeing on transitional periods whose terms favor current and future member states that stand to lose most over the short-term. I look at the scope of these measures using the Eastern enlargement round as an example, and show how both EU members and candidate countries can use them strategically to influence the bargaining outcomes.

While EU members negotiate the terms of accession with the applicants, they also must formulate a common EU position on the various chapters of the *acquis*. This process itself is riddled with conflict because of divergent national preferences of current members. The analysis of how these differences are reconciled is critical for my analytical framework and highlights the shortcomings of the extant literature. Consequently, I trace the accession negotiations surrounding the "Free Movement of Workers" chapter in the Eastern enlargement round. The domestic debates about the liberalization of the European labor markets reveal that EU member states can arrive at very different estimates of the expected costs and benefits from the widening of the Union. States that expect labor market disruptions get involved in complex multilateral negotiations with the supporters of enlargement to strike a deal whose terms will allow them to minimize these disruptions after accession of the candidates.

2.1 Timeline of European Union enlargement

The European Coal and Steel Community (ECSC) was founded in 1951 by six nations: Belgium, France, West Germany, Italy, Luxembourg, and the Netherlands. The pooling of the coal and steel resources of the members and the creation of a common market for them started the economic and political integration of Europe. Since then, the EU has admitted new members in six waves.[1] The first time the EU admitted new members after its foundation was in 1973 when Denmark, Ireland, and the UK acceded to the Community.[2] After this so-called "First Northern Enlargement," the next two expansions were toward the Mediterranean. Greece joined the Union in January 1981 (the first Mediterranean enlargement), with Portugal and Spain following suit in January 1986 (the second Mediterranean enlargement). The second Northern enlargement in 1995 saw Austria, Finland, and Sweden acceding to the EU. The fifth enlargement was the most extensive in the history of the Union, with ten countries being

---

[1] Some scholars speak of five enlargement waves because they include Bulgaria and Romania with the ten countries that joined the EU in May 2004.
[2] Greenland became part of the European Community (EC) with the accession of Denmark but withdrew in 1985, shortly after it achieved internal autonomy. Norway's application failed when a domestic referendum revealed no support for ratification of the treaty. As noted in the introduction, two earlier applications from the UK in 1961 and 1967 were vetoed by then-President of France Charles de Gaulle. In 1961, de Gaulle argued that the accession of Great Britain would alter the nature of the European EC completely and lead to an Atlantic Community under American domination. In 1963, he raised concerns that Britain's economic weakness could inhibit the economic development of the EC. French opposition continued until his resignation and the election of Georges Pompidou in 1969.

admitted at the same time in May 2004. This first Eastern enlargement absorbed Cyprus, the Czech Republic, Estonia, Hungary, Latvia, Lithuania, Malta, Poland, Slovakia, and Slovenia. Three years later, in January 2007, Bulgaria and Romania were granted EU membership rights as well.[3]

These enlargement waves are crucial for the process of European integration. The number of EU members increased steadily from the six founding nations to twenty-seven as of 2007. The process does not appear to have halted: Croatia and Turkey commenced accession negotiations in October 2005, the Former Yugoslav Republic of Macedonia (FYRM) was granted candidate status in December 2005, and several Balkan states – Albania, Bosnia and Herzegovina, Montenegro, and Serbia – are recognized as potential candidates and are waiting to be granted applicant status.

While EU enlargements are often used as an example of how well European integration works, Table 2.1 demonstrates that they did *not* happen without much wrangling. The time-to-accession, measured as the number of months from the formal application for EU membership to accession, varies considerably across enlargement rounds and candidates. Whereas Finland took less than three years to gain entry to the Union, Spain needed nearly nine. At the extreme end, negotiations with Turkey began more than 17 years after its application. Throughout EU's history, expansion was delayed, sometimes indefinitely, either because governments of applicant countries balked at membership (usually when a domestic referendum revealed lack of popular support for joining the Union) or because the EU declared the postponement or failure of accession talks (after a veto by a member or the summary rejection of an applicant by the Council).[4]

As I explain later, the variation in the duration of pre-accession negotiations is largely determined by differences in the fulfilment of various membership criteria and the implementation of the *acquis communautaire*. Since both of these are formal requirements for joining the EU, the official rules of expansion influence not only the course of accession negotiations, but also their outcomes.

---

[3] The accession of these two countries was delayed because of concerns about their ability to fulfill the obligations of membership, especially in the spheres of justice and the fight against corruption.

[4] The Council rejected Morocco's membership application in 1987 without accession negotiations on the grounds that the country was not European.

Table 2.1. *Application and accession of countries to the European Union.*

Country	Application date	Start of negotiations	End of negotiations	Accession/ outcome	Duration (in months)
UK	09.1961	–	01.1963	suspended	–
	05.1967	06.1970	01.1972	01.1973	68
Ireland	07.1961	–	01.1963	suspended	–
	05.1967	06.1970	01.1972	01.1973	68
Denmark	08.1961	–	01.1963	suspended	
	05.1967	06.1970	01.1972	01.1973	68
Norway	04.1962	–	01.1963	suspended	–
	07.1967	06.1970	01.1972	Ratification failed	–
	11.1992	04.1993	04.1994	Ratification failed	–
Greece	06.1975	07.1976	05.1979	01.1981	67
Portugal	03.1977	10.1978	06.1985	01.1986	106
Spain	07.1977	02.1979	06.1985	01.1986	102
Turkey	04.1987	10.2005	–	–	–
Morocco	07.1987	–	–	rejected	–
Austria	07.1989	02.1993	04.1994	01.1995	66
Sweden	07.1991	02.1993	04.1994	01.1995	66
Finland	03.1992	02.1993	04.1994	01.1995	34
Switzerland	05.1992	–	–	suspended	–
Malta	07.1990	07.1997	12.2002	05.2004	164
Cyprus	07.1990	02.2000	12.2002	05.2004	164
Hungary	04.1994	03.1998	12.2002	05.2004	121
Poland	04.1994	03.1998	12.2002	05.2004	121
Slovakia	06.1995	02.2000	12.2002	05.2004	107
Estonia	11.1995	03.1998	12.2002	05.2004	102
Latvia	10.1995	02.2000	12.2002	05.2004	101
Lithuania	12.1995	02.2000	12.2002	05.2004	99
Czech Republic	01.1996	03.1998	12.2002	05.2004	98
Slovenia	06.1996	03.1998	12.2002	05.2004	108
Bulgaria	12.1995	02.2000	06.2004	01.2007	133
Romania	06.1995	02.2000	06.2004	01.2007	138
Croatia	02.2003	10.2005	–	–	–
FYRM	03.2004	–	–	–	–

Source: European Union

2.2 The formal EU enlargement process

Article 49 of the Treaty of Amsterdam, which amended the Treaty on European Union (TEU), states that any European country may apply for membership as long as it embraces the principles of liberty and democracy, and respects human rights and fundamental freedoms, and the rule of law.[5]

These requirements already hint at the exclusiveness of EU membership. Every state which aspires to join the Union must meet many prerequisites before being considered for membership. These prerequisites have been required (with some modifications) since the first enlargement round (Avery 1995, 14), but were not specified explicitly until the Copenhagen summit in 1993 (EU Council 2003). According to the "Copenhagen criteria," before being considered for Union membership, a country must:

(a) have stable institutions that guarantee democracy, rule of law, human rights, and respect for protection of minorities,
(b) have a functioning market economy, and the capacity to cope with competition and market forces in the EU,
(c) possess the capacity to take on the obligations of membership, including adherence to the objectives of political, economic and monetary union, and
(d) adopt the *acquis communautaire* (the entire European legislation) and ensure its effective implementation through appropriate administrative and judicial structures.

Even when a candidate meets all these criteria, the current member states must still agree unanimously that the EU can absorb the new member.

After receiving the candidate's official application for admission, the EU Commission prepares an official opinion about it and formally adopts this opinion by majority vote. The requirements that the applicants have democratic institutions and a functioning market economy are key to EU Commission's opinion about the commencement of accession negotiations.[6] The EU Council then decides unanimously whether to open accession negotiations or to reject the application. In

---

[5] The texts of all treaties can be found at www.europa.eu.int.
[6] In June 2006, the EU members also agreed to take into serious consideration EU's capacity for further expansion (EU Commission 2006a).

The formal EU enlargement process

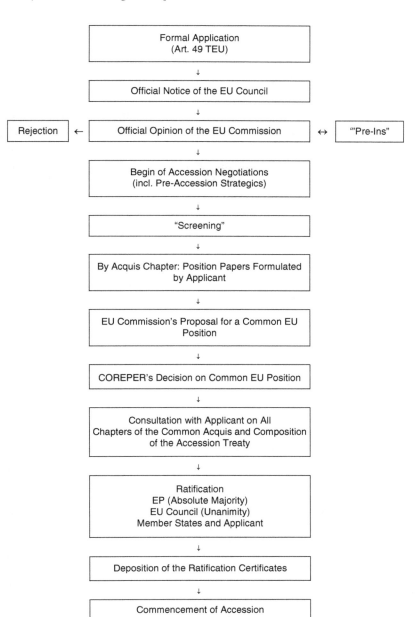

Fig. 2.1 EU enlargement: formal accession process.

the Eastern enlargement, the Council created a middle path by separating the group of applicants into the "ins" (Cyprus, the Czech Republic, Estonia, Hungary, Poland, and Slovenia) and the "pre-ins" (Bulgaria, Latvia, Lithuania, Romania and Slovakia). The Council did not reject the "pre-ins" but decided against opening accession negotiations with them at that stage. The "ins" – countries of the first wave – began formal accession talks in 1998 while the "pre-ins" had to wait until 2000.

Once the Council decides to open accession negotiations, actual enlargement talks concentrate on the full implementation of the *acquis communautaire* as a prerequisite for admission. The *acquis* is the body of common rights and obligations that are binding on all members. It evolves continuously and consists of the treaties, their principles and political objectives, legislation adopted in their application, case law of the European Court of Justice, declarations and resolutions adopted by the Union, measures related to the Common Foreign and Security Policy and Justice and Home Affairs, as well as all international agreements concluded by the Community or by member states among themselves in any field of Union activities. As of 2001, the total stock of the *acquis* on secondary law amounted to 80,000 pages. Its rapid growth continues with approximately 2,500 laws amended annually.

The EU divides the *acquis communautaire* in 31 chapters to facilitate accession negotiations.[7] EU members must formulate a common position on each chapter, and then adopt it unanimously. This position must specify any possible derogations or transitional periods. Formally, the EU Commission proposes a common position to the EU Council, and the EU member governments either accept it unanimously or amend it.[8] This position is then presented to the candidate,

---

[7] The chapters are the Free Movement of Goods, the Free Movement of Persons, the Freedom to Provide Services, the Free Movement of Capital, Company Law, Competition Policy, Agriculture, Fisheries, Transport Policy, Taxation, the Economic and Monetary Union, Statistics, Social Policy and Employment, Energy, Industrial Policy, Small and Medium-Sized Enterprizes, Science and Research, Education and Training, Telecommunications and Information Technologies, Culture and Audio-Visual Policy, Regional Policy and Co-ordination of Structural Instruments, Environment, Consumers and Health Protection, Cooperation in the Field of Justice and Home affairs, Customs Union, External Relations, Common Foreign and Security Policy, Financial Control, Financial and Budgetary Provisions, and Institutions.

[8] According to Avery (2004), the process of formulating a common position starts long before the Commission's first draft.

which prepares its own position paper on the chapter. After that, intergovernmental conferences between the EU and the applicant country are held, with regular meetings at the level of permanent representatives for the member states (COREPER) and ambassadors or chief negotiators for the candidates. When the EU and the candidate states reach a compromise over the exact conditions for the implementations of the chapter, the Commission provisionally closes that chapter. Provisional closure ensures that member states and candidates can re-open the chapter later if further disputes arise. This helps avoid situations in which candidates fail to implement the regulations they have agreed to after the chapter is closed.

The accession treaties incorporate all agreements from the accession negotiations and are drawn up after EU members and applicants have closed all chapters of the common acquis. Following the Council's and the applicant's approval of the treaty, the Commission delivers its opinion, and the European Parliament holds an up or down vote on the treaty by absolute majority. If the treaty is accepted, each member state and acceding country must ratify it according to their own constitutional procedures. When the ratification process is completed, the applicant becomes an official member of the EU.

2.3 Accession negotiations and enlargement outcomes

The EU enlargement process has two distinct phases: the pre-accession decision to grant applicant status, and the accession negotiations. It is necessary to distinguish between the two. The decision to open accession negotiations is an important signal that the EU is committed to enlargement in general. However, whereas it has been difficult to suspend accession altogether once enlargement talks have begun, EU members can defer acceptance indefinitely by refusing to approve the closure of individual chapters. EU members have not shied away from using this instrument whenever they had concerns about losses from enlargement. Using delaying tactics allows them to secure more favorable outcomes without having to take the blame for completely abandoning enlargement. As a consequence, the decision to open accession negotiations is not a binding commitment to accept the applicant.

Recent public debates reveal the importance member states attach to retaining national control over admissions. With the latest enlargement rounds causing increasing levels of distributional conflicts, the EU Commission offered to make it easy to suspend accessions negotiations completely whenever there are serious and persistent breaches of the basic principles of the EU (EU Commission 2006a). Even this was not going far enough for some member states. Many EU members are currently contemplating the implementation of national hurdles designed to strengthen their veto power in the accession process. For instance, then-interior minister of France, Nicolas Sarkozy, proposed that the closure of chapters should require the approval by national parliaments (e.g., *The EU Parliament* 17.02.2006).[9] The use of delaying tactics and the member states' concern with retaining the right to use them amply demonstrate that there exist opportunities to resolve distributional conflicts during the accession negotiations and that governments seize upon these opportunities to ensure that outcomes are not too detrimental to their interests.

I now turn to two aspects of the accession process that I will argue are crucial to understanding the larger context of EU enlargement: the transitional suspension of implementation of the common *acquis*, and the influence of national politics on the formulation of the common position.

2.3.1 Implementation of the acquis communautaire

In general, all applicants have to adopt the common rules of the Union in their entirety. However, current and potential members have considerable wiggle room for negotiating arrangements for the temporary (or, on rare occasions, permanent) suspension of implementation of some EU policies (Article 9 of the Treaty of Accession).[10]

Transitional arrangements between EU members and applicants are the focus of enlargement talks, and are of two types. The dominant type are transitional periods that are to the candidate's *advantage*. These are quite common because usually applicants cannot be

---

[9] See www.eupolitix.com.
[10] Permanent derogations from the common *acquis* are very rare. Two examples are the agreement with Sweden on "chewing tobacco," and the agreement with Denmark on the purchase of certain real estate by foreigners.

expected to apply the whole body of EU rules on the day of accession (Spiesberger 1998, 411).[11] Transitional periods also mitigate the impact of systemic change, help protect higher standards, and motivate active reform policies to complete the applicants' social and economic transition (Lopian 1993, Becker 1999). For these reasons, the EU sometimes grants new members transitional periods in various policy fields. Avery (2004) estimates that the 2004 enlargement round allowed for a total of 322 transitional measures in 17 of the 31 chapters. Given the number of rules incorporated in the *acquis communautaire*, this number is astonishingly low. The sparse use of exemptions reflects the balance between allowing applicants some time to adjust their policies and the desire to accept only those applicants whose policies are already stable and in harmony with the EU's (Plümper et al., 2006).

The other type of transitional periods are those that are to the candidate's *disadvantage*.[12] These are far less common because the implementation of most common policies is relatively unproblematic. The EU has restricted membership rights only in few policy areas. The transitional periods negotiated in favor of EU member states in the 2004 Eastern enlargement talks illustrate the scope and variation of these measures:

(i) Free Movement of Labor
- Arrangements: restrictions on the Free Movement of Labor (including social and tax benefits); Germany and Austria may use further national measures
- Duration: 2004-2011 (with reviews after 2 and 5 years)
- Scope: all acceding states except Malta and Cyprus

(ii) Company Law
- Arrangements: patent holders may prevent the import of a product patented in a member state until patent is obtained in acceding countries

---

[11] A recently published strategy paper of the EU Commission hints that this might change in future enlargement rounds. Instead of relying on the candidates' promise to implement the law after accession, the Commission suggests to make the closure of chapters conditional on the factual implementation of all rules (EU Commission 2006a).

[12] Accession treaties can include transitional periods that are either favorable to the candidates or are at their expense. Typically, they provide for some combination of the two.

- Duration: until patent expires
- Scope: all acceding states

(iii) Agriculture
- Arrangements: direct payments to be phased in, starting at 25% of the present system in 2004, increasing by 5% in the following two years, and then using gradual increments to reach 100% of the applicable EU level in 2013
- Duration: 2004-2013
- Scope: all acceding states

(iv) Transport Policy
- Arrangements: restricted access of non-resident hauliers to the national road transport market
- Duration: up to 5 years
- Scope: the Czech Republic, Estonia, Latvia, Lithuania, Slovakia (2 to maximum of 5 years), Hungary, and Poland (3 to maximum of 5 years)

(v) Regional Policy and Coordination of Structural Instruments
- Arrangements: restricted eligibility for structural aid
- Duration: 2004-2007
- Scope: all acceding states

(vi) Co-operation in the Field of Justice and Home Affairs
- Arrangements: the removal of internal border controls depends on whether all legal, organizational, operational, practical and technical prerequisites are satisfied
- Duration: until prerequisites are satisfied
- Scope: all acceding states

(vii) Other
- Arrangements: Economic Safeguard Clause, Internal Market Safeguard Clause, Specific JHA Safeguard Clause
- Duration: application of new safeguard clauses until 2007, but no fixed end date for existing safeguard clauses after that date
- Scope: all acceding states

The most common restrictions are in the fields of Free Movement of Workers (FMW), Company Law, the Common Agricultural Policies (CAP), Transport Policies, the Common Regional Policies, and Justice and Home Affairs. The scope and duration of these transitional periods depend on the policy field but also vary across enlargement rounds. Unlike permanent derogations that exempt members from the

Accession negotiations and enlargement outcomes 23

implementation of a particular policy, the limitations of membership rights have always been temporary.[13]

Throughout this book, I will use the term *discriminatory* (or *differentiated*) membership to refer to this type of transitional measures. Discrimination denotes the temporary derogation from some aspect of the common *acquis* demanded by one or more member states and agreed upon during the enlargement talks. I prefer this term to the more general *differentiated integration* as it captures more precisely the essence of the measures I wish to focus on. Differentiated integration refers to an asymmetric application of membership rights and rules in favor (or at the expense) of both current *and* new member states. Stubb (1996) discerns three modes of differentiated integration. "Multi-speed integration" is a strategy according to which a core group of EU member states proceed with integration under the assumption that the remaining members will soon follow. The most prominent example of multi-speed integration is the European Monetary Union (EMU). "Variable geometry" is a strategy according to which a core group of EU members proceed with integration under the assumption that the resulting differences are permanent and irreversible. Issues of European defense and peace-keeping within the framework of the Western European Union (WEU), the EUROCORPS, or the EUROFOR provide the best examples in which countries have opted for integration outside of the *acquis communautaire*. Finally, "integration 'à la carte' " is a strategy under which individual EU member states decide in which policy area they would like to participate. The EMU, for example, allows Denmark and the United Kingdom (UK) to opt permanently out of certain regulations.

Discriminatory membership, on the other hand, specifically denotes the differentiation of membership rights to the disadvantage of acceding states. It is thus a special case of differentiated integration, and refers to instances where new member states are *denied* full participation in the *acquis communautaire*. As I mentioned before, these are typically cases of delayed integration into the common market or of phase-ins of monetary transfers which limit membership rights for

---

[13] Some EU members even demanded that objective conditions be specified that, once met, would automatically terminate transitional measures. However, transitional periods have generally been fixed under subjective termination criteria. Permanent derogations, on the other hand, would put pressure on the entire system, and are undesirable (Spiesberger 1998).

newcomers. It is worth noting that in spite of the negative connotation of the label, discriminatory membership helps achieve an outcome that is advantageous to both current and new member states. As the empirical analysis will show, discrimination is not a strategy that allows current members to maximize their gains from enlargement but is rather a tool for solving distributional conflicts.

Scholars typically treat these measures as instruments used non-strategically to facilitate the adaptation processes for the EU and the candidate states (e.g., Mayhew 2000, 13). The goal is to avoid abrupt changes, potential social and economic problems, or strains on the common budget (Becker 1999, Mayhew 2000). The existing explanations of EU enlargement, however, largely ignore the existence of discriminatory membership. I argue that upon closer inspection, the debates between EU members and candidate states as well as the debates within the Union itself reveal that discrimination is a tactic whose effects are much deeper than these scholars are prepared to admit.

2.3.2 The formulation of a common EU position

The second characteristic of the accession process that deserves greater attention is the rule that enlargement talks take place between the candidate and the EU as a unit. EU members have to agree among themselves on a common position for the Union on each issue in the accession talks. The formulation of this common position is usually a difficult and rather lengthy process because fundamental national interests of member states are at stake. With the EU Commission acting as a mediator, EU member governments specify the conditions under which they would be willing to close a given chapter of the *acquis*. Although the negotiations themselves are confidential, the process reveals the differences between relative winners and losers of enlargement within the Union. The enlargement talks are not bilateral – between the EU and the candidate – but at least trilateral – among the relative winners, relative losers, and the applicants.

The negotiations about the implementation of the Free Movement of Workers provision during the EU Eastern enlargement provides a good illustration of the formation of a common position and its relevance to the understanding of the resolution of distributional conflicts caused by enlargement.[14] The positions EU member countries took during these negotiations revealed substantial divergence of preferences on liberalization of their labor markets. Despite being among the strongest supporters of Eastern enlargement, Germany and Austria became serious obstacles when negotiations on the chapter of the "Free Movement of Labor" opened in 2001 (Austrian Government 2000a, 2000b).[15] Politicians in both countries insisted that cheap unskilled labor from acceding states would migrate to neighboring countries and cause a disruption of domestic labor markets. The German Chancellor Gerhard Schröder aptly summarized the fears of the public in one of his speeches:

I am certainly aware of the fears and insecurities here in Oberpfalz, but also in other regions which share a border with the acceding states: concerns about the expected migration of workers, but also of commuters, and concerns about a dumping of wages, social regulations, and environmental regulations. ... You all know about the welfare and wage gap between old and new EU member states. This gap will generate a pressure for migration and adaptation. ... We would have to deal with enforced immigration if the free movement of workers is granted immediately after enlargement

(Schröder 2000).[16]

Many publicized academic studies stoked labor fears of falling wages and rising unemployment with their forecasts of the social adjustments that would be necessitated by the integration in the economic area.[17] Most of these studies assumed that the free movement

---

[14] See Schneider (2006) for a detailed analysis of the Eastern enlargement talks and the liberalization of the European labor market.
[15] See also Schröder (2000).
[16] Translated from: "Natürlich weiss ich, dass es gerade hier in der Oberpfalz übrigens in anderen Grenzgebieten ganz genauso auch Sorgen und Unsicherheiten aufgrund der bevorstehenden Erweiterung gibt: Sorgen vor zunehmender Billigkonkurrenz zum Beispiel, Sorgen vor einem Zustrom an Arbeitskräften, auch von Pendlern, Sorgen vor Lohn-, Sozial- und Umweltdumping. ... Zwischen den bisherigen und den zukünftigen EU-Mitgliedern besteht – Sie wissen es – ein grosses Wohlstands- und damit auch Lohngefälle. Dieses Gefälle wird Migrations- und Anpassungsdruck erzeugen. ... Käme es im Zuge der Erweiterung zu sofortiger voller Arbeitnehmerfreizügigkeit, wären wir mit verstärktem Zuzug auch nach Deutschland konfrontiert."
[17] See, *inter alia*, Bauer and Zimmermann (1999), Böri and Brücker (2000), Hille and Straubhaar (2000), Hönekopp (2000, 2004), Sinn et al. (2001), and Walterskirchen and Dietz (1998).

of Eastern European workers would have a negative impact on the German and Austrian labor markets in particular. In contrast to the sanguine EU Commission, which expected a maximum of 3.9 million migrants in the first decade after expansion (EU Commission 2001), German academic institutes produced gloomy forecasts of up to 6.5 million people migrating from the new member states (Hönekopp 2000, Hönekopp 2004, Sinn et al. 2001). The President of the Austrian Federation of Trade Unions *(Österreichische Gewerkschaftsbund)*, for example, argued that it would be wrong to hope that enlargement would add new jobs to the labor market. In fact, quite the opposite was likely: He expected that between 150,000 and 500,000 job-seekers would flood the domestic labor market (Der Kurier, April 6, 1998).[18] The President of the Chamber of Labor *(Arbeiterkammer)*, Herbert Tumpel, also doubted that the Austrian labor market could cope with the influx of approximately 200,000 job-seekers from the East. Consequently, he called for labor market restrictions until economic power and income in the Eastern neighbors adjusted to the Austrian level (Hinteregger 1998).

Although the published results disagreed on the extent of expected immigration, all studies concurred that Germany and Austria would bear the heaviest burden of migration should the EU grant free movement to Eastern labor.[19] The EU Commission projected that two-thirds of the migrants would settle in Germany, and another ten percent would emigrate to Austria (EU Commission 2001). That migration would be most intense in the frontier regions of Germany and Austria where the labor market conditions were already dire only further aggravated the situation (Sinn et al. 2001). It is not, therefore, surprising that the *Österreichische Gewerkschaftsbund* and the *Arbeiterkammer* fought fiercely for restrictions on the free movement of persons from new member countries, and demanded that these restrictions could only be lifted after the newcomers achieve purchasing power of at least 70% of the EU average. Both organizations strictly opposed transitional periods of fixed duration. Instead, they

---

[18] See Appendix 2.5 for a complete list of all newspaper articles cited in this chapter.
[19] See Böri and Brücker (2001), Brücker et al. (2000), Grosse Hüttmann (2004), Heijdra et al. (2002), Herzog (2003), Hönekopp (2004), Lejour et al. (2001), Sinn et al. (2001).

insisted that objective criteria should determine how long these periods should last. Hans-Werner Sinn, the President of the German Ifo Institute for Economic Research *(Institut für Wirtschaftsforschung)*, argued that the EU should lift restrictions on the free movement of workers only when it can deal adequately with migration pressure (*Financial Times*, February 9, 2004).[20]

This was hardly the common position in the EU. Although Chancellor Schröder's official statement found strong support in Austria and Italy (Schröder 2000), the majority of EU member governments did not share this opinion.[21] The Spanish government strongly opposed any restrictions on the full and immediate implementation of the common *acquis*, and deprecated the German proposal (*Neue Züricher Zeitung*, December 18, 2000; *Der Standard*, June 1, 2001). The Swedish government also aimed at the full liberalization of the Swedish labor market after enlargement. In 1999, the Swedish Premier, Göran Persson, demanded freedom of movement and the avoidance of any kind of protectionism within the EU (Persson 1999). Similarly, the UK and Ireland adamantly refused to make expansion conditional on the extension of transitional periods for the free movement of workers (*Der Standard*, April 19, 2001). Whereas other governments were more moderate in their reactions to the claims made by Germany, Italy, and Austria, most of them preferred to liberalize the EU labor market immediately upon enlargement (*Der Standard*, April 19, 2001).

These differences among the EU member countries indicate that the demand for transitional periods arises from the expectation of negative social consequences from the integration of the labor markets. Whereas German, Italian, and Austrian employers believed that full

---

[20] The German Federation of Trade Unions, *Deutscher Gewerkschaftsbund (DGB)*, had already called for restrictions on the free movement of CEE workers at the early stages of the public debate (DGB 1996).

[21] The protests of the Italian worker organizations were strongest. Like their German counterparts, they forecast strong migration pressures with attendant imbalances in the Italian labor market. It would be employees in regions bordering the new member countries that would have to bear the resulting social costs (*The Times*, December 2, 2003). None of the organizations considered the potential positive effects a more moderate immigration policy would have on the dramatic obsolescence in Italy. To the contrary, high unemployment rates and geographic proximity created strong political pressure for the closing of the Italian labor market to persons from the new member states (Organa 2002).

integration would be beneficial, many employees, especially those in close geographical proximity to the candidate countries, feared that it would be very costly socially because of the strong pressure to adapt to the migration of cheap labor from the newcomers. The expectation of a massive influx of unskilled labor into the economically weak regions bordering the new members was a serious concern for these three countries. Even though numerous empirical studies supported these expectations, public opinion in other member states did not share them.[22] There was no public expression of fear from potential migration of labor from Central and Eastern European (CEE) member states at least until mid-2001. The *Landsorganisation*, Sweden's largest trade association, did expect massive movement of labor following the enlargement. Nevertheless, the association estimated that immigration from the East would have a strong positive effect on the country. Sweden's demographic problem provided the rationale for this assessment: 17% of Swedes were 65 years old or older in 2000. The experts projected that the ageing trend would continue even if the government succeeded in attracting young workers from other countries (Eurostat, 2003, 2005).

The divergence of preferences on the free movement of workers delayed accession negotiations. The German government emphasized the importance of the German interests at stake by repeatedly stressing that the successful conclusion of accession negotiations depended on finding a solution to the labor market problem (*Wirtschaftsblatt*, June 8, 2001; *Frankfurter Allgemeine Zeitung*, April 4, 2001). The need to find a compromise that would avoid further postponement of enlargement became desperate in 2001 when upcoming elections in Germany combined with the impasse the country had reached with Spain on the Common Structural Policy. In return for its support for restrictions on the free movement of labor, Spain had demanded guarantees that its regions would receive the same amount of structural transfers after enlargement as they had before (*Financial Times*, May 15, 2001). Germany firmly rejected any such linkages (*European Report*, May 3, 2001). This unwillingness to concede any ground in order to reach a mutually satisfactory compromise deadlocked the negotiations and delayed the accession of the candidates. To resolve this dispute, most

---

[22] See EU Commission (2001) for a summary of these studies.

EU member states stepped in, backed the German position, and forced Spain to give in (*Observer*, May 22, 2001).[23]

At the Göteburg Summit in June 2001, the EU members finally reached a compromise on a common position that favored German and Austrian interests. Eight of the ten countries that joined the Union in May 2004 had to accept restrictions on the free movement of workers for up to seven years. Malta and Cyprus were exempt and enjoyed full liberalization of labor markets immediately upon accession. The actual implementation allowed for much flexibility because each EU member was free to decide to what extent it wanted to protect its labor market. Possible restrictions ranged from simple registration requirements all the way up to complete protectionism. In 2006, barely two years after enlargement, the EU began looking at possibilities for the early termination of restrictions. In 2009, the EU Commission will decide whether transitional periods are to be shortened or ended altogether. Even then, if a member government expects that the unrestricted movement of workers would destabilize its labor markets, then it may continue the discriminatory policies for up to two more years. In any case, all member states must complete the integration of labor markets by 2011 at the latest (Treaty of Accession 2003, 906ff).

To summarize, the negotiations about the Free Movement of Workers show that (a) the widening of the EU often triggers intense domestic debate because the integration of additional states affects national interests; (b) the exposure to adverse consequences from enlargement varies from member state to member state, with some expecting to be relative winners, and others expecting to be relative losers; and (c) states that fear the consequences from enlargement can block the admission of new members until these distributional conflicts are resolved to their satisfaction.

All of this serves to illustrate the point that EU enlargement is not a bilateral process in which the EU negotiates the terms of accession with applicants as a single monolithic actor. Because domestic interests of member states are at stake, enlargement talks should be treated

---

[23] The EU member states did promise to acknowledge Spain's problems in the Common Structural Policies, and to look for solutions (*Financial Times*, June 8, 2001).

as multilateral negotiations involving different groups of EU members and the candidates. The theoretical framework I present in this book incorporates this insight, which allows it to deliver crisp predictions about the conditions that make enlargement more likely to succeed.

2.4 Conclusion

States seeking to join the EU were often confronted with the unpleasant reality of having to accept restrictions on their rights as EU members in exchange for their admission to the Union. At the very least, they were required to implement the common *acquis*, with the exceptions subject to negotiations, before the EU even decided on their application for accession. In this chapter, I outlined the basic steps in the formal enlargement procedure, and showed the relevance of the rules and practices of accession negotiations for enlargement outcomes.

Accession negotiations give EU members the opportunity to influence the terms under which enlargement takes place. If a member state fears the distributional consequences of integration, e.g., for its access to structural aid or for the stability of its labor markets, then it can delay accession until some acceptable compromise that defrays some of the costs is worked out. The negotiations about the free movement of workers during the Eastern enlargement round illustrate how EU members may come up with very different assessments of the costs and benefits from enlargement. Some of them expected serious disruptions of their labor markets while others anticipated net gains from migration. Those that feared net losses, at least in the short run, refused to approve the accession of candidate states without receiving some protection for their labor markets. Thus, even a traditionally strong supporter of Eastern enlargement like Germany turned into an enlargement skeptic when confronted with the expected costs of massive migration.

In the next chapter, I provide an overview of extant approaches to EU enlargement and argue that they do not account adequately for the enlargement process and as a result fail to explain the Southern and Eastern enlargement rounds, at the very least. I also show that the inability to explain the success of enlargement from a rationalist perspective is entirely due to treating the process as a black box.

2.5 Appendix

EU member positions on the integration of the Eastern European labor markets: newspaper sources

Austrian Government, 2000a: Information Note: The Free Movement of Persons in the Context of Enlargement. Additional Facts on the Austrian Situation relating to the Commission's Information Note of April 17th, 2000. Luxembourg.

Austrian Government, 2000b: Österreich Neu Regieren. FPÖ-ÖVP Regierungsprogramm.

Der Kurier, April 6, 1998. Im ÖGB wachsen Vorbehalte gegen die Ost-Erweiterung, p.2.

Der Standard, April 19, 2001: Wer ist gegen Übergangsfristen: www.ccc-net.at, last accessed: 06.05.2004.

Der Standard, June 1, 2001: "EU-Erweiterung beschleunigen". EU Ratsvorsitzender Göran Persson lobt die Beitrittskandidaten: www.ccc-net.at, last accessed: 06.05.2004.

DGB Arbeitspapier, 1996: Arbeitspapier des DGB zur Osterweiterung der EU, Fortschreibung des DGB-Papiers vom Juni 1996.

EU Commission, 2001: Information Note. The Free Movement of Workers in the Context of Enlargement. Office for Official Publications of the European Community: Luxembourg.

EU Commission, 2004: www.europa.eu.int/eures.

EUObserver.com, May 22, 2001: Top EU leaders reject enlargement subsidies link, www.euobserver.com.

European Report, May 3, 2001: ESC says poor regions should keep cohesion grants after enlargement, Section 2589.

Financial Times, May 27, 2000: Brussels stance irritates EU hopefuls enlargement negotiations. Additional information sought on immigration and border security, p.2.

Financial Times, May 15, 2001: Spain blocks EU agreement on labour, p.11.

Financial Times, June 8, 2001: The lure of enlargement, p.25.

Financial Times, February 9, 2004: Restrictions contradict the ideals of unity. But there are deep cultural fears of being overwhelmed by immigrants, p.13.

Frankfurter Allgemeine Zeitung, April 4, 2001: Schröder verteidigt Übergangsfristen bei EU-Osterweiterung, p.2.

Neue Zürcher Zeitung Folio, December 18, 2000: Europäer werde dagegen sehr: www.nzz.ch, 14.05.2004.

Persson, Göran, March 10, 1999: Discussion at the Swedish Institute for International Relations, in: Livre Blanc Sur L'Élargissement De L'Union

Européenne. Volume II. Rapport Sur Les Positions Des États Membres Et Des États Candidats Sur L'Élargissement De L'Union Européenne.

Schröder, Gerhard, 2000: Speech of the German Chancelor, Gerhard Schröder, at the Oberpfalz regional conference, December 18, 2000, Weiden.

The Times, December 2, 2003: Poor nations will not drag us down, p.12.

Wirtschaftsblatt, June 8, 2001: Persson will EU-Beitrittsverhandlungen beschleunigen.

Workpermit.com, February 27, 2004: Restrictions on working in the EU for new member states. www.workpermit.com, last accessed: 08.10.2004.

3 | A rationalist puzzle of EU enlargement?

Scholars who study European Union (EU) enlargement typically assume that for reasons of Pareto-efficiency only three outcomes are possible: countries either acquire full membership rights, get rejected, or stay out of the Union (e.g., Baldwin et al., 1997, Moravcsik and Vachudova 2003, Schimmelfennig 2001). Whereas this assumption was relatively unproblematic for explaining the two Northern enlargement rounds, scholars had to work hard to explain the Mediterranean enlargements in the 1980s, and were baffled by the successful conclusion of the 2004 Eastern enlargement (Schimmelfennig 2001, 2003). The puzzlement grew even more acute with the latest expansion when Bulgaria and Romania joined the Union in January 2007 *even though* the anticipated costs of admission by far outweighed the gains for several EU members. The failure of extant theories to account for these outcomes spurred scholars into looking for alternative explanations. In his seminal work, Schimmelfennig (2001, 2003) concludes that rational choice approaches cannot offer a satisfactory solution to the puzzle of enlargement. In their place, he proposes an explanation based on the concept of "rhetorical action." According to his theory, the losers of enlargement could not oppose openly the admission of the remaining European states because of normative considerations.

My rationalist explanation of EU enlargement builds upon some of these insights but extends the existing theories to offer a more general framework for analyzing the phenomenon. Instead of solving the puzzle by appealing to non-rational concepts, I argue that the only reason this puzzle exists in the first place stems from the silent assumption that the costs and benefits of enlargement are non-negotiable. As I showed in Chapter 2, however, EU member states and candidates not only can, but in fact do, engage in strenuous negotiations to redistribute the gains and losses occasioned by expansion. Across several waves of enlargement, EU member states devised various strategies to compensate the relative losers among them, effectively buying their approval for the widening of the Union. The admissions process is effectively a means to reaching a trilateral bargain in which the relative winners within the EU assume some of the costs that would otherwise accrue to the relative losers, and in which the EU negotiates certain transitional measures that candidates must agree to before being accepted into the Union. The literature on EU enlargement largely black-boxes the intra-Union negotiations and instead focuses on the bargaining between member states and candidates. I rectify this shortcoming and offer a comprehensive coherent explanation of EU enlargement with two principal elements: (a) I open up the black box of the enlargement process to study how states redistribute the costs and benefits of enlargement among current and future members alike; and (b) I dispense with the assumption that the accession outcome is dichotomous – acceptance or rejection – to study the terms of enlargement bargains that end in successful widening.

3.1 Widening and deepening: two pillars of EU integration

International institutions are "explicit arrangements, negotiated among international actors, that prescribe, proscribe, and/or authorize behavior" (Koremenos et al., 2001, 762). Why states give up sovereignty for the sake of international cooperation is among the main questions that have motivated scholarly research. Work on the enlargement of the EU is deeply embedded in this general literature, especially the strand that deals with European integration. Scholars typically distinguish between "deepening" and "widening" of the Union. Schimmelfennig and Sedelmeier (2002, 502) define "deepening" as the "process of gradual and formal *vertical* institutionalisation" in which the EU member states expand the scope of their common interactions and organizational rules, and increase the number of policies that are decided on the intergovernmental and supranational level. "Widening," on the other hand, is defined as the "process of gradual and formal *horizontal* institutionalisation" in which new states accede and adopt the rules and practices of the Union. Both of these processes propel EU integration forward.[1]

Whereas it is difficult to disentangle these highly interdependent processes, for the purposes of this study I shall limit the scope

---

[1] See Rosamond (2000) for an exhaustive account of the theories of EU integration.

of analysis to the widening phenomenon.[2] Scholars usually rely on the same general theoretical frameworks to explain either process so to understand their findings it is necessary to provide a brief overview of the three main approaches to EU integration: the functionalist/neo-functionalist, the (liberal) intergovernmentalist, and the institutionalist.

3.1.1 Functionalism and neo-functionalism

Functionalism is among the earliest approaches on which theories of EU integration are based (Mitrany 1933, 1965, 1966). Its purpose was not to explain why states might be willing to give up some of their autonomy but to provide a normative prescription about how governments should act to maintain a stable and peaceful international system. The function of international integration then is to enable them to reach these goals (Mitrany 1966, 31).[3]

Neo-functionalism was developed as a less normative and more analytical framework to study regional integration.[4] It is more specific to EU integration because its original goal was to understand and explain the integration of Europe after the Second World War. Briefly, neo-functionalism treats EU integration as a quasi-automatic process in which governments are induced to act and constrained in their actions by actors at the domestic and the supranational levels. Interest groups or political parties at the domestic level and regional institutions (like the EU Commission and the European Court) on the supranational

---

[2] Most approaches focus on either widening or deepening but there are more and more attempts to understand the interrelations between the two (Downs et al. 1998, Laurent and Maresceau 1998, König and Bräuninger 2000, Guerot 2002, König and Bräuninger 2002, 2004, Gilligan 2004, Hausken et al., 2006, Karp and Bowler 2006). Hausken et al., (2006) develop a general theory of widening and deepening of international political unions arguing that members of international organizations face a trade-off when deciding whether to widen or to deepen. Along similar lines, Karp and Bowler (2006) analyze public opinion data on EU widening and deepening and show that domestic preferences are not necessarily consistent towards EU integration.

[3] Federalism (Coudenhove-Kalergi 1926, Spinelli 1972) and transactionalism (Deutsch 1966) are structured along similar lines. I will not spend more time on these approaches because I am interested in explaining the conditions under which EU member states approve the widening of the Union to bolster further integration.

[4] Haas (1958, 1961, 1975), Lindberg (1963), Caporaso (1998), Sandholtz (1984), Burley and Mattli (1993), and Ross (1995).

level are the prime promoters of integration on various dimensions. Governments merely respond to interest group pressure. Functional and political spillovers as well as the increases in common interests then create further demand for integration.

Functionalism and neo-functionalism have been roundly criticized from their inception. One of the major shortcomings shared by both is that they neglect the importance of the state. For instance, neo-functionalism cannot explain the occasions when the national interest of EU member governments trumped common interest by sacrificing the benefits of further integration.[5] Weaknesses like this intensified the search for better theories.[6]

3.1.2 Intergovernmentalism

Intergovernmentalism was developed primarily from Hoffmann's (1964, 1966) critiques of neo-functionalism. Unlike the older theories that assume that actors below and above the national level are central to EU integration, intergovernmentalism sees state governments as its primary agents. In this view, these governments do not simply respond to pressures from the sub- and supranational levels but largely determine the direction and speed of the process themselves (e.g., Mattli 1999, Koremenos et al., 2001). European integration, then, is a product of a sequence of bargains among heads of states interested in maximizing their own welfare and power.[7]

Intergovernmentalism's main assumption that states are primary actors which cooperate only when they share similar interests is also a major focal point for critiques of the theory. Early intergovernmentalist approaches were excessively state-centered, completely neglecting the role of domestic preferences and the institutional

---

[5] The most commonly cited examples are French President Charles de Gaulle's veto of enlargement to Great Britain and the "empty chair crisis" when the French government, which opposed several Commission proposals including a reform of the Common Agricultural Policies (CAP), boycotted the Council of Ministers for six months in 1966.

[6] A full account of this debate is beyond the scope of this study. See Hoffmann (1964, 1966), Nye (1965), Haas (1975, 1976), and Mattli (1999) for some exchanges on the obsolescence of regional integration theory. Rosamond (2000, 74–97) gives a detailed summary of the main critiques.

[7] Moravcsik (1991, 1993), Taylor (1982), Hosli (1993), and Johnston (1995).

environment.[8] In response, scholars have extended the theory to account for domestic and institutional constraints on government behavior.[9] In a seminal work, Moravcsik (1997) offers a two-stage theory of EU integration which draws on the basic insights of intergovernmentalism but at the same time takes domestic preferences seriously to study how they affect the strategies governments pursue and the interstate bargains they strike. He assumes that economic interdependence determines the preferences of actors at the national level, constituting the demand side of integration. Because the government represents at least a subset of domestic society, it is constrained by these interests when negotiating at the international level. The interstate bargains, then, are largely shaped by asymmetric interdependence; that is, they reflect the domestic preferences and the bargaining power of the states. The theory also admits a limited role for supranational institutions as facilitators of cooperation that reduce transaction costs and offer a forum for making credible agreements.[10]

3.1.3 New institutionalism

Scholars criticized even the mature formulations of intergovernmentalism on the grounds that the approach did not go far enough in accounting for the importance of institutions, either as an exogenous or intervening variable between preferences and outcomes (e.g., Keohane 1984) or as an exogenous variable that considerably affects interests and EU integration itself.[11] Pollack (1996, 1997), for example, maintains the assumption that states are the primary actors at the international level but then analyzes how institutions structure individual and collective policy choices. Tsebelis and Garrett (2001)

---

[8] There are other criticisms as well. Pierson (1995), for example, attacked intergovernmentalism for taking a "snapshot view" of EU integration that only allows the analysis of specific bargaining episodes with a clear bias toward successful interstate negotiations. See Rosamond (2000, 130–155) and Mattli (1999) for a more detailed treatment.
[9] Bulmer (1983), Putnam (1988), Moravcsik (1991), and Milner (1997).
[10] Moravcsik (1993, 1997, 1998a, 1998b), and Moravcsik and Nicolaidis (1999).
[11] Garrett (1992), Garrett and Tsebelis (1996), Pollack (1996, 1997), Martin and Simmons (1998), and Tsebelis and Garrett (2001). See Thelen and Steinmo (1992) for a detailed summary of the debate and Schimmelfennig (2003) for an excellent discussion of sociological institutionalism.

develop a general model of the relationship between legislation, policy implementation, and legal adjudication. In their view, "the more difficult it is for new legislation to be passed ... the more discretion bureaucracies and courts have to move policy outcomes closer to their own preferences" (369). There is now a very rich literature on the influences of supranational institutions on EU integration.[12]

3.2 Integration theories and the calculus of EU enlargement

Most of the approaches enumerated in the previous section focus on the vertical integration of policies, or the deepening of the EU. This is but one of the two highly interrelated processes driving integration. The other is horizontal expansion: The enlargement of the EU fosters integration because "newcomers are required (by the terms of the accession agreement) to implement the harmonized policies of the union" (Hausken et al., 2006). The harmonization of policies in turn increases the political and economic benefits for each member state.[13]

Theories of EU enlargement explore (a) why the EU widens, (b) what effect the EU has on domestic policy in candidate countries, (c) how new members affect EU integration in general, and (d) how enlargement affects the distribution of costs and benefits among current members in particular. Even though I necessarily touch upon each of these questions, my study primarily addresses the first. In the sections that follow, I introduce the main approaches to EU enlargement and focus on the theories that seek to answer why the EU widens.

Before I do so, however, it is worth noting that in spite of the intense debate between (liberal) intergovernmentalists and new institutionalists most approaches to EU enlargement necessarily build on some

[12] Marks et al. (1996), Stone Sweet and Sandholtz (1997), Moravcsik (1998a), Schneider and Aspinwall (2001), and Christiansen (2002). Some studies focus on the impact of the EU Commission (Avery 1995, Christiansen 1997, Smyrl 1998, Tsebelis and Garrett 2001), others on the European Court of Justice (Alter 1996, 1998, Garrett et al., 1998, Mattli and Slaughter 1998), and yet others on the EU Parliament (Tsebelis 1994, Moser 1997, Tsebelis and Garrett 2001). There are also studies of the process of EU integration in general, particularly the influence of decision-making rules (Tsebelis 1994, Hosli 1996, König and Päter 2001, König and Bräuninger 2004). Institutionalist work, like its functionalist and intergovernmentalist rivals, is not limited to EU integration. Keohane and Milner (1996), Martin and Simmons (1998), and Koremenos et al., (2001) provide a small sample of applications to other areas.

[13] I discuss these benefits (and costs) later in this section.

form of intergovernmentalism. The reason for this is simple: individual members of the Union can dramatically affect the decision to expand and the accession process itself. Although the EU Commission conducts the accession negotiations with candidate governments and suggests which states to open negotiations with and which states to admit, each member country retains a significant degree of control over these decisions. In particular, the opening of accession negotiations, the closure of individual chapters of the *acquis communautaire*, and the commencement of the final accession stage must be approved unanimously.

This is not to say that the supranational institutions of the EU do not influence the accession negotiations and their outcome. Moravcsik (1998a) and Peterson (2001) separately assess the applicability of contending approaches to EU integration. Both conclude that intergovernmentalism is most useful if one's main goal is to explain the grand bargains – like the ones struck at Intergovernmental Conferences (IGC) – whereas supranational approaches are more useful if one is more interested in explaining everyday legislative processes.[14] These are distinct because at the systemic level the Council of Ministers and the Committee of Permanent Representatives (COREPER) are the primary actors that represent the economic and political preferences of national elites, and the common negotiation position formulated by the member states (Peterson 2001, 295).[15]

Pollack (1997, 126f.) concludes that supranational influence increases if (a) "information is imperfect, uncertainty about future developments is high, and/or asymmetrical distribution of information between the agent and the member states favors the former," (b) "distributional consequences of alternative policy proposals are the smallest," (c) "transaction costs of negotiating alternative policies and the costs of waiting are both high," and (d) the supranational institution "builds policy networks, rallies subnational actors to support its proposals, and pressures member governments to do likewise." When these conditions are met, supranational institutions – the EU Commission in the enlargement case – can affect the processes and their outcomes by constructing focal points, serving as credible mediators for EU members and accession candidates, offering their expertise,

---

[14] See also Sbragia (1993) and Pierson (1998).
[15] See also Avery (1995, 2004), and Moravcsik and Nicolaidis (1999).

or extending bureaucratic capacity.[16] Smyrl (1998) even argues that when the circumstances are right, the EU Commission can force members to accept its own preferences, as it happened with the implementation of the Integrated Mediterranean Programs (IMP):[17]

> Delors succeeded in winning approval for his reform package not because the Member States actively desired it, but because they were determined to avoid the Greek veto of Iberian accession and were forced by the Community's decision-making rules and the urgency of the situation to accept or reject the Commission's proposal as a while (94f.).

Avery (1995, 2004) explicitly investigates the role of the EU Commission in enlargement negotiations. Drawing on his experience as Chief Adviser in the Directorate General for Enlargement of the European Commission in Brussels, Avery argues that the Commission did exert some influence on the accession negotiations by acting as a credible mediator and by proposing solutions that suited all sides at the bargaining table. However, he also finds that this influence was quite limited, more so than in other types of negotiations, for at least two reasons. First, unlike the typical case in which the Commission acts as a negotiator, in the enlargement process it is the President of the Council who fulfills that role. Second, although the Commission drafts the common position, the negotiations between EU members and applicants (and among EU members) usually begin long before the first draft is proposed and each draft must be adopted unanimously by the Council of Ministers (without participation of the EU Parliament).

Historically, the Commission has not been able to do much when its preferences on enlargement were incompatible with those of the EU member states. The members often amended Commission proposals and maintained positions about the specifics of the enlargement process that contradicted the Commission's (Nicholson and East 1987, Ruano 2002). An extreme example of this helplessness occurred during the first Mediterranean enlargement when the Council rejected the Commission's unfavorable opinion on the Greek application. The Commission had proposed a pre-accession period of unspecified duration that was supposed to help Greece overcome its

---

[16] As I noted in Chapter 2, neither the EU Parliament nor the European Court of Justice have much to do with enlargement.

[17] Chapter 7 provides a detailed comparative study of the accession negotiations about the Common Structural Policies (CSP) and the implementation of the IMP.

economic problems. The Council, however, decided to open negotiations immediately (Nicholson and East 1987). To make matters worse, the Commission itself is often split on many issues, which only weakens its influence on accession negotiations. Still, it is important to keep in mind that the EU Commission has facilitated negotiations and as such has contributed to the success of enlargement. I explore some of these issues in Chapter 7 where I show how the Commission can frame accession negotiations and help overcome significant obstacles to enlargement.

I now turn to the theory that explains EU enlargement in terms of Pareto-efficiency. In this view, enlargement succeeds when the net gains it offers are positive. The literature identifying and analyzing the costs and benefits of EU membership is quite extensive.

3.2.1 The gains of EU enlargement

At least since Immanuel Kant, international organizations like the EU have been perceived as institutions that promote peace, stability, prosperity, democracy, human rights, and the rule of law (Kant [1975] 1991).[18] The idea of the European Community is rooted in the desire to foster political stability and economic growth after the devastation of the Second World War. As a result, most approaches to EU enlargement emphasize the political and economic benefits of EU membership. Typically, studies in this vein assume that enlargement increases the gains from membership by integrating more states into a common institutional framework. These gains accrue mainly from the harmonization of policies.

In the realm of economics, EU enlargement is particularly effective in contributing to the economic growth of old and new member states alike. The economic benefits of integration are many: (a) by eliminating tariff and quota barriers to trade, integration reduces transaction costs; (b) by incorporating new and growing markets, integration increases investments and trade;[19] (c) by transforming the legal and regulatory systems underlying the domestic market, integration has

---

[18] For a test of the Kantian triangle – the positive influence of democracy, economic interdependence, and membership in international organizations – see, *inter alia*, Russett et al. (1998) and Russett and Oneal (2001).

[19] Viner (1950), Dunning (1989), Casella (1994), Caves (1996), Brancati (1999), Mattli (1999).

considerable positive effects on labor and capital markets;[20] and (d) by encouraging specialization in the production process, integration leads to more efficient allocation of capital and boosts productivity.[21] Even this partial list shows that EU enlargement can increase the economic welfare of member states by promoting economic integration.

Perhaps more surprisingly, numerous benefits accrue from *political* integration as well. The most common argument is that the admission of new members reduces negative externalities.[22] It is now commonplace to assert that the EU grants membership rights to countries undergoing political and economic transitions to encourage their stabilization.[23] Yarbrough and Yarbrough (2001), for example, claim that this stabilization safeguards the investments of Western European firms. By this logic, EU membership would decrease some of the risks Western European industries are exposed to because it would make macroeconomic policies more predictable, improve the investment climate, and drastically reduce the possibility of expropriation.[24]

By a similar token, *barring* relatively poor countries from membership would have serious deleterious consequences for the political stability of the EU itself (Friis and Murphy 1999, Milbrandt 2001). Poverty-induced migration would rise, crime rates in Western Europe would increase, and the risks of conflict and war would escalate.[25]

These arguments shed some light on the political and economic motivations for expansion, and also help explain why EU members that share borders with the candidate state are more likely to advocate enlargement than countries without common borders.[26] However,

---

[20] Burda (1999), Böri and Terell (2002), Meyer (2002).

[21] Bolton and Roland (1997), Gstöhl (2002), Ruta (2005).

[22] Negative externalities are spillover effects from the economic and political activities of non-member states that are socially costly for the EU (e.g. Pigou 1925, Buchanan and Stubblebine 1962, Cornes and Sandler 1996).

[23] Baldwin et al., (1997), Roland and Verdier (2000), and Yarbrough and Yarbrough (2001).

[24] Baldwin et al., (1997) and Roland and Verdier (2000) make similar arguments.

[25] On migration, see Shevtsova (1992), Böri and Brücker (2000), Böri and Terell (2002), Rudolph (2003), and Kraus and Schwager (2004). On crime and conflict, see Hiemenz and Schatz (1979), and Hollifield (1992a, 1992b).

[26] Moravcsik (1998a) and Schimmelfennig and Sedelmeier (2002) claim that both costs and benefits of enlargement for members are higher the closer they are located geographically to the acceding states. Germany gained tremendously from the reduction of transaction costs to trade after the Eastern expansion but at the same time was most threatened by the mass migration of cheap labor (EU Commission 2001).

using EU enlargement as an instrument to reduce negative externalities might seem like shooting an ant with an elephant gun. Several scholars have argued that association agreements, international aid, and other political instruments would have achieved satisfactory levels of political and economic stability without incurring the costs of expanded membership (Kivikari 2001, Mattli and Plümper 2004).

Incorporating poorer countries into the Union may benefit current members beyond minimizing political and economic risks. Brou and Ruta (2004) show that certain domestic interest groups in richer nations can gain from, and therefore lobby in favor of, EU expansion to poorer nations. Whereas domestic lobbying groups cannot affect policies in a non-member state, they obtain leverage once this state accedes to the Union. If these interest groups expect that the common EU rules would enable them to exert influence on the decision-making internal to such a state, then they will lobby their governments by offering monetary contributions. From this vantage point, it is not at all surprising that members should advocate the admission of less developed countries.

Many authors also point to the decisive role less tangible factors may play in EU expansion. For example, some have argued that EU governments are generally predisposed to admit states that share their norms and values. Schimmelfennig (2002) claims that EU members are more likely to support the accession of democratic countries because they are most likely to conform to the basic values and rules of the EU. The democratic norm increases the probability of application and admission, *and* enforces the exclusion of non-conforming states.[27]

This logic needs to be qualified, however, on theoretical and empirical grounds because the relationship between quality of democratic institutions and EU enlargement is not that straightforward. In particular, whereas the quality of democracy affects the non-member government's decision to apply for membership, it is unrelated to the probability that members would choose that applicant for accession (Schneider 2003, Mattli and Plümper 2004, Plümper et al., 2006). The cause of this non-effect is self-selection at the application stage. Even though both constructivist and rational choice studies have found that

---

[27] Gehring (1995), Fierke and Wiener (1999), Schimmelfennig (2001, 2003), and Sjurson (2002).

states are more likely to apply for EU membership if they are democratic, they have failed to account for the consequences this would have at the approval stage. If applicants tend to be more democratic than non-applicants in the first place, then the EU's choice among candidates cannot be based on their adherence to democratic values. According to Polity IV, the average democracy score of the candidates in the last enlargement round was 9 on a scale from −10 to 10 (Marshall and Jaggers 2003). Only Romania's 2000 polity score of 5 was below the mean. In other words, whereas democracy matters for a state's decision to apply for membership, it is less important for the EU's decision which of the applicant states to admit and which ones to reject. This self-selection into the pool of applicants does not necessarily imply that the quality of democratic institutions has no bearing on enlargement outcomes but it does mean that any such effect would be marginal and occur only through the self-selection at the application stage.[28]

Studies of EU enlargement point to many mechanisms that essentially produce similar results: the Union provides for the enduring political and economic cooperation among members by ensuring the harmonization of their policies. This creates an arena for repeated interaction with effective monitoring and sanctioning capacity, which reduces transaction costs and provides disincentives for unilateral defection. Consequently, it is not just the acceding states that gain from joining the EU. The widening of the Union considerably increases the political and economic benefits for current members as well.

3.2.2 The costs of EU enlargement

The enlargement of the Union creates at least two types of costs: (i) political costs from the decrease in state autonomy and the increase of preference heterogeneity, and (ii) economic costs from the distributional consequences of widening.

The loss of political autonomy that accompanies enlargement can be very costly. The erosion of sovereignty occurs along several dimensions. First, EU legislation is binding on member states for certain

---

[28] Along those lines, Mattli and Plümper (2002, 2004) and Schimmelfennig (2002) have argued that the EU promotes democracy in states that are considering applying for EU membership.

policies. On one hand, committing new members to follow existing rules can be quite advantageous to current members. In just about all enlargement rounds, applicants had to implement the entire body of EU common law, which delivers the benefits of harmonization to existing members (Hausken et al., 2006). On the other hand, this comes at a price. The regulatory needs of the different countries are often incompatible but the EU sets uniform standards. This means that these must reflect some compromise between countries that favor high standards and countries that prefer lower ones (Fink Hafner 1999, Braun 2001, Holzinger 2001).[29]

Second, the admission of new states diminishes the bargaining power of existing members when decision-making rules remain fixed.[30] If the entry of new members changes the "pivotal" position in the Community, then the majority of current members will lose political leverage. If existing members suspect this might happen, they would only agree to the expansion if institutional reforms safeguard their interests or if the economic gains outweigh the political costs.[31]

These costs essentially arise from the loss of political influence as consequence of enlargement (e.g. Koremenos et al., 2001, 791). Member governments may try to minimize them by supporting the accession of a new state only when its admission does not erode their political clout or undermine their political autonomy. However, the governments' ability to achieve their goals depends not only on the formal decision-making rules but also on the interaction among members while attempting to reach a decision. In this process, heterogeneity of policy preferences and the range of policies to be decided upon are both crucial.[32] When there is wide variation in policy preferences, then arriving at a common position can be quite challenging

---

[29] Accordingly, optimal regulatory areas (Holzinger 2001) or concurrent jurisdictions (Casella and Frey 1992) as strictly geographic solutions to these problems seem to be relatively inefficient (Benz 1998).

[30] Fearon (1993), Bueno de Mesquita and Stokman (1994), Raunio and Wiberg (1998), Schneider and Aspinwall (2001), Koremenos et al., (2001), and Baldwin and Widgrén (2005).

[31] Brams (1975), Brams and Affuso (1985), Hosli (1993), Widgrén (1994), Johnston (1995), and Welfens (1995). Some scholars point out that the EU Commission advocates enlargement precisely for this reason: The admission of new states to the Union dilutes the influence of any one member and thus increases the Commission's discretionary leeway (Tsebelis and Garrett 2001).

[32] Alesina et al. (2001), Ruta (2005), and Plümper et al., (2006).

and costly because those favoring different policies must be offered side-payments, which increases log-rolling. Furthermore, the wider the range of policies members must agree on, the less efficient decision-making becomes. Similarly, the more restrictive the rules and the higher the number of members with divergent preferences, the harder it is to find a common position. All of this implies that the utility of harmonization may decline, especially when new members with very different or volatile policy preferences accede to the Union.[33]

It is not surprising, then, that EU members observe very carefully the implementation of the *acquis communautaire* in applicant states. The speed with which the government in a candidate state implements the common body of rules and laws can be an important signal about the similarity of their policy preferences. Presumably, the less political conflict these reforms trigger, the closer aligned the applicant's preferences are to those of the EU. This reassures existing members that this state is less likely to defect or to be an obstacle in the smooth functioning of the system after accession.[34] Because EU members tend to oppose the admission of countries with volatile or very dissimilar policy preferences, they use implementation of the *acquis* to distinguish between acceptable candidates (Schneider 2003, Plümper et al., 2006).[35]

Finally, and perhaps most importantly, EU members oppose the widening of the Union when they expect to be hurt by distributional conflicts after enlargement. Even if all members gain from the accession of new states, these gains are likely to be distributed unevenly among existing members. Historically, advanced industrial countries

---

[33] Heterogeneity of policy preferences may also decrease the value of membership for potential candidates. In a study of the Hungarian debate over EU membership, Navracsics (1997) finds that despite sharing a common desire to join the EU, parties disagreed about some policy areas. Batory (2001), however, finds that neither ideology nor party differences systematically influence the desire to obtain EU membership.

[34] Kydd (2001) reports similar results for North Atlantic Treaty Organization (NATO).

[35] This also may explain why the EU allows so many countries to apply for EU membership: given the conditions for membership, only countries with higher regulatory quality self-select into the pool of applicants. The accession talks then serve to distinguish between "good" and "bad" candidates. Phare (2001), on the other hand, argues that the clustering of negotiations generally provides distributional advantages to countries that cluster.

in the EU have been much more supportive of enlargement than countries with large and inefficient agricultural sectors. Interestingly, the latter seem to have been much more concerned about the possible loss of EU transfers than about potential costs from having to adjust to more intense economic competition or from losing political leverage in EU decision-making. Schimmelfennig (2001), among others, argues that EU Eastern enlargement "threatens to create particularly high costs for poorer, less developed and more agricultural members" (52). EU members with comparative advantage in labor-intense low-skilled production will face competitive pressure when newcomers erode it. When these members also receive a large share of the structural and agricultural funds, distributional conflict can become quite severe. EU members exposed to such distributional costs have been unlikely to support the admission of candidates.[36]

3.3 The puzzle of EU expansion

Rational-choice explanations of EU enlargement typically predict that expansion succeeds when the benefits from admitting new members are larger than the enlargement costs. While this was generally accepted in the fourth expansion to Austria, Sweden, and Finland, it was highly debated whether the two Mediterranean enlargement rounds and EU Eastern enlargement did not leave at least some current members worse off. If for some EU members the expected distributional costs would outweigh the expected benefits, then Eastern enlargement would be rather puzzling.

Scholars in the rational-choice approach addressed these assertions by closely evaluating the various costs and benefits. Based on these evaluations they argued that even for the Southern enlargements and the Eastern enlargement the benefits from enlargement – particularly the integration of markets and the increase in political stability in Europe – outweighed the economic costs and the loss in political autonomy (e.g. Baldwin et al., 1997, Moravcsik and Vachudova 2003). As Baldwin et al., (1997, 168) put it, the benefits from economic and political stabilization are so large that "Eastern enlargement will be a phenomenally good bargain for the incumbent EU15."

---

[36] Schneider (2006, 2007), Plümper and Schneider (2007).

Even though these approaches may correctly demonstrate that the overall enlargement gains were positive, they fall short of acknowledging that some EU members faced relative losses owing to the distributional effect of enlargement. For example, net recipients of structural and agricultural transfers feared that their shares of these funds would decline after enlargement. In 2000, an average of 10.8% of the population of Central and Eastern European (CEE) candidate states was still employed in the agricultural sector compared to an average of 5.6% in the EU countries. Moreover, over two-thirds of CEE regions had a Gross Domestic Product (GDP) that was less than 75% of the EUs (Eurostat). This would make most of these regions eligible for structural aid after enlargement (Bornschier et al., 2003). To accommodate the inevitable demand for these funds without decreasing the benefits of the current recipients, the common EU budget would have had to increase by 60% relative to its 2000 size.[37] However, the net contributors to the common budget strictly opposed any further increases in their contributions, further aggravating the situation and making the fears of the net recipients more acute. Raising the funds would have been inconsistent with *Agenda 2000* anyway. In this measure, adopted by the Council of Ministers at the Berlin Summit in 1999, the EU members agreed to establish a ceiling on the EU budget and to reform the Common Agricultural Policies and the Common Structural Policies.[38] The net recipients therefore expected to suffer rather severe losses if enlargement were to proceed.

Concerns about the costs of widening were not limited to the less industrialized members of the EU. Some of the most economically powerful states expected to incur rather large costs from the integration of markets. As discussed in Chapter 2, Germany and Austria warned that the liberalization of labor markets would cause massive labor migration from the newcomers to several current EU members imposing prohibitively high social and economic costs.

Scholars tend to classify countries into supporters and opposers of enlargement depending on how they expect them fare on the cost-benefit criterion. Traditionally, Austria, Denmark, Finland, Germany, Sweden, and the United Kingdom (UK) are considered the main

---

[37] Courchene et al. (1993), Kim and Tyers (1993), Baldwin (1994).
[38] EU Commission (1997a, 1997b, 1997c, 1999).

… "drivers" of the EU Eastern expansion. Belgium, France, Greece, Ireland, Italy, Luxembourg, the Netherlands, Portugal, and Spain, on the other hand, are usually considered the "brakemen" of enlargement.[39] Even this classification raises doubts about the applicability of cost-benefit analysis. Many scholars lump Germany and Austria with the advocates of Eastern enlargement because both gained from expansion on a large scale and tended to support the accession of those states. This fails, however, to acknowledge that both countries turned into enlargement skeptics during the accession negotiations because they expected serious losses from the integration of labor markets (see Chapter 2).

Schimmelfennig (2001, 2003) picks up on these problems and argues that, according to the rational-choice approach, at least the EU Eastern enlargement should have been vetoed by the potential losers. Existing explanations using this framework can only account for the association of states with the Union (e.g., why the EU granted certain privileges to non-member states without giving them applicant status) but not the decision to admit them to the Union. The puzzle, then, is why Eastern enlargement succeeded even though some EU members expected to incur serious losses from it.

3.4 Alternative explanations of EU enlargement

One possible reaction to the puzzle of EU enlargement is to sidestep it by abandoning the cost-benefit analysis of the rational-choice framework. This is what Schimmelfennig does with his concept of "rhetorical action," which is supposed to link the rational self-interested behavior of states to the collective outcomes in the EU (and NATO). He analyzes the enlargement costs and benefits for current members but argues that in order to connect the members' positions to the final outcome of the enlargement process, one must necessarily take into account normative values and norms.[40]

His argument may be summarized as follows. The Cold War changed the original pan-European vision of the EU to the disadvantage of Eastern European states. However, it was hard for EU members to express this divergence from past official announcements because

---

[39] Friis and Murphy (1999), Grabbe and Hughes (1998), Torreblanca (2001).
[40] Schimmelfennig (1999, 2000, 2001, 2002, 2003).

they could not openly distance themselves from historically developed norms. Proponents of enlargement found it easier to pursue integration with the East because opponents were trapped by rhetorical inconsistencies and as a result could not halt the process. In this view, shared norms constitute the most important prerequisite for membership. The EU (and NATO) were bound to accept countries that made the greatest progress in adopting liberal democratic values.

Schimmelfennig notes correctly that any explanation of EU enlargement must be grounded on the analysis of its potential costs and benefits, which EU members may estimate very differently. For example, while the UK was generally quite supportive of the accession of the ten CEE countries, Spain was rather skeptical because it feared the expected decline in receipts of structural aid, something that was of little concern to the UK.

Whereas I agree with Schimmelfennig that explanation must start with a cost-benefit analysis, I do not believe that one must abandon the rational-choice framework to answer the puzzle of EU enlargement. I argue that EU's Eastern enlargement – and, in fact, all enlargement rounds – can be adequately explained within that framework as long as we account for member states' ability to negotiate the allocation of enlargement gains and losses in a way that would make admitting the candidates Pareo-superior to rejecting them.

Schimmelfennig (2001) provides a cogent summary of his reasoning:

> There are basically two ways in which a state that does not reap net benefits from enlargement can be made to agree to the admission of a new member. On the one hand, enlargement will be possible if the losers are fully compensated through side payments and other concessions by the winners and if these concessions do not surpass the winners' benefits from enlargement. On the other hand, the losers will consent to enlargement if the winners are able to threaten them credibly with exclusion and if the losses of exclusion exceed the losses of enlargement... [However,] neither the CEE countries nor the 'drivers' among the EU members possessed sufficient bargaining power to change the balance of costs and benefits for the 'brakemen' in favor of Eastern enlargement (54).

In other words, the would-be winners of enlargement could not affect the cost-benefit calculations of would-be losers, as required by a rationalist explanation of enlargement. The supposed inability to negotiate the distribution of gains and losses provides the foundation for Schimmelfennig's constructivist explanation, according to

Alternative explanations of EU enlargement

which governments are forced to refer to common norms and values to generate support for enlargement.

In this book, I show that Schimmelfennig's fundamental premise is flawed and it is quite possible to provide a coherent rationalist explanation of enlargement. Union members have at their disposal several instruments that allow them to affect the distribution of gains from expansion. First, enlargement supporters can reallocate the costs and benefits to their own disadvantage. For example, they could increase their contributions to the common budget or agree to limit the amount of funds they receive from it. Second, and more commonly, they can reallocate them at the expense of the candidate by granting it limited rights in areas with distributional conflict. I analyze EU accession negotiations and demonstrate that EU members can, and do, place temporary restrictions on membership rights for newcomers in order to ensure a distribution of enlargement gains and losses that is more favorable to would-be losers.

Furthermore, I show that the phasing-in of membership rights is not meant to maximize the gains for existing members but is merely a tool to solve distributional conflicts and to avoid deadlock in the accession negotiations. This contrasts sharply with the view that outcomes in that bargaining process are determined by the asymmetric power of actors who pursue their narrow material self-interest. Instead of redistributing enlargement gains and losses to make accession the Pareto-superior outcome, transitional periods simply allow current members to maximize their own utility. Moravcsik and Vachudova (2003, 46), for instance, argue that accession outcomes are the result of "asymmetric interdependence." Even though all EU members would gain from Eastern enlargement, the benefits would be much greater for the candidate countries. However, because the candidates were in a weak bargaining position, they had to agree to serious concessions.[41]

I have no quibble with the argument that the concessions candidates have to make depend on their bargaining power. The problem is that the constructivist and the asymmetric interdependence explanations both fail to apply their own insights to the enlargement decision itself. That is, they assume that the decision to widen the Union was

---

[41] Sedelmeier (1998, 2002) shows that applicant countries did have *some* bargaining power because of support they had inside some European institutions. One's weak bargaining position could be improved if supporters within the EU have access to sectoral decision-making and form coalitions with sectoral decision-makers (Sedelmeier 2002, 629).

reached *before* the EU entered accession negotiations. Schimmelfennig explains enlargement with "rhetorical action." Moravcsik and Vachudova (2003, 46, 50), on the other hand, assume that Eastern enlargement was beneficial for all EU members to begin with. In either case, there was no danger that distributional conflicts would endanger expansion or prevent the successful conclusion of negotiations once they were commenced. The basis for this assumption can be found in a statement by the Council of Ministers at the Copenhagen Summit in 1993:

> The associated countries of Central and Eastern Europe that so desire shall become members of the Union. Accession will take place as soon as a country is able to assume the obligations of membership by satisfying the economic and social conditions (EU Council 2003).[42]

Clearly, the decision to open accession negotiations is a signal that the EU is willing to expand. At the same time, however, it also implies that only candidates that can reach an agreement with *all* EU members on *all* 31 chapters of the *acquis communautaire* will be admitted. The decision to start talking is not a binding commitment to enlargement. As I have shown in Chapter 2, each member state can obstruct negotiations and delay accession indefinitely if it is dissatisfied with the provisions of the treaty. During the talks preceding the Eastern enlargement, Germany de facto threatened to stall negotiations until the other members agreed to a seven-year measure to protect labor markets. If EU members were simply pursuing individual gains in accession negotiations, then they could have extracted much larger concessions than they did. The empirical part of this book provides evidence for my interpretation: Discriminatory membership has always been limited to situations in which old members are threatened with relative losses from enlargement.

3.5 Conclusion

This chapter offers a review of the state-of-the-art in political and economic explanations of EU enlargement. The theory I develop in the chapter that follows largely builds on these approaches by explicitly

---

[42] This quote is part of the so-called "Copenhagen Criteria" which lay down the conditions for membership in the European Union. See Chapter 2 for a detailed overview of the prerequisites for membership and the accession process.

Conclusion

incorporating the distribution of costs and benefits from enlargement. My theory specifies the conditions under which enlargement is likely to cause distributional conflicts and social tensions, and explains how accession negotiations can resolve them.

While useful as foundation for further theoretical development, existing rational-choice approaches do not provide an adequate explanation for all EU enlargement rounds. In particular, their assumption that expansion provides net benefits to all EU members is contradicted by the distributional conflicts in the Southern and Eastern enlargement rounds. Some scholars have tried to resolve the puzzle from a constructivist perspective, which acknowledges the uneven effects enlargement has on member states. However, the assumption that motivates the entire line of reasoning – that it is impossible to negotiate the distribution of gains and losses – is contradicted by the intense bargaining during the accession talks.

In this book, I offer a rationalist solution to the puzzle of EU enlargement, which extends and improves upon existing theories in several ways. First, I analyze the structure and the process of the multilateral accession negotiations to derive implications about the conditions under which EU members would be more likely to approve expansion. Second, I take policy preferences seriously and treat the EU as a group of heterogeneous members that negotiate the terms of accession with a group of heterogeneous applicants. Third, I account for the institutional context that endows each member with a veto over enlargement – it is this feature that turns distributional conflicts into potentially fatal obstacles to enlargement. Fourth, and perhaps most important, I treat enlargement outcomes as endogenous to the negotiations. Most studies assume that the distribution of enlargement costs and benefits is given exogenously and is not open to negotiation. Consequently, they consider only two extreme outcomes – accession or rejection – instead of taking stock of the actual terms of enlargement. Because of this blind spot, scholars were confounded by the Southern and Eastern expansions, and will have trouble explaining any future enlargement rounds in terms of Pareto-efficiency.

As long as we admit the possibility that EU members and candidates can negotiate the distribution of gains and losses from enlargement, we can explain EU enlargement in rational-choice terms. Discriminatory membership can be one such re-distributional tool that defrays some of the expected costs for relative losers in the Union at the expense of the newcomers and helps avoid the collapse of accession talks. This approach accounts for the actual process of expansion, and in doing so provides a more general and more parsimonious explanation of EU enlargement.

4 | *A theory of discriminatory membership*

In the 1980s, France and Italy opposed the unconditional accession of Spain and Portugal to the EU. There was widespread concern in both countries that Spanish and Portuguese participation in the CAP would be seriously damaging to their agricultural sectors. Spain's accession alone would increase the Community's agricultural area by 30% and its farm workforce by 25%. Community agricultural production would rise sharply by 25% for vegetables, 48% for fresh fruit, and 59% for olive oil. Wine of Spanish vintage would constitute nearly a quarter of European Union (EU) output. Even though France supported Spanish membership in principle, it opposed any substantive talks until both sides could agree on a common basis for negotiations.

The bargaining model presented in this chapter clarifies why distributional conflicts can hinder the widening of the EU despite overall political and economic gains. It also helps understand the conditions that make successful enlargement more likely. In general, EU members that foresee distributional conflict have incentives to oppose the unconditional accession of a new state. This is a potential stumbling block to enlargement because the admission of the applicant must be approved unanimously. These tensions need not be fatal, however, if the net gains from enlargement are positive. In that case, it is possible to settle these disputes by redistributing some of these gains from the applicants and/or the relative winners within the EU to the relative losers.

The bargaining model builds on a more general framework that accounts for the costs and benefits of EU membership. This helps derive the conditions that make differentiated membership, an instrument that redistributes enlargement gains at the expense of the candidate, superior to alternative strategies like full membership, intra-Union redistribution, or non-membership. EU members and applicants do not have to forego the overall gains from enlargement when distributional conflict arises during the accession negotiations.

Such conflict does not necessarily imply that widening will fail or that candidates will never obtain full membership rights. Redistribution of enlargement gains can resolve that conflict, and the manner in which it does so depends on the candidate's bargaining power. The more favorable the applicant's position is, the more likely are relative winners among the members to defray the costs for the relative losers. Conversely, a weak bargaining position makes it more likely that the applicant would have to bear most of these costs. In addition, the size of the total benefit for current EU members also influences how redistribution is achieved. The larger the gains from enlargement for current members, the more willing the relative winners will be to internalize some of the costs to ensure the accession of the candidate.

The rest of the chapter is organized as follows. The following section lays out the basic assumptions of the theory. Section 4.2 presents a model of the distributional effects of EU enlargement that helps explain how EU members manage the accession of new states in the shadow of conflicts it causes. Section 4.3 derives the hypotheses that I will investigate empirically.

4.1 Basic assumptions of the theoretical model

The theory I present in this chapter builds on the standard political economy models developed by Drazen (2000) and Persson and Tabellini (2002), among others. I assume that governments care about staying in power and are therefore interested in strategies that maximize the likelihood that they survive in office.[1] While negotiating the conditions under which candidates would agree to join the Union and members would agree to accept them, governments compare the available options, rank-order them according to their preferences, and choose the strategy that makes it most likely that they will retain office. Actors bargain over the terms of international cooperation and reject any agreement that they do not consider sufficiently beneficial. In other

---

[1] I abstract away from ideological or partisan preferences, and further assume that the government will behave as a benevolent social planner only when doing so would improve its chances of retaining office. It may seem restrictive to assume that governments only care about staying in office. However, this has no serious substantive effect on the theoretical results. Furthermore, any policy that a government may wish to implement for ideological or partisan reasons requires that it be in power anyway, thereby inducing strategically a preference for actions that allow it to do so.

words, cooperation must arise in the context of a non-cooperative game in which each actor seeks to maximize its own payoff. Finally, I assume that governments discount the future; that is, gains and losses that accrue today loom larger in their calculations than those that will accrue in the future.

To succeed, EU enlargement must be Pareto-optimal for members and candidates alike; that is, it must make no participant worse off and some participants strictly better off relative to any alternative. Clearly, no state that expects to lose from joining the Union would even consider membership. The Norwegian public, for example, decided to stay out because the expected costs to the fishing sector were too high to justify accession. Such outside options not only influence the decision to seek membership but also affect the bargaining power of the applicant during the enlargement talks.[2] On the EU side, observe that while members have an incentive to invite an applicant to join when they expect positive net benefits from enlargement, accession must be approved unanimously. Any member that expects to be a relative loser can veto the application. This veto power ensures the Pareto-optimality of successful enlargement within the Union.

The necessity of Pareto-optimality creates the puzzle of EU enlargement. Numerous EU members expected relative losses from the Eastern expansion and existing rational choice theories failed to predict that they would support it anyway.[3]

4.2 The calculus of EU enlargement

The assumptions of the model make it clear that the theory fits squarely in the larger framework based on the benefits EU members obtain and the costs they pay for belonging to the Union. I already discussed in some detail the literature on the positive and negative aspects of membership in Chapter 3. Here, I will summarize them as a reminder that whenever members have to decide whether to accept or reject a candidate, they will take all these factors into account.

---

[2] See Mattli (1999), Mattli and Plümper (2002, 2004), and Plümper et al., (2006) for a demand-side explanation of EU enlargement. In this work, I study when EU members accept a candidate that has already applied to join the Union.
[3] Among those who expected to fare badly were Spain, France, Greece, Italy, Ireland, Portugal, Belgium, the Netherlands, and Luxembourg. See also Chapter 3.

The fundamental goal of the Union, as enshrined in Article 6 of the Treaty on European Union (TEU), is to promote peace, democracy, the rule of law, and respect for human rights. This reflects the roots of the organization in the Second World War; in particular, the desire of all Europeans to prevent killing and destruction on such a scale from ever happening again. The notion that the value of an international organization is in its ability to help achieve lasting peace among nations dates back to Immanuel Kant. His vision of the "perpetual peace" was based on international law and organizations in addition to representative democracy and economic interdependence (Kant [1975] 1991).

Within the scope of this overarching goal, the EU offers its members the numerous benefits that accrue from cooperation within the European institutional framework. First and foremost, individual states profit from the harmonization of policies. The resulting policy coherence yields economic and political gains by reducing transaction costs, increasing synergy and positive spillover effects, and even offering the possibility to redistribute welfare at the international level. For example, structural aid programs and agricultural subsidies can transfer wealth from the more advanced industrial countries to the agriculturally-bound economically and structurally weak fellow members. By increasing the levels of international political and economic cooperation, such policies lead to growth and stability in Europe. European integration can account for about 0.8% of economic growth of EU member states (Henrekson et al., 1997). Ireland was among the countries that gained tremendously from structural aid after joining the Community in 1973. Its Gross Domestic Product (GDP) leapt from about 60% of the EU average upon accession to over 110% of that average in 2004.[4] More recently, the goal to stabilize politically the Eastern region of Europe was a major impetus behind the Eastern expansion (Friis and Murphy 1999).

Two inter-related mechanisms serve to secure and increase the benefits of cooperation. Members can widen the Union to incorporate a larger number of states into the general economic and political institutional framework. Within that framework, members

---

[4] Ireland's success owes much to the political acumen of its government but also to demographic factors. The Irish are relatively young and well-trained, production costs are low, and research support is high.

have implemented institutional monitoring with sanctioning abilities to cope with incentives to defect and free-ride.[5] For instance, the Community can deprive a member of its vote in the Council of Ministers when this member is in serious and persistent breach of the common rules and principles (Articles 6(I) and 7(I, II) of the TEU). Various other institutional rules, such as penalizing members that fail to implement common EU law, serve a similar purpose. With its effective monitoring and sanctioning capacities, the Union provides members with disincentives to defect which ensures that they will live up to their obligations. The Union reduces, and even resolves, the problem of collective action "by providing stable negotiating forums, pooling activities, elaborating norms, and acting as a neutral information provider, trustee, allocator, or arbiter" (Schimmelfennig and Sedelmeier 2002, 509). The common rules and standards help coordinate expectations of members, reduce uncertainty, and increase the credibility of their commitments. Moreover, the Union facilitates agreements on issues of common interest by providing opportunities for issue-linkage and side-payments.[6]

Despite the major gains from international cooperation policy harmonization can yield, EU members can come into serious conflict when they have divergent preferences on a common policy or a distributional issue. The efforts to create a common foreign policy provide the best example of a conflict that did not arise because of distributional implications but because of heterogeneous policy preferences. Governments are particularly sensitive to this area because it impinges directly on domestic security. Disagreements about how much authority member states should retain derailed the original attempt to establish a European Defense Community (EDC) in 1954, and have hindered progress ever since.

The negotiation of the common budget for the 2007–13 period, on the other hand, is a good example of distributional conflict. Whereas most members agreed that the budget would have to be consolidated,

---

[5] States tend to defect from cooperation because the international system lacks effective governance structures (Olson 1965, Schelling 1996, Hampton 1987, Heckathorn 1996). The most commonly cited example is the failure to collaborate in the Prisoner's Dilemma (Axelrod 1984).

[6] The seminal work on collective action is Olson (1965); see also North (1993). For issue-linkage and uncertainty reduction, see, *inter alia*, Stein (1982), Oye (1985), and Abott and Snidal (1998).

they disagreed on precisely *how* to do that. Even now, 40% of the common budget is allocated to agricultural subsidies. The UK, which has a small and efficient agricultural sector, demanded that this share be reduced. Not surprisingly, this met with the determined opposition of the main beneficiaries of the Common Agricultural Policies (e.g., France), which rejected any reduction of subsidies for their farmers. Distributional conflicts among EU members are likely to arise when they have to decide on budget reforms or when widening of the Union is expected to change their net receipts. Every enlargement wave has been the occasion for such conflicts. When Spain and Portugal sought to join the EU, Greece in particular fought for an increase of the common budget that would enable it to retain its level of structural aid.

Clearly, different common EU policies vary in how prone they are to distributional conflict. Buchanan (1965) offers one useful method of categorizing policies based on their consumption characteristics.[7] We can think of policies as being rival, neutral, or complementary in consumption. This characteristic then determines the net benefits members receive as a function of the total number of beneficiaries. In areas where policies are neutral or complementary, enlargement will not have distributional effects. Only in areas where policies are rival will enlargement cause tensions or even distributional conflicts among members.

A common policy that yields to each member constant benefits that do not depend on the total number of beneficiaries is *neutral*. If increasing the number of beneficiaries also increases the marginal utility for each member, then the policy is *complementary*. Some examples of policies in the latter category are the common EU market and the various environmental and technical standards. Consider the environmental standards that each EU member must adhere to. When implemented, these standards enhance the quality of the environment not only within each country, but also across countries. Increasing

---

[7] Buchanan (1965) refers to the "consumption" of public goods. Even though the EU policies are not "consumed" by member states, I find Buchanan's terminology helpful, and will use it throughout. More generally, my theory builds on the economic theory of clubs. Some prominent examples are Olson (1965), Fratianni and Pattison (1982, 2001), Padoan (1997), Cornes and Sandler (1996), Frey (1997), and Fratianni (1998).

The calculus of EU enlargement 61

the number of members that observe these regulations creates positive externalities and reduces pollution in all states. In addition, the requirement that standards be uniform decreases transaction costs and makes it more likely that more governments would agree to implement them.

When increasing the total number of beneficiaries decreases the marginal utility for each member, the policy is *rivalrous*. For example, if more members have to share the benefits from a common fund (or one member draws a larger share), then congestion can occur. In the EU context, members receive agricultural subsidies and structural transfers from the EU. If the size of the budget is held constant, the addition of more members eligible to draw from these funds will decrease the receipts of existing members. Rivalrous policies then are fertile grounds for distributional conflicts.

I should note that categorizing EU policies according to their consumption characteristics is not as clear-cut as it might seem at first. Take the integration of common markets, like the labor market for example. With its reduction of transaction costs, this integration facilitates the migration of individuals, which decreases unemployment. The policy is then complementary. However, if labor migrates in very large numbers, it can disturb the existing EU market, causing hardship to immigration targets. This makes the policy rivalrous. Recall that in the Eastern enlargement some members were rather skeptical about liberalization of labor markets precisely because they expected that the influx of cheap labor from the newcomers would affect adversely their domestic markets. This may be an extreme case, but it does illustrate how important it is to scrutinize very carefully each common policy field to determine its consumption characteristics. Still, the categorization is a simple and useful way to distinguish among EU policies, so I will retain it while acknowledging its shortcomings.

4.2.1 *The emergence of distributional conflicts*

The accession of new states to the EU may cause tensions among members when it has asymmetric distributional consequences or when it is likely to increase policy preference heterogeneity. The increased complexity of decision-making, however, affects all members equally. Therefore, the distributional effects of enlargement are more likely to cause disagreement about which candidates to admit and under what conditions. Even when all members benefit from enlargement, as may have been the case in the first and fourth enlargement rounds, the gains may be unevenly distributed among them. Historically, intra-Union financial transfers have constituted the fault line between supporters and opposers of expansion. The beneficiaries of these transfers have been concerned with the loss of this benefit more than with any other potential losses like declining influence in future EU decisions or costly adjustments to more intense economic competition.

As shown in Chapter 2, every enlargement round gave rise to distributional conflicts. In the second enlargement to the South, for example, the Mediterranean member states feared that Spain's and Portugal's accession would drastically reduce their share of structural transfers. During the accession negotiations, the Greek Prime Minister repeatedly threatened to delay enlargement until appropriate safeguard measures were introduced to protect his country's access to financial aid, and even demanded compensation remedies in the form of an increase of structural transfers for some regions of Greece.[8] Luxembourg also required that some conditions be attached to the accession of these two countries because of expected disruptions to the domestic labor market resulting from the influx of cheap labor from the newcomers.

Although several members project relative losses from enlargement, others expect relative gains. In the Eastern enlargement, the aggregate gains accrue from the political and economic stabilization in accession countries, which reduces poverty migration to the West, and the complete abolition of trade barriers and capital controls (Mattli and Plümper 2002, 552–556). The benefits from market integration and political stability are larger for economically advanced states that are geographically close to the acceding states: they gain from enlargement and because they do not receive transfers from the EU, they do not have to worry about diminished access to these funds (Baldwin et al., 1997, Mayhew 2000). These countries have strong incentives to support the admission of the Central and Eastern European (CEE) candidates. All else equal, countries that do not expect relative losses from distributional conflicts should advocate the accession of new applicants.

---

[8] See also Chapter 7 for the debates on the Integrated Mediterranean Programs (IMP).

The calculus of EU enlargement 63

I have previously developed a formal model of distributional conflicts in the EU enlargement process (Schneider 2007). Here, I simplify the results to illustrate the potential for distributional conflict and how it affects EU members' evaluation of enlargement; interested readers are encouraged to read the original article. The member's utility function incorporates the benefits from cooperation and policy harmonization as well as the budgetary and political costs. In other words, it models the gains and losses from EU membership that I outlined in the substantive discussion above. We can now formally represent the heterogeneity of preferences when members are exposed to distributional conflicts in a given policy area.

Figure 4.1 shows how the utility of EU members changes when more states join the Union.[9] The number of acceding states is on the *x*-axis, and the resulting payoff to EU members is on the *y*-axis. Note that this figure is for illustration purposes only: I have considerably simplified the model. First, I divided EU members into recipients of the European Agricultural Guidance and Guarantee Funds (EAGGF) under the Common Agricultural Policies (CAP) and recipients of the European

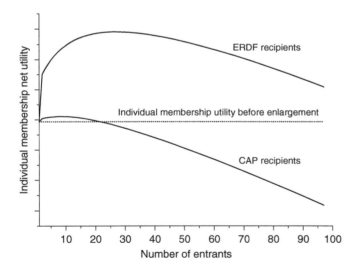

Fig. 4.1 The impact of enlargement on EU member states.

[9] See Schneider (2007, 87–93) for the parameter values used in this example.

Reconstruction and Development Funds (ERDF). Second, I assumed that applicants become CAP beneficiaries. As a result, the utility of a member that is a CAP beneficiary will be different from the utility of a member that is not a CAP recipient. Given these assumptions, we can investigate the consequences of accession while holding everything else constant. The dotted line represents the utility of EU members before enlargement. This is their reservation value because this is the payoff they expect to receive if widening does not occur. When the admission of new states results in an expected utility below their reservation value, EU members reject enlargement.

The graph illustrates the differential effect of expansion on members' utilities. All EU members strictly benefit from adding up to seven new states although the gains to states that do not receive EAGGF subsidies are larger and increase faster. Adding more states decreases the benefits to countries that receive direct payments under the CAP, and at twenty-two new members, their expected utility from enlargement becomes less than their reservation value. From this point on, these members would block any further enlargement. Even though the rising number of contributors would have a positive effect on the common budget, this is insufficient to offset deleterious effect of a rising number of recipients. As a result, members eligible for agricultural funds become embroiled in conflict over their distribution.

This example clearly shows why distributional conflicts are important for the outcome of the expansion process. Because enlargement must be approved unanimously in the Council of Ministers, it will fail if any EU member expects to be worse off in the wider Union relative to its current situation. It is true that new member contributions to the common budget can countervail the decline in benefits. However, in the Eastern enlargement all CEE candidates were relatively poor, which means that they would become net recipients of structural *and* agricultural transfers. As a result, existing beneficiaries of EU transfers expected relative losses despite the political and economic benefits.

As discussed in Chapter 2, the accession of some candidates will not cause distributional conflict. In the Eastern enlargement talks, Germany was much less concerned about the impact the accession of Malta and Cyprus would have on its domestic labor market. Both countries were small, economically advanced, and enjoyed low rates of unemployment. Wages were higher than in any other candidate state. In fact, they nearly reached the EU average, and exceeded gross wages in Portugal, Greece, and Spain. With the exception of Slovenia, all other applicants were far below the European average. All of this made mass labor migration from Malta or Cyprus very unlikely, which meant that their accession posed no threat to the domestic labor markets of current EU members.

To summarize, despite its overall positive political and economic effects, the widening of the EU often triggers distributional conflicts among member states. Because enlargement requires the unanimous approval of current members, potential losers can always block the admission of new states if gains are not redistributed to compensate them for their losses. Hence, distributional conflict can be a serious hindrance to successful enlargement. The goal of enlargement talks, then, is to locate a Pareto-efficient agreement that would ensure that nobody is worse off after expansion. Since EU members that expect net gains already support enlargement and a candidate's application for membership is a strong signal that it expects to benefit from joining the Union, these negotiations naturally center on improving the expected payoffs for the enlargement laggards. The question then becomes how to increase their benefits sufficiently – so they expect at least as much as their reservation value – while simultaneously ensuring that this is not prohibitively costly to the supporters and the candidates.

4.2.2 The resolution of distributional conflicts

So far, we have considered the conditions under which some EU members would prefer blocking enlargement to the unconditional admission of candidates. Because they are faced with the prospect of suffering relative losses, they would refuse to grant full membership rights to the applicant. Without redistribution of enlargement gains from relative winners within or without the Union to themselves, these relative losers would not agree to widening at all.

Intra-Union redistribution occurs when members expecting net gains from enlargement transfer some of their benefits to members expecting net losses. The "drivers of enlargement" can defray some of the expansion costs by contributing more to the common budget or agreeing to smaller transfer payments. Alternatively, would-be members may be asked to shoulder a disproportionate share of the burden. If they agree to limitations on their membership rights in the area in which there is distributional conflict, then the "brakemen of enlargement" may approve their accession. In the area of CAP, the first option would have current members raising their budget contributions so that net recipients of direct agricultural payments would receive the same amounts after enlargement. The second option would qualify access to these funds for newcomers either by making them ineligible to receive any payments or restricting the amounts available to them. Clearly, if new members have only limited claims to agricultural subsidies, then the main EAGGF recipients among the current members would not have to worry about losing their benefits in that policy area. If applicants are at least as well off inside the Union even with these restrictions as they would be if they remained outside, then Pareto-optimality would be achieved. In that case, they would still be willing to join and because former losers would not veto their accession, enlargement would succeed.

Historically, even though EU member states have used both options to help enlargement along, saddling newcomers with the costs tends to happen more frequently. Still, there have been several occasions in which the "drivers of enlargement" inside the Union have given up some of the gains to resolve distributional conflicts. For example, in 1984 the UK requested, and received, a rebate from its contributions to the common budget. The problem was that the UK had never received much of the CAP, which traditionally claim's the lion's share of common spending, even though it had been one of the poorest countries in the Union. The reason was that only a small fraction of the British population worked in the agricultural sector, and most farms were large relative to those in other EU countries. The negotiated compensation, the "British rebate," was to return two-thirds of the amount by which United Kingdom (UK) contributions to the budget exceeded EU expenditure returning to the Kingdom.

Another example involves the Common Structural Policies (CSP). The ERDF facilitates the adjustment of relatively under-developed European regions to the rest of the Union. Only poor and structurally weak regions are eligible for these funds. During the second Mediterranean expansion, the EU agreed to establish the Integrated Mediterranean Funds, mostly to compensate Greece for the decrease in structural aid it would receive after the accession of Spain and Portugal. The intra-Union redistribution occurred when Germany agreed to raise its long-term budgetary contributions to finance agricultural subsidies and the ERDF. Generally, budgetary expansion were quite common before *Agenda 2000*.

This changed in 1999 at the Berlin Summit when the Council of Ministers voted to cap the budget and reform the CAP and the CSP. The resulting *Agenda 2000* provides for a decline in total appropriations from €92 billion in 2000 to €90.6 billion in 2006, and a budget cap of 1.27% of the EU Gross National Product (GNP).[10] The spending on the CAP declined to €41.2 billion in 2006. The reform drastically curtailed the possibilities for intra-Union redistribution of enlargement costs, which had far-reaching implications for accession negotiations. Consequently, distributional conflict has gotten much more acute. To give just a few examples, when the structurally weakest EU members (Spain, Greece, Italy, and Portugal) threatened to delay Eastern enlargement unless they were compensated for the expected loss in structural aid, the Union responded by shifting the burden on the CEE candidates. The Eastern Europeans would receive about €137 per capita in 2006, considerably less than the €231 per capita structural aid that would go to Spain, Greece, and Portugal (EU Commission 2003). The same happened with the Common Agricultural Policies: New members would not receive full subsidies upon accession. Instead, these would be phased-in over ten years, starting at 25% of the transfers they would be entitled to (EU Accession Treaty, 2002).

Distributional conflicts emerged in policy areas unrelated to the budget as well. For instance, restrictions were requested, and granted, for the free movement of labor in every enlargement wave except the second Northern enlargement in 1995. When the UK joined the European Community (EC) in 1992, it was forced to agree to limitations on the free movement of its workers to the Netherlands, Belgium, France, Germany, and Luxembourg. The Netherlands requested the transitional period because it feared a large influx of workers from the UK, which was still relatively weak economically. British GDP was about 72% of the EU average by the time of accession. The countries that were most attractive to British labor because of short distances and other socio-economic factors were precisely the ones that were granted exceptions. A similar pattern obtained in the two Southern enlargement waves. All three Mediterranean countries had to accept

---

[10] EU Commission (1997a, 1997b, 1997c, 1999).

limited access to the European labor market for up to seven years. By the same token, Germany and Austria strongly opposed the immediate liberalization of the labor markets in the Eastern enlargement. In that case, they secured protection for their domestic labor markets for a transitional period.

These brief examples illustrate how EU enlargement negotiations focus on attaining Pareto-efficiency, and show some of the possible outcomes of the enlargement process. The most straightforward expansion happens when there is no objection to granting newcomers full membership rights. States accede to the Union unconditionally when no subset of current members expects a net loss from enlargement. This happened when Austria, Finland, and Sweden joined in 1995 (there were some minor tensions about the Common Fisheries Policies).

If some members do expect relative losses, then members and candidates try to negotiate the allocation of enlargement gains. Expansion succeeds when newcomers agree to qualifications to their membership rights, when the "drivers of enlargement" defray some of the costs for the losers, or both. The specifics of the outcome depend on the bargaining power of the participants. Typically, candidates have unattractive outside options and this puts them at a disadvantage at the bargaining table. Consequently, they are forced to agree to differentiated membership rights. As long as this discrimination does not make joining the Union worse than the reservation value of remaining outside, it may be possible to achieve Pareto-optimality.

Discriminatory membership cannot ensure Pareto-optimality if the most severe discrimination an applicant is prepared to accept while still retaining its willingness to joint the Union is insufficient to meet the reservation value of the "brakemen." In that case, EU widening will succeed if, and only if, the supporters of enlargement within the Union agree to redistribute some of their gains. The Eastern expansion – the integration of CEE members into the Common Agricultural Policies in particular – is a good example of this mixed strategy. The ten new members will receive a disproportionately small share of EAGGF subsidies for ten years after their accession. For their part, current members compromised on a reform of the CAP that reduces the costs incurred by net contributors to the budget.

It is worth noting that sometimes it is not possible to locate a Pareto-efficient deal. In these cases, enlargement must fail, as it has on several

The calculus of EU enlargement 69

occasions. Norway and Switzerland have not yet managed to negotiate a deal with the EU that would also be acceptable to their citizens. Both have opted to remain outside the Union. Norway, for example, wanted to keep its twelve-mile fishing limit indefinitely. The government did accept a transitional period of ten years but the citizens found this unsatisfactory, and rejected enlargement in a referendum (53.5% to 46.5%). The EU itself rejected Bulgaria and Romania in 2004, and only admitted them after they successfully fulfilled all membership criteria.

In general, all else equal, whenever the "brakemen" condition their approval for widening on the receipt of side-payments, the probability that newcomers will join the Union unconditionally declines. At the same time, supporters of enlargement among the EU members have no wish to see prospective membership for a newcomer degraded so much that it abandons its application. The more important enlargement is to relative winners inside the Union, the more likely are they to redistribute some of their gains to compensate the relative losers. By similar logic, the more important enlargement is to the candidate, the more likely it is to get saddled with a disproportionate share of these costs as the price of joining the Union.

4.2.3 The transitional nature of discrimination

Even though there have been many instances in which applicants were forced to accept some restrictions of their membership rights, the Union has never asked for permanent limitations. There are several reasons why this should be so and why even temporary qualifications of these rights over the so-called transitional periods have been sufficient to tilt the balance of costs of benefits in favor of enlargement. To begin with, differentiated membership has been transitory because permanent derogations are incompatible with EU law. Legally, EU members cannot forever restrict the rights of new members to avoid the costs of widening. Of course, candidates would probably be much less keen on joining the Union if there was no prospect of acquiring full membership rights at some point after accession.

On the other hand, even temporary differentiation can be enough for governments that discount the future. To see that, suppose that some EU member believes enlargement is so unattractive that its expected payoff from the unconditional accession of a candidate is less than its reservation value. Logically, this member will reject unconditional expansion. Suppose now that the candidate offers to accept some temporary restrictions (e.g., phasing-in of agricultural subsidies). This increases the member's expected payoff from the conditional accession over the transitional period. If the period is long enough, the costly grant of full membership rights is far in the future. Because the government cares more about the short and medium term, the overall expected payoff from accession with transitional qualifications may exceed the reservation value. Under these circumstances, this government will agree to admit the new member and the Union will negotiate differentiated membership over the required transitional period. In general, when the expected benefits from enlargement are lower than the expected costs from unconditional accession but higher than the expected costs from discriminatory accession, then candidates will be given differentiated membership and enlargement will succeed.[11]

The underlying logic is straightforward: when newcomers are discriminated against, enlargement benefits accrue immediately but full costs need only be paid after the transitional period. Even when EU members discount the future only moderately, the expected gains will increase and the expected losses will decline. For instance, restricting the access of CEE member states to the EAGGF subsidies for a decade allows France and other beneficiaries of the CAP to obtain all the gains from enlargement over that decade while deferring the costs far into the future. Governments have limited time horizons, which leads them to overvalue their short-term payoff. It is because of this that the gradual phasing-in of full membership rights can be sufficient to buy off the "brakemen" of enlargement.

There are other reasons why transitory discrimination may be sufficient to compensate relative losers. To begin with, EU members do not necessarily expect that they will remain losers over time. Accession to the EU requires substantial policy changes, such as the elimination of tariffs and non-tariff barriers within the Union, the adoption of the common external tariff, and whatever else is necessary to implement the free movement of goods, services, people, and capital. Baldwin et al., (1997) conservatively estimate that the CEE members will experience a 1.5% increase in real income as a result of their accession to

---

[11] See also Plümper and Schneider (2007, 575) for a graphical depiction how phasing-in of membership rights affects EU members' calculus of enlargement.

the EU. Breuss (2002) projects that by 2009 real GDP of the Czech Republic will gain approximately 5% to 6%, while that of Hungary and Poland will see increases of 8% to 9%. Most studies predict that per capita income in old and new members will converge, investments will increase sharply, and production will shift from large primary sectors to industry and tertiary sectors.

The European Commission assessed the impact of Eastern enlargement on new member states two years after accession (EU Commission 2006b). Its findings largely bear out these expectations: the new members made significant progress in implementing the *acquis communautaire* in national legislation; economic and legislative convergence occurred in most areas. Economic growth was approximately 3.8% per annum between 1997 and 2005. The opening of the financial sector to foreign investment, the substantial regulatory reforms, and the improved modes of supervision all resulted in efficiency gains for the financial system.[12]

Progress also occurred in areas where conflicts between current and future members had been most intense: the liberalization of labor markets and the agricultural sector. Barely two years into membership, labor market conditions improved drastically in the new member states. Employment reversed its downwards trend in 2004, and then expanded by 1.5% the following year; the average unemployment rate dropped by 0.8% over that period (EU Commission 2006b, 53).[13] The inclusion of the newcomers into the framework of the EU Social Agenda provided further opportunities for improvement because the Agenda promotes employment, social cohesion, and the modernization of the European social model. These factors are all relevant in estimating the expected migration from the new members. These positive results caused some members to revise their projections, which lowered their estimate of the threat CEE workers posed for domestic labor markets. This substantially reduced the incentive to clamor

---

[12] The EU Commission has drawn positive conclusions about the impact of enlargement on acceding states for past enlargement rounds as well. The notable exception is Greece, which experienced a decline in wealth over time. According to comparative studies, this is most likely the result of "inappropriate fiscal policies and strategies to attract foreign direct investment (e.g., re-nationalisation of public companies in the 80s)" (EU Commission 2006b, 47).

[13] These estimates largely correspond to the Commission's forecasts in 2001 (EU Commission 2001).

against labor market liberalization. In 2006, Greece, Spain, Portugal, and Finland decided to lift their restrictions on the free movement of labor, while Belgium, Denmark, France, Italy, the Netherlands, and Luxembourg weakened theirs.

Enlargement has also led to re-structuring and efficiency gains in areas covered by the Common Agricultural Policies. The major EAGGF beneficiaries expected the Greek accession in 1981 to increase their short-term costs, and managed to secure their position with a five-year transitional period for the CAP. However, Greece was already on its way to convergence with the EU simply from being associated with the Community. The size of its agricultural sector had been 51.7% in 1961 but had dropped by 9.6% by 1975. After joining the Union, policy reforms decreased the number of farmers and increased agricultural prices to EU levels by the mid 1980s, well before the termination of the transitional phase (Pezaros 2004, Chatzopoulou 2006). Although still far above average, the size of the agricultural sector shrank from 32% in the accession year to 15.8% in 2002.

The developments in the agricultural sector after the Eastern enlargement fit the overall trend. EU membership has caused considerable convergence among old and new member states. The share of agricultural Gross Value Added (GVA) in GDP has declined by 1% per annum, and the share of the labor force employed in the sector has gone down by 1.8%, while average real incomes have gone up by 70% (EU Commission 2006b, 100ff.). These changes loom large in the calculations of direct payments for member states. The shrinking of the agricultural sector decreases the burden for the CAP, and ameliorates conflicts about the distribution of agricultural funds among the main beneficiaries.[14]

Another reason why transitory discrimination may be sufficient to compensate relative losers is that political leaders in EU member states expect to stay in power only for a limited time. The debates about the liberalization of the labor market reveal that EU governments mostly worry about their domestic audiences while negotiating the terms of accession. Labor market restrictions were imposed at the accession of

[14] The increase in the average income amply demonstrates a basic dilemma for the Union. On one hand it promotes economic development and growth. On the other hand, it gives farmers an incentive to stay in the primary sector. This directly increases direct payments through the CAP, which lowers competitiveness and intensifies distributional conflicts among EU member states.

Portugal and Spain to protect Luxembourg. The seven-year transition period was abandoned when the expected mass migration did not take place. The forecasts about the Eastern enlargement were generally positive except for the short-term disruptions expected in Germany and Austria. The German government insisted on a transitional period in large part because it was facing re-election and was particularly sensitive to the widespread fears of German workers. In securing some protection for the domestic labor market, the German government was less concerned about potential (and unlikely) long-term costs than about obtaining voter support in the short run. These political calculations are based on two assumptions. First, voters tend to discount the past when assessing government performance. That is, decisions made a long time ago do not matter as much as recent policies.[15] In that respect, even though labor market liberalization was a major topic in the present electoral campaign, the German government did not expect it to be that important for future elections because of the encouraging migration forecasts. Second, many politicians who were in power when the EU admitted the CEE countries have lost elections since. If enlargement causes frictions in the long-term, it will be their successors that will have to deal with the electoral consequences.

To summarize, EU members do not demand permanent derogations from the *acquis communautaire* because transitional periods are sufficient to alter the balance of costs and benefits in favor of enlargement. They are sufficient because governments tend to discount the future, the economic and political structural reforms tend to decrease the expected costs, and political parties in power tend to overemphasize short-term strategic considerations.[16]

4.3 Hypotheses on expansion and differentiated membership

We can derive several testable implications from this theory of differentiated membership. EU members that expect net losses from enlargement should request some sort of compensation in the accession negotiations. The probability that some member will

---

[15] Drazen (2000) provides an accessible introduction to political-economy accounts of voting behavior.
[16] I should note that discounting future losses may not magically make transitional periods Pareto-efficient. Perhaps the best example is the problematic Turkish accession to the Union and possible permanent derogations from the common *acquis*.

oppose unconditional expansion depends on the likelihood of post-enlargement distributional conflict or negative consequences for domestic markets. In other words, members that receive large agricultural subsidies will oppose the unconditional accession of countries that would also need large chunks of these funds; current net recipients of structural transfers from the EU will oppose the unconditional accession of relatively large and comparatively poor countries with underdeveloped infrastructure; countries with high unemployment will oppose the unconditional accession of relatively poor neighbors with abundant cheap labor. When such conflicts arise, the relative losers of enlargement will delay accession talks and demand some compensation.

Hypothesis 1 *All else equal, EU members are more likely to demand discrimination against a new member (or some other compensation) in a given policy area if they expect that its accession will cause distributional conflict in that area.*

If distributional conflicts arise, then the likelihood of unconditional enlargement will decline, *ceteris paribus*. This happens because relative losers will not agree to accession without being adequately compensated. Because enlargement must be approved unanimously, failure to redistribute the gains in favor of the "brakemen" will prolong accession negotiations and may even cause their breakdown. The theory states that the resolution of this conflict will involve some type of redistribution between the relative winners and the relative losers. There are at least two general strategies EU members may use: either the applicant accepts discriminatory membership rights or the "drivers of enlargement" transfer some of their gains to the losers. If neither strategy can achieve a Pareto-optimal deal, enlargement will not succeed. Therefore, the probability that a candidate accedes with full membership rights decreases in the presence of distributional conflict.

Hypothesis 2 *All else equal, a candidate is less likely to receive full membership rights when some EU member expects relative losses from enlargement because of distributional conflict in a some policy field.*

At the same time, distributional conflict will increase the odds that acceding states will have to bear some of the costs of enlargement by accepting a phasing-in of their membership rights.

Hypothesis 3 *All else equal, a candidate is more likely to receive discriminatory membership rights when some EU member expects relative losses from enlargement because of distributional conflict in some policy field.*

Finally, even though the theory focuses on the differentiation of membership rights for acceding states, the redistribution of enlargement gains *within* the Union should lower the probability that these states will be discriminated against.

Hypothesis 4 *All else equal, a candidate is less likely to receive discriminatory membership rights when EU members agree to redistribute enlargement gains and losses within the Union.*

The more the "drivers of enlargement" value the accession of a candidate, and the more desirable the applicant's outside options, the greater the odds that they will coordinate on some intra-Union redistribution to keep the applicant interested in EU membership. For instance, the EU agreed to increase the area in which the Common Fisheries Policies would apply to avoid the breakdown of negotiations with Norway and Ireland in the early 1970s. It is not just rich applicants that have valuable outside options.[17] EU accession was quite controversial in Greece, where the left-wing opposition boycotted the ratification of the treaty.[18] This and the resulting threat of political instability placed Greece in a relatively strong bargaining position even though only France actively supported its membership. Greece managed to avoid transitional periods of twelve years for the Free Movement of Workers and eight years for the Common Agricultural Policies.

---

[17] The EC did not accept the EFTA states' demand for permanent derogations from the *acquis* in several policy fields.

[18] The treaty was ratified by a majority but 104 of the 300 deputies were absent (Nicholson and East 1987).

4.4 Conclusion

This chapter offers a rationalist account of how EU members and applicant states use accession negotiations to achieve enlargement. The continuing widening and deepening of the EU showcases the far-reaching benefits of membership. Nevertheless, the gains and losses from EU expansion are distributed unevenly among EU member states. Under certain conditions, political and distributional conflict decreases the value of expanded membership for some members. Because enlargement has to be approved unanimously, such conflict can become a serious obstacle to the success of accession negotiations. The literature has not given a satisfactory explanation why enlargement succeeds *despite* distributional conflicts.

The theoretical model in this chapter begins with this observation and provides for several mechanisms through which accession talks can influence the outcome of the enlargement process. If the accession of a candidate triggers distributional conflict or causes political tensions within the Union, then the opponents and supporters of expansion have to resolve these conflicts before accession can take place. The theory assumes that EU members and candidates bargain over the allocation of enlargement gains. When aggregate gains are positive but some members expect net losses, granting newcomers differentiated membership rights is one way in which losers can be induced to agree to expansion.

In the following chapters, I subject the theoretical hypotheses to empirical tests. I study the conditions under which EU members demand transitional periods for the full application of the common *acquis* to the disadvantage of acceding states, and the conditions under which current and new members agree to implement discriminatory measures.

5 | EU enlargement, distributional conflicts, and the demand for compensation

European Union members and candidates must agree on the implementation of thirty-one common EU policies over the course of enlargement. Most of the time, negotiations on individual chapters go through smoothly. Occasionally, however, an EU member would deliberately delay accession negotiations by vetoing the provisional closure of a particular chapter. The most common reason for such delaying tactics is the need to secure some derogation from the *acquis communautaire*. As I showed for the Eastern enlargement in 2004 (Chapter 2), EU members and candidates sometimes compromise on the full applicability of the common *acquis* by granting only restricted membership rights to newcomers.

I now analyze the five successful EU enlargement rounds prior to 2004 in an attempt to assess empirically the correlation between membership applications, distributional conflicts, and enlargement outcomes. There are three specific questions that I investigate in this and the next two chapters of this study:

(1) Why do European Union (EU) members oppose the unconditional accession of some applicants, or, more specifically, why do they demand that new members be given restricted rights in some policy areas? (This chapter.)
(2) If distributional conflicts arise during the accession negotiations, how are they resolved so enlargement can succeed? (Chapter 6.)
(3) What is the relationship between the imposition of discriminatory membership and the intra-Union redistribution of enlargement costs? (Chapter 7.)

The separate examination of each stage of the accession process should provide a fairly strong test of the theory in Chapter 4. I begin with the analysis of the origins of distributional conflicts and the effect they have on strategy choices of members during the enlargement talks. I then analyze how EU members and applicants cope with the delaying tactics of the relative losers from enlargement, and study how it affects the negotiated outcomes. In Chapter 6, I focus on the probability that acceding states are forced to agree to discriminatory membership rights. In Chapter 7, I go one step further to examine the trade-off between discriminatory membership and the redistribution of enlargement costs among Union members.

To test the first component of my theory, I conduct an empirical study of the emergence of distributional conflicts in three policy areas: the Common Agricultural Policies (CAP), the Common Structural Policies (CSP), and the Free Movement of Workers (FMW). Recall that hypothesis 1 requires me to test whether EU members are more likely to oppose the unconditional accession of a new state when they expect disruptions of the common market or distributional conflicts in some policy area. The hypothesis is stated in fairly general terms and the sources of conflict normally differ across issue areas. For example, how much a state receives from the European Agricultural Guidance and Guarantee Funds (EAGGF), and indeed whether it receives anything at all, depends on the size of its agricultural sector, and its agricultural production, among other things. Generally, this will have very little to do with policies that affect, say, the free movement of workers. It is therefore necessary to look at each policy area separately.

I use the distributional rules within the Union to identify the factors that determine the gains and losses current members and candidates should expect from enlargement in a given policy area. I then study whether members that expect accession to be relatively costly are more likely to resort to delaying tactics in the negotiations. The policy area-specific theoretical predictions are as follows: (a) The accession of countries with large and inefficient agricultural sectors should be very costly to members that receive large agricultural subsidies CAP; (b) The accession of poor countries with underdeveloped infrastructure should be very costly to members eligible for structural subsidies (CSP); (c) The accession of countries with an abundant low-paid labor force should be very costly to members with high unemployment, especially when they are geographically close to the newcomers (FMW).[1]

The empirical analysis takes these predictions and tests whether the demand for discriminatory membership is related to such fears. The

---

[1] As I discuss in the following sections, the EU Commission conducted a study to assess the potential of labor market disruptions and found that members that expect high unemployment were generally opposed to the labor market liberalization for their relatively poor neighbors.

main results demonstrate that a member will demand that a newcomer be restricted in its access to agricultural and structural transfers when both parties are important beneficiaries of these funds. Analogously, a member that expects serious disruptions in the domestic labor market will oppose the full liberalization of the labor markets for the newcomer. Overall, the expectation of distributional conflict in a given policy area drives the demand for differentiated membership in that area. France, for instance, refused to allow the newcomers from Central and Eastern Europe full access to direct payments in the CAP because it was afraid that its own subsidy would decline precipitously. There are no (or negligibly little) spillover effects across issue areas. Whether a member or a candidate is a main CAP beneficiary depends on the size and efficiency of its agricultural sector. This does not affect the expectation about likely negative consequences from labor market integration.

These findings have significant implications for the study of EU enlargement. The fundamental idea is that EU enlargement does not affect EU members equally and we must distinguish between relative winners and relative losers from enlargement. The differences between these two groups then determine the negotiation outcomes. Members that expect net losses from enlargement in some policy area oppose the accession of states without some qualifications of their rights in that area. In the extreme, they can threaten to veto the unconditional accession altogether. The negotiations among EU members as well as between the EU and the candidates then proceed along those conflict fault lines. In Chapter 6 I show that either EU members and applicant states resolve these conflicts or else widening fails. Even without going into a deeper analysis of enlargement outcomes, these results are sufficient to establish the importance of member state heterogeneity for the fate of expansion.

5.1 Research design

The theory predicts that the expected utility of expansion for some EU members will depend on the characteristics of a specific candidate. For instance, a member's demand for differentiated rights in labor policy for a given candidate depends on that member's assessment of the likely disruptions of its domestic labor market that would be caused by extending full liberalization to that particular candidate. The theory distinguishes not only among different EU members, but also among different applicants. For example, Germany and Austria, but not Spain and the UK, sought to protect their labor markets from the Central and Eastern European (CEE) candidate states, and no one sought discrimination against Malta or Cyprus. This implies that we should look at each pair of states composed of one member and one candidate, or a *member–candidate dyad*.

Furthermore, the theoretical model postulates that the causes of distributional conflict differ across issue areas. For instance, the expected costs and benefits from enlargement when it comes to agricultural subsidies depend on the sizes of the agricultural sectors of the member and the candidate as well as the amount of funds the member receives prior to the accession of the new country. These factors do not influence the expected severity of labor market disruptions because the latter are mostly determined by migration pressures arising from anticipated social costs caused by the free movement of labor. This means that we should look at each policy area separately.

The most appropriate unit of analysis, therefore, is the member–candidate dyad in a specific policy area, the *policy dyad*, for each enlargement round. I look at all enlargement rounds prior to 2007.[2] There are 18 dyads in the first enlargement round, 9 in the second, 20 in the third, 36 in the fourth, and 150 in the fifth, for a total of $N = 233$ dyads per policy area.

I study three different areas: Common Agricultural Policies, Common Structural Policies, and the Free Movement of Workers. These are ideal cases for analysis because they tend to be among the most conflict-ridden. As I discussed in Chapter 4, the common EU policies vary in their proneness to conflicts. For some policy areas, expansion may make no difference to some members or may even be entirely beneficial.[3] For other policy areas, however, expansion affects members unequally and may thus provoke distributional conflicts between the net beneficiaries and the relative losers. The three policy areas I examine fall in that category. It should be noted that it is not *necessary* for distributional conflicts to occur. The fate of enlargement is only jeopardized when one or more members expect net losses in some policy area after the accession of some candidate. Most EU policies are not

---

[2] This excludes Bulgaria and Romania. Furthermore, Norway, Switzerland, and Malta had to be dropped because of insufficient data.

[3] The economic theory of clubs refers to such policy areas as neutral or complementary in compensation (Buchanan 1965).

subject to debate during negotiations and do not present obstacles to enlargement. Serious distributional conflicts only happened in the Free Movement of Workers, the Common Agricultural Policies, Transport Policies, the Common Fisheries Policies, and the Common Structural Policies.[4] But even there, it was not the case that all EU members demanded compensation or that all candidates were subjected to discriminatory measures. There is significant variation in the dependent variable across policy fields, dyads, and enlargement rounds.

The most conflict-riddled policy areas are the hardest test cases for the theory because the odds of distributional conflicts are short and the theory distinguishes between states that accede unconditionally and states that were forced to accept differentiated membership. If the empirical analysis fails to uncover a positive correlation between a member's request for discrimination and its expectation of serious distributional conflict, then my theory would not be supported. Instead, the alternative theory of asymmetric interdependence – the claim that EU members deliberately exploit their bargaining leverage to maximize their own gains – would be supported. Recall that my theory predicts that because the accession of new states affects current members in varying degrees, only members that expect relative losses from enlargement should demand compensation.

5.1.1 Dependent variables

For each policy dyad, the dependent variable measures whether the EU member officially requested discrimination against the candidate in that policy area. As discussed in Chapter 2, distributional conflicts become apparent when accession negotiations focus on the implementation of the common *acquis*. For each of the thirty-one chapters of the common law, the EU and the applicant bargain over possible temporary deviations from the rules. I traced the accession negotiations for each policy dyad to see whether the EU member demanded transitional periods for the specific candidate and/or some other form of compensation. Usually, such demands are made openly in public. Sometimes, however, the reports of the Council summits or the EU Parliament,

---

[4] I exclude Transport Policies because Austria was the only country that demanded and received special treatment there. I also do not analyze the Common Fisheries Policies because I could not obtain enough information to code the dependent variable.

among others, record the tensions occasioned by accession. To collect all the necessary information, I conducted a systematic content analysis of documents from the EU Parliament, summaries from the relevant EU Council summits, reports of the EU Commission, various scholarly secondary sources, and several official interviews. In addition, I searched the international newspapers in the *Lexis-Nexis* database. I analyzed these documents and recorded all information about EU member positions during accession negotiations for each of the three policy areas.[5]

The dichotomous dependent variable then summarizes whether a specific EU member ever made an official request for differentiation of rights in a given policy area for a specific candidate or demanded compensation because of expected hardship due to that candidate's accession to the Union. For the CAP, the analysis is limited to EAGGF subsidies, and discrimination means that the newcomer is denied full access to agricultural subsidies. For the CSP, discrimination means that the newcomer is denied the full amount of structural aid it would normally be eligible for. For the FMW, discrimination means that labor from the newcomer is not permitted to take employment freely or receive social benefits in a member state. For each policy dyad, the dependent variable takes a value of 1 if such a demand was ever officially made, and 0 otherwise.

Over the five enlargement rounds, EU members requested qualification of candidate rights for one of the three policy areas in about a third of the cases. With the exception of the Northern enlargement, the probability that EU members would demand some form of discrimination was high and steadily increased from one enlargement to the next. In the first Northern enlargement to include the UK, Ireland and

---

[5] The EU Parliament compiles information about the positions on expansion of EU members and candidates (European Parliament 1999). The most important secondary sources are Hasenpflug (1977), Wallace (1978), Tsoukalis (1981), Donges (1982, 1983), Nicholson and East (1987), Avery (1994), Francisco (1995), Deubner (1997), Preston (1997), Burda (1998), Hinteregger (1998), Burda (1999), Böri and Brücker (2000, 2001), Böri and Terell (2002), Grosse Hüttmann (2004), Heijdra and Keuschnigg (2000), Heijdra et al. (2002), Heijman (2001), Mayhew, (2000, 2002, 2003), Organa (2002), Price (1999), Redmond (2000). Among the people officially interviewed for various newspapers were Fischer (1998), Persson (1999), and Kok (2001). *Lexis-Nexis* includes over 11,000 news sources from all over the world. I used keyword searches to find the relevant articles.

Denmark, members opposed unconditional membership in only 1% of the cases. This jumped to 23% in the enlargement talks with Greece, which doubled to 46% in the second Mediterranean enlargement, and then rose again to 75% in the Eastern enlargement round. Despite the clear overall trend, there is significant variation among member state behavior across rounds. Whereas Luxembourg requested protection of its labor market when Spain and Portugal applied for membership, it did not do so in the Eastern enlargement. In the latter case it was Germany and Austria that provided the strongest impetus behind these demands. In general, CAP is the area where discrimination demands are most common. Members have sought to limit candidate access to agricultural subsidies in nearly 90% of the cases. In comparison, requests for discrimination occurred in about 50% of the cases when it came to European Reconstruction and Development Funds (ERDF/ESF), and only 16% of the cases when it came to labor market liberalization.

5.1.2 Model specification

The linear multivariate regression model is inappropriate when the dependent variable is dichotomous. Using some variant of the common Ordinary Least Squares (OLS) model would violate several assumptions that are required to ensure that the estimates are unbiased and consistent.[6] The *probit* model offers the proper specification that accounts for the S-shaped relationship between the explanatory variables and the probability of distributional conflict (Bliss 1935).[7]

Before specifying the model, it will be useful to introduce some simplifying notation. Some explanatory variables (e.g., EU budget contributions) are specific to the EU member state in the dyad, others (e.g., regime type) are specific to the candidate state, and yet

---

[6] Linear regression models will also produce out-of-bounds predictions for the dependent variable. Long (1997) discusses how the assumptions of the linear model are violated when the underlying relationship is not linear.

[7] An alternative to the *probit* is the *logit*, in which the logits of the binomial probabilities are modeled as a linear function of the explanatory variables. I estimated a logistic regression and the results do not differ from the *probit* findings. As a robustness check, I also estimated a rare-events *logit* model, *relogit*, as recommended by King and Zeng (2001) for cases where the dependent variable takes one of the values far more frequently than the other. As expected, the standard errors were slightly larger but the substantive results remain the same.

others (e.g., distance between capital cities) are specific to the dyad itself. Let M denote the $N \times m$ vector of explanatory variables that are member-specific, K denote the $N \times k$ vector of variables that are candidate-specific, and D denote the $N \times d$ vector of variables that are dyad-specific. The respective coefficient vectors are then denoted by β, γ, and δ. Finally, let $z \in \{CAP, CSP, FMW\}$ index the policy area for which the equation is being specified. The probability of the demand for discrimination in a policy area is then given by

$$\Pr(Y_z = 1) = \Phi(\alpha_z + \beta_z M_z + \gamma_z K_z + \delta_z D_z).$$

I estimate a separate *probit* model for each policy area.[8] This effectively assumes that the models are independent and requires some further investigation because it might not necessarily be the case. For example, it could be that the demand for compensation in one policy area could have spillover effects in another area. If that is the case, the error terms of the three equations will be correlated. Estimating independent *probit* models would then produce inefficient (but still unbiased) estimates. To deal with that possibility, I estimate a *probit* specification of the Seemingly Unrelated Regression (SURE) model (Cappellari and Jenkins 2003). This allows me to account properly for the possible contemporaneous correlation among the error terms of the three equations (Zellner 1962).[9] In the *probit* specification of SURE, the error terms of the individual *probits* are assumed to be distributed according to the multivariate normal distribution with zero mean and a covariance matrix whose off-diagonal elements represent the correlations between pairs of equations (the diagonal elements are all set to 1). Table A-1 in the appendix shows the results of this estimation. In general, these do not differ much from the estimation results from the independent *probit* specification. In fact, Likelihood Ratio tests do not always support rejection of the null hypothesis of uncorrelated error terms (e.g., model 3). In other words, in some cases it appears that the error terms are not correlated, which implies that the independent *probit* specification is more appropriate. Although the analysis will generally refer to the results of the independent *probit* estimations, I will discuss the differences between specifications whenever appropriate.

---

[8] All estimations performed with Stata 10. The replication data set and all programs are available upon request.
[9] See also Plümper and Schneider (2007) who use alternative estimation techniques to account for correlated errors across equations.

The use of *probit* models also makes interpretation of the coefficients harder. In linear regression models, a change in the independent variable has the same effect on the dependent variable "regardless of the value of that variable at the start of its change and regardless of the level of the other variables in the model" (Long and Freese 2001, 88). In regression models with limited dependent variables, on the other hand, the "effect of a change in a variable depends on the values of all variables in the model and is no longer simply equal to one of the parameters of the model" (Long 1997, 5). Whereas it is still straightforward to interpret the direction and statistical significance of the estimated coefficients, it is much more difficult to assess their substantive effects. To facilitate analysis of these effects, I will generate predicted probabilities for several values of the main explanatory variables while holding the other variables constant at given sample values. I will also provide some predictions the model generates for specific actual cases from the data set. For example, I will look at the prediction for the probability of discrimination in the Free Movement of Labor for the Germany–Cyprus dyad and compare it to the prediction for the Germany–Poland dyad. Such examples also help evaluate how well the models fit the data.

I also assume that the observations are independent across EU member states but not necessarily independent within groups of member states. In other words, if a member delays accession negotiations for some candidate, it might be more likely to demand discrimination against another candidate as well. The regressions account for the potential clustering within groups (Froot 1989, Williams 2000). Finally, I use the robust Huber–White sandwich estimator to control for potential heteroscedasticity across EU members (Huber 1967, 1981, White 1980).

5.2 Free movement of workers

The Free Movement of Workers is guaranteed by Article 39 of the European Community (EC) Treaty. The necessary regulations to implement it are specified in Council Regulation (EEC) No 1612/68 of October 15, 1968 (Official Journal L 257, October 19, 1968). The right to free movement prohibits nationality-based discrimination in employment practices and in determining eligibility of social benefits:

Any national of a Member State is entitled to take up and engage in gainful employment on the territory of another Member State in conformity with the relevant regulations applicable to national workers. He is entitled to the same priority as the nationals of that Member State as regards access to available employment, and to the same assistance as that afforded by the employment offices in that State to their own nationals seeking employment. His recruitment may not be dependent on medical, occupational or other criteria which discriminate on the grounds of nationality.

[... A national of one Member State working in another member state is] entitled to the same social and tax benefits as national workers. A national of one Member State working in another is entitled to equal treatment in respect of the exercise of trade union rights, including the right to vote and and to be eligible for the administration or management posts of a trade union. He may be excluded from the management of bodies under public law and from the exercise of an office under public law. He has the right of eligibility for workers' representative bodies within the undertaking.

Labor migration is costly to EU members when it disturbs their labor markets causing diminishing wages and increasing rates of unemployment (EU Commission 2001, 2). Members expect serious losses from enlargement when migration is likely to trigger social and political tensions. It is therefore important to examine the likelihood of migration itself and the probability that it actually disturbs the domestic labor markets.

5.2.1 Variables and data sources

The variables used to test the relationship between the emergence of distributional conflicts and the probability of discrimination demands must measure the potential for labor migration from a candidate to a member and, more importantly, the likelihood that this migration will create adaptation pressures and high social costs in the member country. There are many studies that forecast labor migration and estimate the probability of market disturbances, especially for the fifth enlargement round.[10] The EU Commission itself summarized and evaluated the most influential forecasts in 2001 (EU Commission 2001). These studies are general and there has never

---

[10] See, *inter alia*, Böri and Brücker (2001), Brücker et al. (2000), EU Commission (2001), Grosse Hüttmann (2004), Heijdra et al. (2002), Herzog (2003), Lejour et al. (2001), and Sinn et al. (2001).

been an attempt to forecast the effect of the accession of a particular candidate on a specific member's labor market. However, the EU Commission did emphasize the factors that increase the potential for migration and market disruptions. I draw on these insights for my dyad-specific empirical analysis.

The income gap between the countries, and the labor market situation in the source and target countries were among the factors the EU Commission considered crucial for migration forecasts. In addition, "geographical proximity, emigration traditions and the existence of ethnic or family networks, ethnic and political problems, cultural and linguistic differences, and expectations about economic and social progress in the home country" were important as well (EU Commission 2001, 7).

It was not possible to find information about the average wages for the candidate countries of the 1972, 1981, and 1986 enlargement rounds. Instead, I use per capita Gross Domestic Product (GDP) in Purchasing Power Standards (PPS) as a suitable alternative. The variable, *Candidate GDP*, measures the applicant's GDP per capita as a percentage of the EU average (EU = 100). It varies considerably from 31% to 130%. Not surprisingly, the two Mediterranean and the Eastern enlargement rounds saw the accession of most economically weak candidates. Still, the Irish GDP was about 55% of the EU average upon accession, and the British GDP in 1973 was roughly the same percentage of the EU average as the Spanish in 1986, as well as the Cypriot and the Slovenian in 2004. Data provided by the statistical office of the EU (Eurostat).

The rates of unemployment in the member state and the candidate country also affect the potential for migration and labor market disruptions. *EU Member Unemployment* and *Candidate Unemployment* measure the share of the workforce in the respective country that is currently unemployed. Southern countries seem to be afflicted the worst. Spain's unemployment rate, for example, never fell below 10%. In the mid 1990s when the Northern European countries applied for EU membership, the country had to cope with an unemployment rate of over 18%. Data from Eurostat.

Other factors also influence migration and the pressure for social adaptation (EU Commission 2001, Sinn et al. 2001). The mass influx of workers becomes more likely if there is already a network of nationals from the same country in the target state. For example, the existence of such networks in Luxembourg (over 30% of foreigners were Portuguese) increased that country's incentive to seek labor market protection during the negotiations over the accession of Spain and Portugal. Unfortunately, it is not generally possible to obtain nationality data about the foreigners in member states. As an approximation, I control for the overall number of foreigners instead. The variable *EU Member Share of Foreigners* measures the fraction of the EU member's population that is composed of foreigners. The data show that despite considerable variation in the share of foreigners across members, Germany and France have always been most attractive to migrants. Data from Eurostat and OECD (2004).

A member country that neighbors a candidate is more severely affected by likely migrations. The variable *Distance Between Capitals* takes into account geographical proximity by measuring the distance, in thousands of kilometers, between capital cities of the two dyad members. This is admittedly a crude measure of migration propensity. Other relevant factors would be the costs of travel, the existence of a separating body of water, and so on. Data from John Haveman and the *International Trade Data* web site.

Workers are also more likely to emigrate if the industrial sector in their home country is large (EU Commission 2001). Immigration of this relatively highly-skilled labor is generally even more worrisome than the migration of low-wage workers. The variables *EU Member Industry Employment* and *Candidate Industry Employment* measure the percentage of workers employed in the respective country's industrial sector. The data reveal a downward trend in industrial sector employment in member states and candidates alike. On the average, between 20 and 30 percent of the workforce is in the industry. The only outlier is the Czech Republic which still employed about 40% of its labor in the industrial sector in 2001. Data from Eurostat.

I also control for several other relevant factors. The variable *EU Member Population Over 65* measures the percent of the EU member's population aged 65 years or older. Ageing populations face serious challenges in maintaining an active workforce. Consequently, when the proportion of old people is high, the country should be less likely to demand restrictions on the free movement of labor. On the average, EU member countries had populations where over 15% of the people were 65 or older in 2000, and these numbers are expected to rise. Data from Eurostat.

The variable *EU Member Exports to Candidate* captures how important the candidate country is to the EU member in economic terms. It measures the size of exports from the member to the applicant as a percentage of the member's GDP. The higher the exports, the more important is the accession of the candidate to this member because the concomitant decline in transaction costs would be more pronounced. The larger gains from economic integration should decrease the probability of a demand for transitional restrictions. Data from the *Direction of Trade Statistics* of the International Monetary Fund (IMF) (IMF various years).[11]

The variable *EU Member Budget Contributions* measures the member's contribution to the common EU budget as a percent of the total contributions. Net contributors generally try to avoid increases in their long-term contributions and as a result resist attempts to expand the budget. Consequently they are more likely to demand differentiated membership for newcomers. This dynamic was most obvious in the Eastern enlargement when Germany, along with several other net contributors, opposed any increases in the CAP funds to finance expansion. Data from the EU Budgetary Vade-Mekum (EU Commission 2003).

The closer the applicant's regime type to the democracy of the member state, the less intense the political conflicts, and the lower the likelihood of a discriminatory demand. The variable *Candidate Democracy* measures the level of democracy in the applicant state. It ranges from 6 to 10, with higher numbers representing the extent of consolidation of democratic institutions. A fully democratic polity has three essential elements: fully competitive political participation, institutionalized constraints on executive power, and guarantees of civil liberties to all citizens in their daily lives and in political participation. (In contrast, in a fully autocratic system, political participation is suppressed, the chief executive is chosen by an elite group, and there are no constraints on the exercise of power.) Theoretically, this variable can range from -10 to $+10$ but the truncation of values in the data set reflects the self-selection of democracies into the applicant pool (Mattli and Plümper 2002, Plümper et al., 2006). All candidates were already relatively stable democracies at the time of their application. Data from the Polity IV project (Marshall and Jaggers 2003).

---

[11] The results remain unchanged if we use imports instead of exports.

Finally, the variable *Expected Size of the EU* measures the total number of member states the Union would have provided all applicants in the current round are admitted.[12] This captures the functional aspects of distributional tensions: the larger the EU, the less likely are losers to get compensated for at least two reasons. First, more members imply higher transaction costs and increased difficulties in coordinating and reaching agreements. Second, more members also generally imply more countries being eligible for the common funds, which means more intense conflict over the distribution of these funds. As I argued before, the variable should affect the likelihood of conflict in the CAP and CSP but not in the FMW.[13]

Table A-2 in the appendix provides descriptive statistics for all variables.[14]

---

[12] Note, the results are not affected by including Bulgaria and Romania in the last enlargement round.

[13] It is important to control for the functional aspect of distributional conflicts. I expect that larger expansions should increase the risk of distributional conflict, especially over agricultural and structural funds, but they should not by themselves explain the emergence of such conflicts. As robustness checks, I estimated models with dummy variables for each enlargement round as well as models with a variable counting the number of previous rounds. Because the results are essentially the same, I do not present them here.

[14] As the discussion of FMW conflicts in Chapter 2 suggests, there might be other factors that influence the emergence of distributional conflicts. During the Eastern enlargement, the German social-democratic government was particularly sensitive to potential labor market problems because accession negotiations on that chapter took place right before the elections to the Lower House of the German Government (*Bundestag*). The government's concern about losing votes from the very public debates could explain Germany's strong protectionist stance about migration from the East. The same electoral logic could affect other policy areas as well. Governments of relatively poor member states, for example, would be more concerned about the distribution of structural aid after enlargement if negotiations were right before elections. Elections may also strengthen the EU member's bargaining power vis-à-vis the candidate states and other members. I do not include a variable for upcoming domestic elections in the empirical model because its effects are not straightforward without a fully specified theoretical model. For example, if elections do increase the government's leverage during the pre-election period, then they would have incentives to shift elections closer to (or further away from) the negotiations of domestically relevant topics. Alternatively, if elections occur according to a predefined calendar, they would have incentives to schedule negotiations during suitable periods. This means that elections and negotiations should be modeled as endogenous processes. I leave this for future research because my theory does not explicitly account for such complex relationships.

5.2.2 Estimation results

Table 5.1 presents the results from the estimations of three *probit* models. Model 1 is the baseline and incorporates all variables of central theoretical interest. Models 2 and 3 add several control variables as robustness checks.

Overall, the models fit the data well. The Wald test is highly significant for all three specifications, which means that it is highly unlikely that the joint impact of the variables is zero.[15] Model 2, the best of the three, predicts 87% of the outcomes correctly. The fit with actual cases is very good as well. For instance, the estimated probability that Germany would demand restrictions on the free movement of labor for Poland and the Baltic countries is almost one. The estimated probability that France would demanded these restrictions for the United Kingdom (UK) is nearly two-thirds. Luxembourg, on the other hand, is not predicted to be very likely to demand protection against Cypriot workers – the estimated probability is close to zero.

To get a better sense of Model 2's fit with the data, I calculate the expected probabilities and then generate a predicted value for the dependent variable, setting it equal to 1 if the probability is at least 50%, and 0 otherwise. Table 5.2 tabulates these against the actual values. This contingency table shows that the model predicts correctly 67% of the demands for discrimination and over 97% of the cases with no demand. The model generally under-predicts demand, which is not surprising because it only happens in about 15% of the cases. Given the sparsity of the model, the fact that it predicts correctly about 93% of the outcomes should be encouraging.

The estimated coefficients support the theoretical claims. The signs of all statistically significant coefficients are in the hypothesized directions. EU members are unlikely to demand restrictions for the free movement of workers for relatively rich candidates because migration is expected to be much lower from such places. However, they become increasingly likely to demand differentiation for candidates with high unemployment rates because excess labor is very likely to migrate to new markets after accession. It does not seem to make a

---

[15] Although I present the pseudo R^2 as well, it is mostly for the sake of completeness as it is not a reliable measure of fit for *probit* models. See Kennedy (2003) and Long (1997) for the uses and misuses of R^2.

Table 5.1. *Free movement of workers: probit model for the likelihood of demands for discrimination.*

	Model 1	Model 2	Model 3
Candidate GDP	−0.042**	−0.039*	−0.035**
	(0.010)	(0.014)	(0.008)
Candidate unemployment	0.064*	0.071†	0.050
	(0.029)	(0.038)	(0.034)
EU member unemployment	0.040	−0.082	−0.011
	(0.102)	(0.104)	(0.101)
Distance between capitals	−0.634	−0.837†	−0.459
	(0.408)	(0.463)	(0.344)
EU member share of foreigners	0.272**	1.078*	0.249**
	(0.077)	(0.428)	(0.066)
Candidate industry employment	0.077*	0.101*	0.076*
	(0.026)	(0.035)	(0.026)
EU member industry employment	0.119**	0.196*	0.198*
	(0.036)	(0.056)	(0.079)
Candidate democracy		−0.134†	
		(0.084)	
EU member exports to candidate		−0.006†	
		(0.004)	
EU member budget contributions		−0.407*	
		(0.200)	
EU member population over 65		1.738†	
		(0.997)	
Expected size of the EU			0.122
			(0.098)
Constant	−5.556*	−6.725*	−10.648*
	(2.162)	(2.610)	(4.427)
N	214	214	214
Wald χ^2	331.49**	3463.38**	401.55**
Pseudo R^2	0.42	0.53	0.46

† $p < 0.1$, * $p < 0.05$, ** $p < 0.001$. Robust standard errors in parentheses.

Free movement of workers 93

Table 5.2. *Free Movement of Workers: model fit.*

		Predicted demand		
		No	Yes	Total
Actual demand	No	176	5	181
	Yes	11	22	33
	Total	187	27	214

difference whether the EU member itself has high rates of unemployment. This is somewhat surprising because domestic concerns about the potential influx of foreign workers should be especially acute when unemployment is high. EU members also become less likely to demand discrimination the farther away the candidate is in geographical terms. However, the effect is rather weak statistically: the variable *Distance Between Capitals* is only marginally significant in the second model and is insignificant in the first and third models.[16] As expected, EU member's strategy choice is predicated on other factors as well. Countries with large proportions of foreigners in their populations are more likely to demand transitional periods for the free movement of workers. The larger the industrial sector in either the member or the applicant state, the greater the chances that the EU member will demand differentiated membership for the candidate. In general, then, the main explanatory variables lend considerable support to the theory. Almost all variables identified as driving expectations of massive labor migration and severe labor market dislocations are significant predictors of calls for discrimination by EU members.

The control variables are all statistically significant in Model 2 but not overwhelmingly so. In fact, in the SURE version of this model reported in Table A-1 their significance is very marginal and two of the variables, *EU Member Exports to Candidate* and *EU Member Population Over 65* fail to clear the standard thresholds at all. With these caveats in mind, we can briefly look at the substantive effects. Candidates whose democratic regimes are more institutionalized are less

---

[16] Note that standard errors are higher in the multivariate probit SURE estimations reported in Table A-1 in the appendix.

likely to face demands for discrimination, as are candidates to whom the EU member exports more. Both effects are in the expected direction. This is not so for the other two control variables. It appears that EU members that contribute more to the common budget are less likely to demand differentiated rights for candidates. This could be because these countries also have the highest vested interest in the Union as a whole and might tend to support equal rights upon accession as a matter of principle. It also seems that countries with higher proportions of elderly people are more likely to demand discrimination. This may be the result of preferences over social matters conflicting with preferences over economic ones. If older people are systematically more concerned with preserving the social and cultural character of their nation, then they might oppose the free movement of people from other countries, especially when these are "more" foreign on these dimensions. These speculations must remain tentative, however, because the variables do not appear to have much of an impact in the SURE model and because exploring their influence in detail is beyond the scope of this project.

It is worth emphasizing that the inclusion of these controls does not decrease by much the statistical significance of the major explanatory variables. Only one of them, *Distance Between Capitals*, becomes insignificant, and only in Model 3 where I include the expected size of the EU as the control (which itself is insignificant as well). In other words, the findings from this empirical analysis largely support the theoretical claims about the Free Movement of Workers. EU members are more likely to oppose unconditional admission of a candidate when they expect high social and economic costs from its integration in their labor markets.

5.2.3 Predicted probabilities

As I noted above, it is not easy to interpret the substantive significance of the explanatory variables because in *probit* models the marginal effects do not equal the coefficients. Even statistically important factors may turn out to change the dependent variable by very little. Since we want to assess the strength of their effects, I set the explanatory variables to various theoretically interesting and empirically relevant values to create hypothetical dyads, and then calculate the predicted probability that the EU member in that dyad demands the discrimination of the candidate. By controlling the variation of these hypothetical dyads, I can then see how much any specific change in one variable (or a set of variables) affects the probability of such a demand. I also conduct a similar analysis for some actual dyads to gauge the fit of the model in the sense of its ability to predict the outcomes in real situations.

I begin by taking a quick look at some hypothetical dyads that resemble actual cases. Although not as good a test of model fit as the contingency table, this can nevertheless give some rough idea about scenarios in which we would have some fairly strong priors about the outcome. For instance, it should be highly unlikely for a member with the characteristics of Luxembourg in the early 1970s to demand transitional protection of its labor market from a candidate with the characteristics of Denmark. This is so because both economies were doing very well with GDPs above the European average, and foreign nationals constituted small shares of the workforce in both countries. Even though the two countries had relatively large industrial sectors (44% for Luxembourg and 38% for Denmark) and are geographically close, neither faced high unemployment rates. The model conforms to these expectations – the predicted probability is less than one percent (0.61%).

The situation is markedly different if we consider a 2001 dyad comprising Luxembourg and a candidate with the characteristics of Slovenia. Luxembourg still had low unemployment (although it was about 2% higher than in the 1970s), high GDP, and now an even smaller industrial sector. Slovenia, on the other hand, had high unemployment (about 6.6%), relatively low GDP (about 70% of the EU average), and a large industrial sector. Even though Slovenia is further away from Luxembourg than Denmark, the model predicts that the odds of Luxembourg demanding labor protection against Slovenia are nearly 51%.

Of course, a discrimination demand should be nearly certain when the member's economy is wobbly and the candidate has large potential for labor export. Take, for instance, the dyad comprising France and Poland in 2001. The French unemployment rate was substantially higher than Luxembourg's (9.3%) and there were considerably more foreigners living there. Poland, on the other hand, appeared poised to export its abundant workforce: unemployment ran over

16%, GDP was less than 41% of the EU average, and the industrial share was about 31%. The model estimates that the likelihood of France demanding labor protections against Poland was a whooping 96%. These simple comparisons demonstrate how important it is to account for distributional conflict when trying to understand the outcome of EU accession negotiations.

Turning now to a more systematic approach, I estimate the conditional effects of the most interesting explanatory variables – the candidate's GDP, the number of foreigners in the EU member state, the unemployment rates, and the sizes of the industrial sectors – on the probability that the EU member in the hypothetical dyad demands discrimination against the candidate. Table 5.3 presents the results of varying each of the main variables separately while holding all others at some predetermined level. In this case, I created three hypothetical scenarios that differ in their proneness to discrimination. To do this, I separated the variables in two sets: those that increase the probability of such demands, and those that decrease it. For the scenario that is not very likely to generate a discrimination demand, I set the variables in the first set to their values at the 25th percentile in the sample, and the variables in the second set to their values at 75th percentile. For the scenario that is very likely to generate such a demand, I do the reverse: all positively-related variables are set to the values at the 75th percentile, and all negatively-related variables are set to the values at the 25th percentile. For the moderate case, all variables are set to their median values. I use Model 2 for the predictions but the substantive results do not change if we use any of the other models.

The most striking finding that emerges from examining Table 5.3 is that although individual conditional effects do exist, they are quite weak. As we move down each column, the predicted probabilities increase but not by very much. Take, for instance, the hypothetical scenario that is moderately prone to discrimination demands. As the share of foreigners in the EU member's population increases from 0.17% (25th percentile in the sample) to 0.65% (median), the probability that it will demand labor protection increases from 0.11% to 0.56%. If the share rises further to 1.39% (75th percentile in the sample), the probability of discrimination also goes up to 4.09%. If the share of foreigners is very large (the maximum of 7.34% in the sample), then the probability of discrimination leaps up to 100% (not shown in the table). Observe, however, that in the high-risk

Table 5.3. *Free movement of workers: predicted probabilities of demands for discrimination (%).*

	Scenario proneness to discrimination		
	Low	Moderate	High
	EU member share of foreigners		
25th percentile: 0.17	0.23	0.41	93.93
	(0.00, 0.03)	(0.00, 2.97)	(17.20, 100.00)
Sample median: 0.65	0.23	0.97	94.90
	(0.00, 0.05)	(0.02, 4.74)	(21.92, 100.00)
75th percentile: 1.39	0.24	4.93	95.91
	(0.00, 0.09)	(0.63, 15.62)	(28.01, 100.00)
	Candidate GDP		
75th percentile: 76.2	0.23	0.17	91.57
	(0.00, 0.03)	(0.00, 1.33)	(4.84, 100.00)
Sample median: 56	0.38	1.02	94.41
	(0.00, 0.36)	(0.03, 4.83)	(15.16, 100.00)
25th percentile: 40.7	0.55	4.01	95.92
	(0.00, 1.81)	(0.16, 15.25)	(28.01, 100.00)
	EU member industry employment		
25th percentile: 25.3	0.23	0.26	92.27
	(0.00, 0.03)	(0.00, 1.81)	(6.09, 100.00)
Sample median: 28.7	0.29	1.02	94.32
	(0.00, 0.10)	(0.03, 4.83)	(14.15, 100.00)
75th percentile: 32.5	0.40	4.78	95.92
	(0.00, 0.63)	(0.44, 15.48)	(28.01, 100.00)
	Candidate industry employment		
25th percentile: 27.3	0.23	0.43	93.90
	(0.00, 0.03)	(0.00, 2.37)	(12.39, 100.00)
Sample median: 31	0.27	1.02	94.93
	(0.00, 0.07)	(0.03, 4.83)	(18.78, 100.00)
75th percentile: 35.3	0.35	2.71	95.92
	(0.00, 0.26)	(1.32, 11.18)	(15.87, 100.00)
	Candidate unemployment		
25th percentile: 6.3	0.23	0.69	94.37
	(0.00, 0.03)	(0.00, 3.64)	(15.79, 100.00)
Sample median: 9.1	0.25	1.02	94.91
	(0.00, 0.04)	(0.03, 4.83)	(18.30, 100.00)
75th percentile: 15.7	0.32	2.91	95.92
	(0.00, 0.20)	(1.85, 12.18)	(28.01, 100.00)

95% confidence intervals in parentheses.

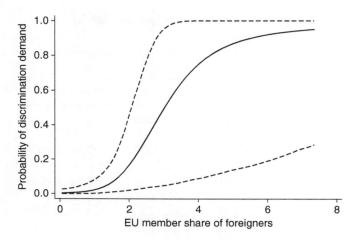

Fig. 5.1 Free movement of workers: effect of EU member share of foreigners on discrimination demand. Solid line shows predicted probabilities; dashed lines show 95% confidence intervals.

scenario, discrimination demand is certain regardless of how many foreigners are in the country. In other words, the combined effect of the other variables can swamp the individual contribution of the foreigner share.

Figure 5.1 gives a more detailed view of the effect of this variable for all values in the sample. The solid line plots the expected value of the predicted probability of discrimination and the dashed lines plot the 95% confidence interval around that prediction (all other variables held at their sample medians). Note the dramatic increase in the expected probability that the EU member will ask for temporary differentiation when foreigners constitute 2 or more percent of its population. One should be cautious about putting too much into that result, however. As the wide confidence interval clearly shows, there is a lot of uncertainty about predictions in the upper range because of the sparsity of observations with states that have such high numbers of foreign nationals.

Turning now to the two variables measuring the size of the industrial sector in the EU member and the candidate states, Table 5.3 shows that the high-risk hypothetical scenario over-determines the probability of discrimination demands. Taking a less extreme baseline, however, generates some interesting observations. Figure 5.2 shows

Free movement of workers

how the expected probability of discrimination demand in the dyad is affected by the size of the industrial sector of the EU member (Figure 5.2(a)) and the candidate (Figure 5.2(b)). In both cases, the more people are employed in industry, the more likely is the member to

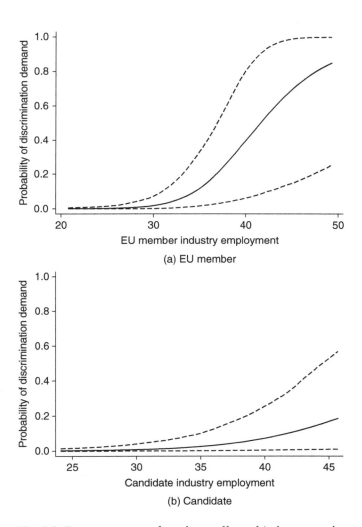

Fig. 5.2 Free movement of workers: effect of industry employment on discrimination demand. Solid line shows predicted probabilities; dashed lines show 95% confidence intervals.

demand transitional limitations on the candidate's labor market rights. However (and perhaps not surprisingly), the EU member's behavior is much more heavily influenced by the size of its own industry. For instance, when this sector employs 40% of the workforce in the EU member state and 31% in the candidate state (the sample median), the expected likelihood of a discrimination demand is about 40%. Conversely, when industry employs 40% of the workforce in the candidate state and about 29% in the EU member state (the sample median), the expected likelihood is less than 10%. At the extreme, as the fraction of the workforce employed by industry in the EU member state approaches one half, the probability that this member will demand differentiation exceeds 80%. The corresponding value at the extreme upper end of employment in the candidate state is less than 20%. In other words, the impact of the size of the *domestic* industrial sector is roughly four times that of the foreign sector.

The other two variables, *Candidate GDP* and *Candidate Unemployment Rate*, have marginal influence on the likelihood of discrimination demands, as can be readily seen in Figure 5.3(a) and Figure 5.3(b). Consider first the weak effect of candidate's wealth depicted in Figure 5.3(a). Although there is some discernible impact for poor applicants, the lower bound of the confidence interval is extremely close to zero meaning that one cannot be very confident of the substantive significance suggested by the expected value of the predicted probabilities. Still, some observations are worth making. For example, candidates with GDP per capita around half that of the EU average can expect somewhere between 5% and 10% likelihood of being asked to accept temporary limitations (again, in the moderate-risk scenario). The richer the candidates, the less of an impact their wealth has and the more confident we become of its vanishing effect (as shown by the steadily decreasing width of the confidence interval). As before, if we consider the high-risk scenario, then the effect of GDP is entirely swamped by the other variables, as shown in Table 5.3: the decrease is so negligible that it does not even register in the predictions.

Similarly, the higher the unemployment rate in the candidate country, the more likely is the EU member to ask for differentiation. The lower bound of the confidence interval, however, is very close to zero across the entire range of variation of the explanatory variable, which makes even this weak effect somewhat uncertain. It is only when unemployment rates become extremely high (e.g., above 15%) that the

Free movement of workers 101

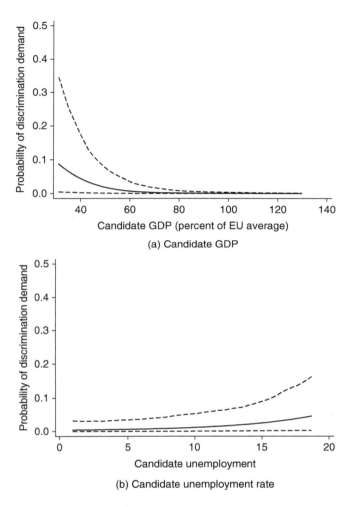

Fig. 5.3 Free movement of workers: effect of candidate GDP and unemployment rate on discrimination demand. Solid line shows predicted probabilities; dashed lines show 95% confidence intervals.

likelihood of discrimination demands increases visibly to somewhere around 5%.

To summarize, each of the main explanatory variables exerts discernible impact on the probability that the EU member demands transitional exemptions for its labor market liberalization with respect to the candidate. However, the individual effects tend to be quite weak, which raises an important point. In theory, the EU member will take into account all of the relevant factors simultaneously when projecting the consequences of enlargement for its labor market situation. This suggests that it might make more sense to examine the *joint* effect of these variables. To this end, I created three configurations of these variables to reflect situations in which the EU member should expect negligible, moderate, or severe adverse consequences for its labor market. To model a hypothetical scenario in which there should be little fear of the unconditional accession of the candidate, I set *Candidate GDP* (which lowers risk) to its value at the 75th percentile in the sample, and the four other variables (which increase risk) to their values at the 25th percentile. For the hypothetical scenario in which there should be extreme fear, I set the candidate's wealth to the 25th percentile and the risk-inducing variables to their 75th percentile values. Finally, for the moderate scenario, all five variables are held at their sample medians. As before, the other explanatory variables are set to one of the three predetermined levels used for Table 5.3. This creates nine hypothetical scenarios, and the predicted probabilities for each are displayed in Table 5.4.

As predicted by the theory, taking the five main statistically significant explanatory variables as a group yields very crisp and large substantive effects on the probability that the EU member will ask for

Table 5.4. *Free movement of workers: joint effect (%)*.

Adverse consequences	Scenario proneness to discrimination		
	Low	Moderate	High
Negligible	0.23	0.00	52.58
	(0.00, 0.03)	(0.00, 0.04)	(0.00, 100.00)
Moderate	0.73	1.02	84.21
	(0.00, 4.34)	(0.03, 4.83)	(0.09, 100.00)
Severe	3.96	65.99	95.92
	(0.00, 57.84)	(22.33, 96.10)	(28.01, 100.00)

95% confidence intervals in parentheses.

transitional measures for the free movement of labor against the candidate. Even in the least conflict-prone hypothetical baseline scenario EU member's expectation about the likely consequences of unconditional accession matter: the likelihood of discrimination demand increases from less than one-quarter of a percent to nearly four percent. Taking the baseline case with moderate conflict makes for an even sharper difference. A member who expects moderately adverse labor market consequences is only about 1% likely to ask for discriminatory measures. However, a member who expects severe hardship is nearly 66% likely to ask for such measures under otherwise identical circumstances. Finally, recall that the individual variables had almost no separately discernible effect in the scenario that is highly prone to conflict. Taken as a group, however, reveals a substantial impact: the probability that the EU member will ask for discriminatory measures leaps from about 53% when it expects negligible consequences for its labor market to almost 96% when it expects severe consequences.

5.2.4 Conclusion

The empirical analysis of the Free Movement of Workers lends substantial support to my theoretical claims. Member states appear to assess the likely impact the candidate's unconditional accession will have on the value of their membership in the Union. Expectations about labor migration and attendant societal adaptation pressures seem to drive EU member calls for transitional periods restricting the free movement of workers from certain candidate countries. The larger the projected migration to the target EU member and the higher the potential costs of such immigration for society, the more reluctant its government will be to approve the admission of the source candidate without some safeguard measures. As the theory predicts at the higher level of abstraction, if EU members expect enlargement to cause distributional conflicts or political tensions, then they are likely to demand transitional discrimination against certain candidates to reduce these losses. One possible objection to this claim could be that the findings are specific to this particular policy area and do not generalize beyond it. I now turn to the first of two additional policy areas whose study will allow me to refute this objection and to increase the confidence in my results.

5.3 Common Agricultural Policies

Every year the common *acquis* is augmented by 2,500 pages of new EU law, indicating that the EU is constantly expanding its competencies in policy-making. The Common Agricultural Policies (CAP) have always been among the most important policy areas. Presently, the CAP accounts for nearly half the common EU budget; still a sizeable share even if it is down from 1970 when the EAGGF peaked at 87% of the budget. The EC Treaty states that the objectives of the Common Agricultural Policies are:

a) to increase agricultural productivity by promoting technical progress and by ensuring the rational development of agricultural production and the optimum utilization of the factors of production, in particular labor, b) to ensure a fair standard of living for the agricultural community, in particular by increasing the individual earnings of persons engaged in agriculture, c) to stabilize markets, d) to assure the availability of supplies, and e) to ensure that supplies reach consumers at reasonable prices (Article 33, EC-Treaty).

In pursuit of these general objectives, the EU governments founded the Common Organization of Agricultural Markets (COAM) to create common rules for competition, provide for the coordination of various national market organizations, and serve as a European market organization. The CAP is financed from the EAGGF. In 1964, the Community split the EAGGF into two sections: the Guidance Section and the Guarantee Section. The Guidance Section contributes to structural reforms in agriculture and to rural development, while the more important Guarantee Section funds the COAM. The latter includes expenditures that encourage exports of agricultural products, and the purchase and storage of agricultural surplus. The funds are distributed through direct payments to EU farmers. In the early years of the CAP, farmers were offered subsidies and guaranteed prices that were supposed to provide them with incentives to produce. Several reforms targeted decoupling of production from subsidies in an attempt to create a more competitive and market-oriented agricultural sector. Because of these reforms, production no longer determines the amount of subsidies even though farmers continue to receive direct payments to maintain income stability.

The allocation of agricultural subsidies among EU member states has always been a source of friction, but tensions are most likely to erupt into conflict during accession negotiations. Candidates have had

Common Agricultural Policies 105

to accept restricted eligibility for agricultural subsidies on several occasions even before the Eastern expansion. However, it is during the last enlargement round that this conflict exposed the fault lines most clearly: none of the candidates will be granted the full agricultural subsidy it is eligible for in the first decade of membership.

It will be useful to get some idea how the allocation of agricultural subsidies affects the conflict proneness of accession negotiations. Unfortunately, information about the amount of subsidy EU members should expect after enlargement cannot be obtained prior to enlargement. Consequently, I predict the effect of the EU Eastern enlargement on each member's share of EAGGF. This prediction is possible because we know the size of the agricultural sector of each state, which turns out to be one of the most important factors driving the state's share of these funds. The Gross Value Added (GVA) of the agricultural sector is one measure of its size. This is highly correlated with the amount of subsidies allocated under the EAGGF (0.94 pairwise correlation coefficient). Columns two and three in Table 5.5 show the GVA and EAGGF allocation for each member in 2000.

I assessed the expected effect of the Eastern enlargement on the EU members' shares of agricultural subsidies as follows. I created a data set for the members and candidates in 2000. For each country, I recorded its GDP per capita as percent of EU average, population (in thousands), GVA of the agricultural sector (in millions of Euros), and the size of the industrial sector (in percent of workforce employed). I then estimated an Ordinary Least Squares (OLS) model for the EU members with the amount of EAGGF subsidy (in millions of Euros) as the dependent variable. Using the estimated coefficients on the four explanatory variables, I then predicted the size of the subsidy for both members and candidates.[17] Using the partially out-of-sample predictions, I calculated a projected size of an unconstrained budget after expansion by adding all expected subsidies. The fourth column in Table 5.5 shows the results. The number in parentheses after the expected subsidy is this subsidy's percent share of the total predicted budget. The model projects that the budget would have to grow from

---

[17] For the EU members, the predictions also serve as a test of model fit. With a few exceptions, the predicted subsidies are close to the actual ones. Ireland is an outlier because its subsidy is about twice the size one would expect based on its agricultural sector. Belgium, Italy, Sweden, Luxembourg, the Netherlands, and Portugal, on the other hand, would be expected to receive higher subsidies.

Table 5.5. *Common Agricultural Policies: actual and estimated EAGGF subsidies, 2000.*

	Agriculture GVA (€ mil)	EAGGF subsidy (€ mil)	Projected subsidy and share of unconstrained budget	Projected subsidy with a constrained budget	Expected subsidy deficit
Austria	2692	1019	895 (1.9%)	748	−147
Belgium	2796	955	1070 (2.2%)	894	−175
Denmark	3454	1305	1018 (2.1%)	851	−167
Finland	1516	728	679 (1.4%)	568	−111
France	31661	8982	7477 (15.5%)	6252	−1225
Germany	17497	5642	5494 (11.4%)	4594	−900
Greece	8210	2597	2235 (4.6%)	1869	−366
Ireland	2842	1678	818 (1.7%)	684	−134
Italy	28220	5031	6739 (14.0%)	5635	−1104
Luxembourg	127	21	67 (0.1%)	56	−11
Netherlands	9303	1397	2407 (5.0%)	2013	−394
Portugal	2692	652	1240 (2.6%)	1037	−203
Spain	23072	5469	5445 (11.3%)	4553	−892
Sweden	1611	798	874 (1.8%)	731	−143
United Kingdom	10810	4059	3875 (8.0%)	3240	−635
Candidates	–	–	7902 (16.38%)	6608	−1295
Total	–	40331	48233 (100%)	40331	−7902

Source: Eurostat and own calculations

€40,331 million to €48,233 million if it were to accommodate the candidate states. This sets the expectations for the shares of direct payments each member would receive after enlargement if the common EU budget sets no constraints on CAP expenditures. This, of course, creates no distributional friction aside from the thorny problem of generating additional contributions to fund the larger budget.

Agenda 2000, however, set the stage for conflict because it constrained the budget such that despite projected higher demand for EAGGF, an increase in available funds would be highly unlikely. EU members agreed not only to freeze the budget but even to scale it back to its 1999 levels by 2006, which implied further reductions of agricultural expenditures.[18] To estimate the effect of this budgetary ceiling, I took the percent share of each country's subsidy calculated in the previous step, and then computed the subsidy this share would yield if the budget were limited to its 2000 level. Naturally, this results in reductions across the board for all countries, as shown in the fifth column. The average subsidy loss is expected to be about 16%.

Finally, I subtracted the projected subsidy assuming an unconstrained budget from the projected subsidy assuming a constrained budget to compute the deficit each member would have to suffer because of enlargement. This difference is of particular interest because it clearly reveals the extent of distributional conflict after enlargement given budgetary constraints. It also shows how *Agenda 2000* ensured that every expansion would intensify existing conflicts about the distribution of common funds. The subsidy deficit is especially troublesome for the main beneficiaries. France, the most extreme case, would receive about €1,225 million *less* if expansion occurred under *Agenda 2000*. The next two most impacted members would be Italy, with a loss of €1,104 million, and Germany, with a loss of €900 million.

The brief exercise illustrates the potential for conflict in the CAP. Members have a clearly defined interest in estimating the effect of enlargement on their benefits from common policies, and in opposing unconditional accession of candidates when the expected costs are too high. In this section I analyze whether such conflicts occur during accession negotiations. I study empirically the factors that determine whether EU governments request asymmetric allocation

---

[18] EU Commission (1997a, 1997b, 1997c, 1999).

of agricultural subsidies. I identify several such factors and then use them to predict the probability of discrimination demand. EU members are expected to ask for discrimination against a candidate if they are among the main beneficiaries of agricultural subsidies, if the candidate will receive a large share of these funds, and if the total funds available fail to increase with the accession of more net recipients.

5.3.1 Variables and data sources

Recall that the dependent variable codes whether the EU member in the dyad officially requested differentiated membership for the candidate state. For the present analysis, this refers to requests for asymmetric allocation of agricultural subsidies.[19] The CAP has traditionally been among the policy areas that occasion the most heated debates in the Union. Frictions occur not only between the main beneficiaries and candidates but also among the beneficiaries and the net contributors who have become progressively less willing to fund an ever-increasing budget. All of this results in escalating demands for discrimination. In the last enlargement, limitations for new member access to agricultural subsidies were requested in over 60% of the cases compared to about 45% in 1986 when the heavily agrarian Spain and Portugal joined the Union.

The main explanatory variables must capture the expected distribution of agricultural funds after enlargement as well as how important these subsidies are to the EU member states. The most direct measure would be the allocation of EAGGF after expansion but this information is not available. Instead, I use the GVA of the agricultural sector. The variables, *Candidate Agriculture GVA* and *EU Member Agriculture GVA*, measure the GVA at factor costs in millions of Euros for the respective country. As Table 5.5 shows, it is extremely highly correlated with the size of the EAGGF subsidy for existent members, which makes it eminently suitable as a proxy. Data from Eurostat.

The variable *Expected Size of the EU* is coded as described in the previous section. When the Union has more members, each must either contribute more to the common budget or receive less CAP funds.

---

[19] I focus on direct payments but there are other types of discrimination (e.g., export constraints on some agricultural products) under the CAP.

Common Agricultural Policies

In contrast to the Free Movement of Workers, however, the larger the EU, the more likely members should be to demand discriminatory allocations of agricultural subsidies.

The variable *EU Member Budget Contributions* is also coded exactly like it is for the FMW area. It is designed to capture the EU member's willingness to approve budget increases to accommodate the higher costs of agricultural subsidies after enlargement. Net recipients of agricultural transfers may even prefer to support budgetary expansions instead of membership restrictions because this reduces the net contributors' leverage in seeking further far-reaching reforms. Net contributors, on the other hand, should be less likely to agree to budget growth and more likely to call for discrimination that would help them avoid a possible ramping up of their contributions to finance policies under the CAP. In the enlargement talks with the CEE countries, the net CAP beneficiaries asked that the EAGGF funds be increased because most candidate countries were still relatively agrarian. In their discussions of possible Pareto-optimal strategies with the net contributors, they coordinated on restricting the allocation of subsidies for the new member states.

In addition to these main explanatory variables, I include several controls. Even though the GVA of the agricultural sector proxies the amount of subsidies a candidate would receive, it does not capture the importance of this sector to the candidate's economy. The variable *Candidate Agriculture Employment* measures the percentage of workers employed in the agricultural sector. The more agrarian the applicant country, the more pressure there will be for it to gain access to EAGGF subsidies upon accession. This should make member states more likely to call for temporary restrictions. Data from Eurostat.

As discussed previously, capping the budget intensifies distributional conflicts because it forces net beneficiaries to accept deep cuts in their subsidies. This increases their incentives to seek transitional limitations for candidates and makes discrimination more likely. If, on the other hand, the budget is allowed to grow to accommodate the demands of the new members, then it is more likely that applicants will gain unconditional access to CAP funds. The variable *EAGGF Budget Ceiling* is coded as 1 if the budget is capped, and 0 otherwise.

The last three controls, *Candidate GDP, Candidate Democracy,* and *EU Member Exports to Candidate,* are all measured as in Section 5.2.1, and their expected effects are the same. Table A-3 in the appendix provides descriptive statistics for all variables.

5.3.2 Estimation results

Table 5.6 presents the results from the estimations of three *probit* models. Model 1 is the baseline and incorporates all variables of central theoretical interest. Models 2 and 3 add several control variables as robustness checks.[20]

Overall, the models fit the data reasonably well. The Wald test is highly significant for all three specifications, meaning that it is very unlikely that the variables do not have any impact as a group. Model 2, the best of the three, predicts 75% of the outcomes correctly. Table 5.7 tabulates the actual outcomes against the model's predictions (as before, I code the predicted outcome as discrimination if the estimated probability is at least 0.50). The model predicts correctly 79% of cases without discrimination and 71% of cases with discrimination. About 24% of its predictions for no discrimination turn out to be wrong, and as do roughly 25% of its predictions for discrimination.

The estimated coefficients support the theoretical claims. All main explanatory variables are statistically significant and their effects are in the hypothesized directions. As the positive coefficients on the GVA variables indicate, EU members that receive large agricultural subsidies tend to fear the unconditional accession of applicants that are expected to receive substantial shares of these subsidies as well. As a result, members become more likely to demand that eligibility for EAGGF subsidies be phased in for these applicants. Furthermore, as the theory predicts, these net contributors to the budget also get entangled in these distributional conflicts. The higher the member's budget contributions, the more likely is it to request transitional limitations of candidate access to subsidies in order to avoid further increases in the budget.

---

[20] I excluded *Expected Size of the EU* from Model 3 because the EU capped the EAGGF only prior to the last enlargement round. Including both variables would induce serious collinearity problems.

Table 5.6. *Common Agricultural Policies: probit model for the likelihood of demands for discrimination.*

	Model 1	Model 2	Model 3
Candidate agriculture GVA	0.091*	0.065†	0.104*
	(0.034)	(0.040)	(0.039)
EU member agriculture GVA	0.051*	0.065*	0.062*
	(0.019)	(0.024)	(0.021)
Expected size of EU	0.160**	0.156**	
	(0.037)	(0.042)	
EU member budget contributions	0.037†	0.033†	0.034†
	(0.020)	(0.019)	(0.018)
Candidate agriculture employment		0.038*	
		(0.013)	
EU member exports to candidate		−0.007	
		(0.013)	
Candidate democracy		−0.025	
		(0.024)	
Candidate GDP		−0.012*	
		(0.005)	
EAGGF budget ceiling			2.189**
			(0.492)
Constant	−4.316**	−3.779**	−2.522**
	(0.828)	(1.000)	(0.545)
N	214	214	214
Wald χ^2	36.05**	40.53**	28.67**
PseudoR^2	0.32	0.38	0.36

† $p < 0.1$, * $p < 0.05$, ** $p < 0.001$. Robust standard errors in parentheses.

Table 5.7. *Common Agricultural Policies: model fit.*

		Predicted demand		Total
		No	Yes	
Actual demand	No	90	24	114
	Yes	29	71	100
	Total	119	95	214

The findings also strongly support the hypothesis that the expected size of the EU matters greatly. The larger the Union is expected to be after enlargement, the more likely are members to demand discrimination against the newcomers in the Common Agricultural Policies. It is instructive to compare this result with the corresponding finding for the Free Movement of Workers in Section 5.2.2. Recall that the expected size of the EU had no statistically discernible impact on the likelihood of demands for discrimination in the FMW. This difference is anticipated by the theory, which predicts the effect based on the consumption characteristics of the policy areas. Because the CAP gobbles up the largest chunk of the common budget, an expansion of the Union without a corresponding increase in the funding for the EAGGF will reduce the subsidies for net beneficiaries. In contrast, expansion does not automatically trigger labor market disruptions in member states. This happens only when the economies of both the applicant and the member have certain features. (In fact, EU widening may even be positive to some members because it may not cause adaptation pressures.)

It is also interesting to note that it is not just the expected subsidy for the candidate that influences the likelihood of discrimination demands but also the size of its agricultural sector as well. Applicants that are largely agrarian are expected to fight hard for relative large agricultural subsidies, and as a result EU members tend to be wary of their unconditional accession. Including the size of the agricultural sector of the member state reveals no statistically discernible effect (which is why I excluded it from the final estimation). In other words, the size of the EAGGF subsidy, as proxied by the agricultural GVA, is an adequate predictor of its behavior. As expected, capping the budget for such subsidies produces a serious increase in the likelihood of discrimination demands. As with the FMW, wealthier candidates pose less of a threat to CAP beneficiaries, which reduces the probability of transitional qualification of their rights. (Democratic institutions and member exports to the candidate fail to clear the traditional standard for statistical significance.)

These findings highlight the important role agricultural subsidies play in EU member's evaluation of the desirability of unconditional enlargement. The larger its subsidy, the more likely it is to demand some restrictions for new members. The larger the subsidy the candidate will receive, the more likely are the existing beneficiaries to request qualifications of its access to the EAGGF. The larger the number of new members, the more conflicting claims the budget has to accommodate. This makes existing members very likely to ask for discriminatory rights for the newcomers, especially when the budget cannot grow because of a legally mandated ceiling. These results are robust to different model specifications and do not change substantively if we vary the sets of controls or if we use a SURE model instead of the independent *probit* models for the estimation.[21]

5.3.3 Predicted probabilities

As in Section 5.2.3, I assess the substantive strength of the effects of the four principal explanatory variables by creating hypothetical dyads and calculating predicted probability that the EU member will demand the discrimination of the candidate.

I begin with a quick look at dyads that resemble actual cases for which we would have some fairly strong priors. For instance, it should be highly unlikely for a member with the characteristics of Sweden in 2001 to demand transitional protection of its agricultural subsidies from a candidate with the characteristics of Cyprus. Both countries had very small agricultural sectors: the Swedish employed 2.9% of the workforce and the Cypriot employed 5.4%. Sweden's share of EAGGF was less than 2%, and Cypriot GVA was low, meaning that direct payments through the EAGGF were relatively unimportant to either country. The model confirms our expectations and predicts that the probability of discrimination demand is vanishingly small at 0.04%.

The situation changes considerably when we consider a member who is a significant beneficiary of EAGGF subsidies. Even though Germany employed a relatively small fraction of its workforce in the agricultural sector (about 2.6%), the GVA of that sector was more than ten times larger than the Swedish. Germany also claimed nearly 14% of the EAGGF subsidies. Consequently, it was far more concerned about the Cypriot accession than Sweden. The model predicts that the likelihood of Germany demanding transitional discrimination against Cyprus in the CAP will be about 35%. The predicted probability more than doubles to 87% if the candidate has the characteristics of Poland, whose agricultural production was almost sixteen times

[21] Table A-1 in the appendix shows the results of the SURE estimation.

larger than the Cypriot and where nearly 19% of the workforce were still employed in the agricultural sector.

Turning now to a less impressionistic approach, I estimate the conditional effects of the principal explanatory variables in dyads that differ in their propensity to distributional conflicts. The methodology is analogous to the one I used in Section 5.2.3 for the FMW. Table 5.8 presents the results.[22]

Discrimination demands become somewhat likely even in moderately conflict-prone scenarios if either the EU member's or the candidate's GVA is at the respective sample median (about 48% in both cases). These demands become very likely if the member's GVA is at the 75th sample percentile (approximately 72%). Comparing the strength of the effect of the two, it is evident that the behavior of the EU member is closely conditioned on its own subsidy. Take, for instance, the highly conflict-prone scenario and observe that whereas increasing the candidate's GVA from the 25th to the 75th sample percentile produces an increase in demand risk of roughly one and a half percentage points, an analogous increase in the EU member's GVA results in a jump of about 14%.

The reason for this difference becomes clearer when we look at the predicted probability of demand for discrimination as a function of agricultural GVA for all sample values of the explanatory variable. Figure 5.4(a) plots the expected probability and its 95% confidence interval for the EU member, and Figure 5.4(b) does the same for the candidate. Despite the uncertainty evidenced by the relatively wide confidence intervals, the overall trend is evident: higher GVAs are associated with higher probabilities of discrimination demands. For the EU member, changing the GVA from the sample minimum to the sample maximum more than doubles that probability with a nearly 50% jump. For the candidate, the corresponding increase of 10% is modest by comparison. However, the difference comes mostly from the fact that at the high end, EU member agriculture GVA is triple that of the candidate. This makes the change of the explanatory variable much larger, which accounts for the stronger substantive effect. If we consider an increase from the sample minimum to about €10 million, the probability of discrimination rises from about 40% to roughly 55%

---

[22] Note, for *Expected Size of the EU* I analyze the actual historical enlargement scenarios.

Common Agricultural Policies

Table 5.8. *Common Agricultural Policies: predicted probabilities of demands for discrimination (%).*

	Scenario proneness to discrimination		
	Low	Moderate	High
Candidate agriculture GVA			
25th percentile: 0.35	2.63	46.66	91.97
	(0.12, 10.15)	(19.34, 73.01)	(75.83, 99.01)
Sample median: 0.87	2.80	47.94	92.47
	(0.14, 10.67)	(20.70, 73.66)	(77.61, 99.08)
75th percentile: 10.2	3.21	50.73	93.46
	(0.19, 12.46)	(23.86, 74.94)	(80.06, 99.28)
EU member agriculture GVA			
25th percentile: 2.69	2.63	45.28	79.40
	(0.12, 10.15)	(17.63, 72.03)	(53.00, 95.49)
Sample median: 3.79	2.95	47.94	81.31
	(0.17, 11.15)	(20.70, 73.66)	(56.93, 95.89)
75th percentile: 13.98	9.21	71.91	93.46
	(2.04, 22.28)	(48.96, 89.70)	(80.06, 99.28)
Expected size of the EU			
6	0.21	0.66	11.55
	(0.00, 1.98)	(0.00, 5.10)	(1.03, 34.56)
9	0.48	1.41	20.86
	(0.00, 3.57)	(0.00, 8.10)	(5.33, 45.13)
12	1.11	3.10	34.99
	(0.01, 5.95)	(0.11, 13.35)	(16.88, 55.92)
15	2.63	6.75	52.60
	(0.12, 10.15)	(0.78, 21.05)	(35.46, 69.09)
25	29.62	47.94	93.46
	(8.26, 57.82)	(20.70, 73.66)	(80.06, 99.28)
EU member budget contributions			
25th percentile: 1.4	2.63	45.18	86.36
	(0.12, 10.15)	(17.69, 71.14)	(62.27, 98.17)
Sample median: 3.6	3.01	47.94	87.95
	(0.15, 11.45)	(20.70, 73.66)	(66.77, 98.37)
75th percentile: 14	5.93	60.82	93.46
	(0.47, 21.05)	(30.92, 84.02)	(80.06, 99.28)

95% confidence intervals in parentheses.

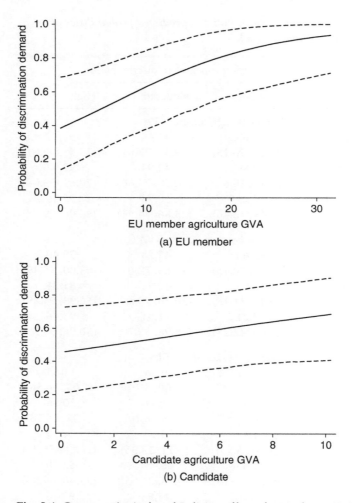

Fig. 5.4 Common Agricultural Policies: effect of agriculture GVA on discrimination demand. Solid line shows predicted probabilities; dashed lines show 95% confidence intervals.

in both cases. Hence, the marginal strength of the effect seems roughly similar but in practice the demand for discrimination is more responsive to the EU member's own agricultural GVA simply because it will tend to be much higher than the candidate's.

Common Agricultural Policies

Table 5.8 also suggests that the expected size of the Union has a strong substantive effect, especially when it comes to a very large widening. In the moderately conflict-prone scenario, expansions to 6 to 15 members are likely to be unconditional (risk is less than 7%) but there is nearly 48% chance that the unconditional widening to 25 members will be opposed. The risk increases dramatically in the highly conflict-prone scenario. Here, even a moderately large unconditional expansion to 15 member states is likely to be opposed (53%), and a huge expansion of the CEE variety is nearly certain to be opposed (94%). Of course, the expected size of the EU does *not*, by itself, guarantee distributional conflict. In the scenario where the other variables make conflict unlikely, even the largest unconditional expansion will probably not cause much consternation – the likelihood of a discrimination demand is about 30%.

Figure 5.5 plots the effect of the expected size of the EU on the probability of discrimination demands while holding all other variables at their sample medians. As the narrower confidence intervals indicate, we can be quite sure that large expansions to about 15 members are extremely unlikely to generate demands for transitional qualifications in these moderately conflict-prone baseline situation.

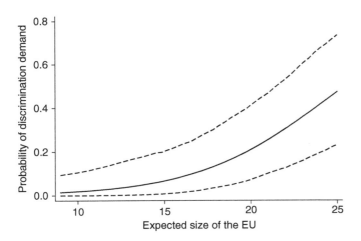

Fig. 5.5 Common Agricultural Policies: effect of expected size of the EU on discrimination demand. Solid line shows predicted probabilities; dashed lines show 95% confidence intervals.

Although the expected probability climbs to nearly 50% for expansions to 25 new members, the confidence intervals also widen. This reflects the uncertainty of the estimate that comes from the sparsity of such observations (there is only one such enlargement in the sample). Still, the lower bound of the confidence interval (20%) exceeds the upper bound for moderate enlargements (10–15%). Hence, we can be relatively certain that there will be a significant difference between these two types of enlargements. Furthermore, at the higher end, the upper bound is close to 80%, which implies that there is a good chance of the EU member asking for discrimination against the candidate.

Finally, Table 5.8 suggests a substantively weak effect of EU member budget contributions. Even though the variable is statistically significant and affects the probability of discrimination demands in the expected direction, the overall influence is not very strong. For example, changing the contribution size from the 25th to the 75th sample percentile results in a less than 7% increase in demand risk in the highly conflict-prone scenario, a little over 15% in the moderately conflict-prone scenario, and merely 3% in the low conflict-prone scenario. Even these differences are not very convincing because of the wide confidence intervals around the estimated probabilities. Figure 5.6 clearly shows this for the moderately conflict-prone

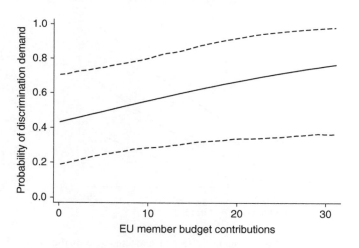

Fig. 5.6 Common Agricultural Policies: effect of EU member budget contributions on discrimination demand. Solid line shows predicted probabilities; dashed lines show 95% confidence intervals.

Table 5.9. *Common Agricultural Policies: joint effect (%).*

	Scenario proneness to discrimination		
Adverse consequences	Low	Moderate	High
Negligible	2.63	5.06	13.40
	(0.12, 10.15)	(0.36, 18.42)	(1.88, 34.99)
Moderate	35.54	47.94	68.92
	(12.32, 62.30)	(20.70, 73.66)	(36.77, 90.63)
Severe	74.63	83.78	93.46
	(52.45, 90.88)	(64.57, 95.26)	(80.06, 99.28)

95% confidence intervals in parentheses.

scenario. Despite the overall positive trend, the extreme width of the confidence intervals makes strong conclusions undesirable.

As in the case of the Free Movement of Workers, the principal explanatory variables are supposed to work as a group in affecting the member's propensity to demand discrimination. As before, I created three sets of hypothetical scenarios that vary in the degree of adversity the EU member expects after the unconditional accession of the candidate. In this case, this is very straightforward because all four variables increase the risk of discrimination demands. Consequently, I vary them jointly from the values at their 25th sample percentiles (negligible adversity) to the median values (moderate adversity) to the values at their 75th sample percentiles (severe adversity). Table 5.9 shows the predicted probabilities for each of the nine hypothetical scenarios.

The *joint* effect of the main explanatory variables is very large. If the expected consequences are negligible, then there is no risk of discrimination demands being made regardless of how conflict-prone the scenario otherwise may be. With moderately adverse consequences, these other factors begin to matter: in the low and moderately conflict-prone scenarios, the expected probability is still less than 50% but in the highly conflict-prone scenario it is nearly 69%. Moving to a situation in which the EU member expects severe hardship makes demands for discrimination either very likely (75% when other variables ameliorate the situation slightly) or nearly certain (94% when the other variables contribute to the adversity). In the latter baseline scenario, changing the expected hardship from moderate to severe increases the risk of a discrimination demand by nearly 80%. As the theory would predict, the explanatory variables have a very strong substantive effect as a group even if the individual effects tend to be relatively weak when considered separately.

5.3.4 Conclusion

The empirical analysis of the Common Agricultural Policies lends substantial support to my theoretical claims. EU members appear to assess the probable impact a candidate's unconditional accession will have on their agricultural subsidies. Expectations about serious reductions in the size of their EAGGF subsidies seem to drive EU member demand for transitional periods that would restrict the candidate's eligibility for these funds. Members that enjoy high subsidies are more likely to call for qualifications of a candidate's rights to EAGGF money, especially when the candidate itself is likely to be eligible for a large share of these funds. The situation is especially aggravated when it is impossible to expand the budget to handle these additional claims.

The model's predictions accord well with the historical record: France was more likely to demand restrictions for Poland than it was for Hungary, and both probabilities were higher than the likelihood that Italy would require protection against Poland's unrestricted participation in the CAP. In contrast, Luxembourg was in general well-disposed to the unconditional accession of new members and was very unlikely to ask for protection of its agricultural subsidy. These findings buttress the empirical support of the theory provided by the analysis of the Free Movement of Workers policy area. I now turn to the third, and last, policy area – the Common Structural Policies – in order to make that support even stronger.

5.4 Common Structural Policies

The Common Structural Policies (CSP) account for about one third of the EU budget in 2000–06 and are generally considered the second most important policy area after the CAP. The CSP were started in 1957 to

promote throughout the Community a harmonious, balanced and sustainable development of economic activities, a high level of employment and of

social protection, ... the raising of the standard of living and quality of life, and economic and social cohesion and solidarity among Member States
(Article 2&3 EC-Treaty).

EU members are interested in reducing economic and social disparities among the European regions.[23] Although the fundamental goal remains the same, the means of its implementation – the Common Structural Policies – has changed substantially over time. The seven original Objectives were reduced to three in 2000. Objective 1, which consumes about two-thirds of the total allocation to ERDF/ESF, promotes the development and structural adjustment of less developed regions. These are regions whose GDP per capita is less than 75% of the EU average, or that are very remote, or that have very low population density. Objective 2, which accounts for up to 11.5% of the total funds, provides assistance to regions undergoing economic or social changes, to rural areas in decline, to fishery-dependent areas in depression, and to urban areas in straits. Objective 3 picks up regions that do not qualify for funding under Objective 1 and targets human resource development.

In this section I study empirically the conditions under which EU governments request asymmetric allocation of European Reconstruction and Development Funds (ERDF) and the European Structural Funds (ESF). EU members are expected to ask for transitional qualifications of the candidate's access to the ERDF/ESF if they are among the main beneficiaries of structural subsidies, if the candidate will receive a large share of these funds, and if the total funds available for regional programs fail to increase with the accession of many qualifying candidates.

5.4.1 Variables and data sources

Although Eurostat provides some data at the regional level, their quality and availability is quite poor. For example, there is no information about Spain and Portugal. Fortunately, aggregate data will be adequate for the analysis I have in mind.

The best indicator of the candidate's eligibility for structural transfers is its per capita GDP and its relationship to the EU average.

---

[23] Council Regulation (EC) No 1260/99; Official Journal L 161 of 26.06.1999.

As I noted above, the largest share of the ERDF/ESF is allocated under Objective 1 according to which a region qualifies if its GDP is no more than 75% of the EU average. As in the previous sections, the variable *Candidate GDP* measures the candidate's per capita GDP in PPS as a percentage of the EU average. Eye-balling these data reveals that over 75% of CEE regions would qualify for structural aid under this criterion. Under both Objective 1 and Objective 2, candidates with substantial fractions of their workforce employed in the agricultural or industrial sectors are more likely to receive structural assistance. I include the variables *Candidate Agriculture Employment* and *Candidate Industry Employment* to capture this. These variables are as described in the previous sections.

According to the theory, EU members that receive large structural transfers should be far more interested in ensuring that candidates obtain limited rights to these funds. The variable *EU Member ERDF/ESF Amount* is a proxy for the importance of structural aid to the member state and measures the amount of money, in billions of Euros, that the member received right *before* enlargement. Traditionally, the largest recipients have been Ireland, Spain, Greece, and Portugal. Data from the EU Commission (2000a).

I also include several controls, the codings of which have all been previously described. The larger the *Expected Size of the EU*, the harder will it be to compensate the net recipients. The higher the *EU Member Budget Contributions*, the more concerned will it be about possible budget increases. In both cases, the probability that the EU member will ask for differentiation of membership rights for the candidate should increase. The distributional conflict will become much more intense if the budget cannot grow to accommodate the increased demand for structural aid that comes with expansion. The variable *ERDF/ESF Budget Ceiling* is coded as 1 if the structural budget is capped (as it was in 2000) and 0 otherwise. The last two controls, *EU Member Exports to Candidate* and *Candidate Democracy*, are all measured as in Section 5.2.1, and their expected effects are the same. Table A-4 in the appendix provides descriptive statistics for all variables.

5.4.2 Estimation results

Table 5.10 presents the estimations of three *probit* models. Model 1 is the baseline and incorporates only the variables of main theoretical

Table 5.10. *Common Structural Policies: probit model for the likelihood of demands for discrimination.*

	Model 1	Model 2	Model 3
Candidate GDP	−0.009*	−0.011*	−0.004*
	(0.004)	(0.005)	(0.002)
Candidate industry employment	0.031*	0.045**	0.044*
	(0.014)	(0.013)	(0.014)
Candidate agriculture employment	0.026*	0.026**	0.037*
	(0.010)	(0.010)	(0.017)
EU member ERDF/ESF amount	0.744**	0.719*	0.730*
	(0.231)	(0.235)	(0.233)
EU member budget contributions	−0.123*	−0.124*	−0.126*
	(0.063)	(0.062)	(0.063)
Expected size of the EU	0.072	0.049	
	(0.055)	(0.053)	
EU member exports to candidate		−0.135*	−0.133*
		(0.066)	(0.067)
Candidate democracy		0.044	0.011
		(0.028)	(0.029)
ERDF/ESF budget ceiling			0.936†
			(0.563)
Constant	−2.994**	−2.930*	−2.743**
	(0.746)	(0.933)	(0.579)
N	214	214	214
Wald χ^2	45.86**	43.97**	46.01**
Pseudo R^2	0.40	0.43	0.43

†$p < 0.1$, *$p < 0.05$, **$p < 0.001$. Robust standard errors in parentheses.

interest. Models 2 and 3 add several control variables as robustness checks.[24]

Overall, the models fit the data quite well. The Wald test is highly significant, meaning that the variables have a discernible statistical effect as a group. Model 2, which I use for all interpretations in this section, predicts correctly 85% of the observed outcomes. Table 5.11

---

[24] As before, I exclude *Expected Size of the EU* from Model 3 because of collinearity problems. There is no indication that this introduces omitted variable bias.

Table 5.11. *Common Structural Policies: model fit.*

		Predicted demand		
		No	Yes	Total
Actual demand	No	145	2	147
	Yes	30	37	67
	Total	175	39	214

tabulates the actual outcomes against the model's predictions (as usual, the predicted outcome is coded as discrimination if the estimated probability is over 50%). The model predicts correctly 99% of cases without discrimination and 55% of cases with discrimination. The relative lack of success in the latter case is mitigated by the fact that when discrimination is predicted, the model will be wrong in only 5% of the cases. In general, the model over-predicts no discrimination: 175 cases (82%) as opposed to the actual 147 cases (69%). Still, given the high level of data aggregation and the parsimoniousness of the model, the fit is satisfactory.

The estimated coefficients strongly support the theoretical claims. Except for the expected size of the EU, all principal variables are statistically significant across the three specifications, and except for *EU Member Budget Contributions,* their effects are in the hypothesized directions. EU members are more likely to demand differentiated rights for a candidate when it is relatively under-developed (low GDP compared to the EU average), and when its agricultural or industrial sectors employ substantial fractions of its workforce. The propensity to make such requests also increases for EU members that receive larger amounts of structural transfers.

The one anomalous finding concerns the effect of the size of the budget contributions. Contrary to expectation, the more the EU member contributes to the common budget, the less likely it is to ask for qualifying the candidate's access to structural aid. Recall that in the CAP, net contributors were *more* likely to ask for differentiated rights. One possible explanation is that net contributors are more concerned about CAP increases than they are about ERDF subsidies. That may be caused by the different consequences of the two subsidies: whereas structural aid fosters economic growth in poor regions, the EAGGF, with their protectionist flavor, have usually been seen as a political instrument. For example, direct payments to farmers redistributed income from relatively wealthy industrial nations to France and poorer agrarian states. Unlike EAGGF transfers that tend to hinder the industrialization of backward states, structural aid usually contributes to economic development. This implies that the most industrialized countries – which also tend to be the main net contributors to the EU budget – could actually profit when structural transfers produce economic growth and political stabilization in less advanced member states, or when they promote more intense economic cooperation and reduce the transaction costs to trade.

Unlike the situation with the CAP, the expected size of the Union has no statistically discernible impact on the likelihood of discrimination demands. This could be simply because the budget for structural aid has remained relatively stable over time and has not been subject to potential sharp increases like the budget for agricultural subsidies. This should not be too surprising: after all, the goal of these structural transfers is to improve the economy of the affected regions to the point that they would no longer qualify for such aid. Unlike the EAGGF, which produces incentives to maintain one's subsidy indefinitely, the ERDF has a built-in dynamic which should eventually disqualify the recipient. This characteristic of the ERDF also probably accounts for the relatively weak effect that capping the budget has. Although doing so is going to make distributional conflicts more intense, as expected, the statistical significance of the variable barely clears the 10% level.

Of the remaining control variables, the quality of the candidate democratic institutions does not seem to affect EU member's propensity to ask for transitional restrictions. The trade relationship between the member and the candidate, however, does. The more the EU member exports to the applicant, the less likely it is to demand discrimination against it. This is because the EU member has a clearly defined interest in promoting the economic well-being of its trading partner, and the ERDF transfers are meant precisely for this purpose.

These findings support the hypothesis that EU member demand for differentiation of a candidate's rights to structural aid is determined by the member's eligibility for these funds and the likelihood that expansion would reduce the amount it receives. These results are robust to different model specifications and do not change substantially if we use a SURE model instead.[25]

5.4.3 Predicted probabilities

As in Section 5.2.3 for the Free Movement of Workers and Section 5.3.3 for Common Agricultural Policies, I create hypothetical dyads and compute predicted probabilities of demands for discrimination of access to structural funds. Looking at several dyads that resemble actual cases can serve as a quick check on our intuitive priors. For instance, a member with the characteristics of Denmark in the early 1980s should be extremely unlikely to ask for compensation for the accession of a candidate with the characteristics of Portugal. With its relatively high GDP, Denmark has never been among the main recipients of structural aid, and as such should not be very concerned about Portugal's entry to the Union. Indeed, the model confirms our expectations by predicting that the probability of discrimination demand will be negligible at 0.04%. The propensity to ask for differentiated membership increases considerably if the candidate is relatively poor (63% in the French–Estonian dyad) or if the EU member is among the main beneficiaries of structural aid (86% in the Greek–Latvian dyad).

Table 5.12 presents the results of a somewhat more systematic analysis. As before, I create hypothetical baseline scenarios that vary in their conflict-proneness, and then examine the effect of changing each of the principal explanatory variables given the contexts these scenarios create. I use Model 2 but the substantive results remain the same if we use any of the other specifications.

The first, and perhaps most striking, finding that emerges from the inspection of this table is that *EU Member ERDF/ESF Amount* has a consistently strong effect on the risk of discrimination demand for scenarios that are at least moderately prone to conflicts. When all other factors ameliorate distributional conflict, even a main beneficiary is unlikely to ask for differentiation of so unoffensive a candidate (probability is 6%). The low propensity for discrimination persists in the moderately conflict-prone scenario as long as the EU member receives structural transfers that amount to no more than the sample median

---

[25] Table A-1 in the appendix shows the results of the SURE estimation.

Table 5.12. *Common Structural Policies: predicted probabilities of demands for discrimination (%).*

	Scenario proneness to discrimination		
	Low	Moderate	High
Candidate GDP			
75th percentile: 129.7	0.69	21.74	88.59
	(0.00, 6.47)	(2.05, 59.07)	(66.46, 98.71)
Sample median: 56	0.94	27.06	91.72
	(0.00, 8.79)	(4.53, 62.70)	(72.33, 99.33)
25th percentile: 40.7	1.21	31.77	93.50
	(0.00, 10.98)	(7.30, 66.52)	(75.76, 99.62)
Candidate industry employment			
25th percentile: 27.3	0.69	22.70	88.97
	(0.00, 6.47)	(2.89, 58.08)	(65.75, 98.82)
Sample median: 31	0.92	27.06	91.34
	(0.00, 8.43)	(4.53, 62.69)	(70.93, 99.29)
75th percentile: 35.3	1.28	32.75	93.50
	(0.00, 11.19)	(7.16, 68.38)	(75.76, 99.62)
Candidate agriculture employment			
25th percentile: 6.5	0.69	25.49	89.89
	(0.00, 6.47)	(3.88, 61.15)	(69.94, 98.87)
Sample median: 8.7	0.76	27.06	90.68
	(0.00, 6.92)	(4.53, 62.69)	(71.22, 99.06)
75th percentile: 18.4	1.12	34.70	93.50
	(0.00, 9.81)	(8.30, 70.61)	(75.76, 99.62)
EU member ERDF/ESF amount			
25th percentile: 0.1	0.69	23.84	56.50
	(0.00, 6.47)	(2.92, 60.61)	(21.60, 87.33)
Sample median: 0.27	0.80	27.06	60.89
	(0.00, 7.65)	(4.53, 62.69)	(26.09, 89.08)
75th percentile: 2.23	6.11	75.03	93.50
	(0.10, 29.75)	(53.28, 91.74)	(75.76, 99.62)
EU member budget contributions			
75th percentile: 14	0.69	7.58	56.11
	(0.00, 6.47)	(0.01, 43.28)	(17.20, 90.87)
Sample median: 3.6	2.68	27.09	90.66
	(0.18, 10.37)	(4.53, 62.70)	(72.20, 98.80)
25th percentile: 1.4	4.43	35.37	93.50
	(0.47, 14.10)	(8.04, 70.42)	(75.76, 99.62)

95% confidence intervals in parentheses.

(27%). However, if the member is among the main beneficiaries, it is very likely to seek protection for its subsidies (75%). The situation is further aggravated if the other variables make the candidate's unconditional accession especially problematic. In this case, discrimination becomes likely even if the member receives relatively little aid (57%) and nearly certain if it receives a lot of it (94%).

Figure 5.7 illustrates this effect very well for the moderately conflict-prone scenario. Although we cannot be very sure of the precision of our predictions for members that receive small amounts of ERDF/ESF transfers (note the relatively wide confidence intervals for aid of less than about €2 billion), we can say that the effect is quite large and significant for members who receive more substantial amounts. In fact, our confidence in the model's prediction grows with the amount of money the member gets under the CSP. Observe further that the model predicts that members that receive more than roughly €1.5 billion in structural transfers are likely to demand differentiated membership for the newcomers. At the very least, this set would include six of the EU member states: Spain, Portugal, Italy, Germany, the UK, and Greece.

In contrast to this sharp prediction, the effect of the candidate's wealth is quite weak. This is immediately evident from inspection of

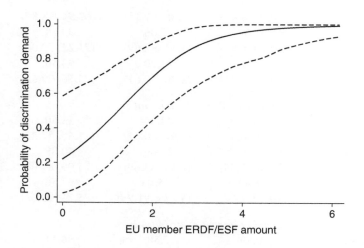

Fig. 5.7 Common Structural Policies: effect of EU member ERDF/ESF amount on discrimination demand. Solid line shows predicted probabilities; dashed lines show 95% confidence intervals.

Common Structural Policies 129

Table 5.12: even some of the poorest applicants with per capita GDP around 41% of the EU average are unlikely to be forced to accept transitional limitations for their access to CSP funds as long as the baseline context is at most moderately conflict-prone. Although demands for discrimination of wealthier candidates are even less likely, the model will predict no such demands for both scenarios. The effect is also negligible when the other variables create very high propensity for distributional conflict: both rich and poor candidates are very likely to face discriminatory measures (89% and 94%, respectively).

Figure 5.8 illustrates the weakness of this effect graphically. Observe that the confidence intervals are quite wide and remain relatively static throughout the entire range of the explanatory variable. In other words, we are quite uncertain about the expected probability of discrimination demand regardless of candidate wealth, and we cannot even say much about the differences between very rich and very poor candidates. There is an overall downward trend, which is captured by the statistical model, but we should be wary of putting too much into the interpretation of its substantive effect. The findings for the fractions of the candidate's workforce employed in its industrial and

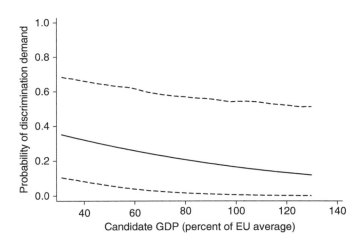

Fig. 5.8 Common Structural Policies: effect of candidate GDP on discrimination demand. Solid line shows predicted probabilities; dashed lines show 95% confidence intervals.

agricultural sectors are very similar, both in terms of their weakness and associated estimation uncertainty.

The effect of the EU member's contributions to the budget is only slightly stronger. Even the smallest contributors – who are the most prone to ask for discrimination – are not likely to do so unless the baseline case is already highly conflictual. In that case, the effect can be quite serious. For instance, while relatively large contributors will also probably make such demands (56%), the smallest are nearly certain to do so (94%). Figure 5.9 graphs the predicted risk of discrimination demands for the moderately conflict-prone scenario. Note the uncertainty of the model's predictions for relatively small contributors, and their improvement for the larger ones. In general, this variable is also of marginal substantive interest.

However, the theory does not concern itself with the individual effects of the principal explanatory variables but rather with their joint impact on the probability of discrimination demands. As before, I created three hypothetical scenarios that vary in the degree of adversity the EU member expects after the unconditional accession of the candidate. The methodology is the same as the one used for the FMW and

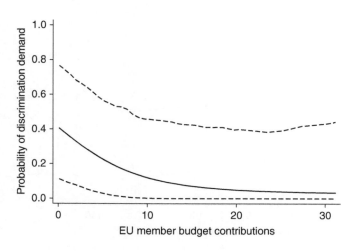

Fig. 5.9 Common Structural Policies: effect of EU member budget contributions on discrimination demand. Solid line shows predicted probabilities; dashed lines show 95% confidence intervals.

Common Structural Policies

Table 5.13. *Common Structural Policies: joint effect (%).*

Adverse consequences	Scenario proneness to discrimination		
	Low	Moderate	High
Negligible	0.69	4.23	5.20
	(0.00, 6.47)	(0.00, 31.48)	(0.00, 38.23)
Moderate	7.55	27.06	31.07
	(1.21, 21.02)	(4.53, 62.70)	(5.20, 68.76)
Severe	72.55	92.08	93.50
	(27.74, 98.24)	(72.40, 99.43)	(75.76, 99.62)

95% confidence intervals in parentheses.

CAP cases. Table 5.13 shows the predicted probabilities for the nine scenarios that combine these with the three baseline contexts.

The joint effect of the main explanatory variables is very large, especially when members are threatened by severe losses. In these cases, the scenario's conflict-proneness hardly matters: the probability of a discrimination demand is close to 73% even when all other variables make the candidate's unconditional accession unproblematic otherwise. Note, on the other hand, that members are unlikely to ask for differentiated rights irrespective of the conflict characteristics of the baseline scenario even if they are moderately threatened (31% risk in the worst case). In other words, while the joint effect is indeed dramatic at the high end of expected adversity, it does not make itself felt before that. In fact, our estimates remain very uncertain in all but these exceptional cases.

5.4.4 Conclusion

The empirical analysis of the Common Structural Policies lends satisfactory support to my theoretical claims. Member states appear to estimate the consequences an unconditional accession of a candidate will have on their ability to receive their customary amounts of structural aid. The larger the benefit of ERDF/ESF transfers, the more likely is the EU member to request transitional periods for the candidate's eligibility for these funds. This propensity is stronger if the candidate's economic characteristics make it more likely to qualify for a large share of the structural budget. The model's predictions accord well with the historical record. The estimated probabilities suggest that the most determined opposition to the unconditional accession of the CEE countries should come from Spain, Greece, and Portugal. In contrast, Ireland, which used to be among the main beneficiaries of structural transfers, was quite reluctant to ask for the differentiation of membership. Not surprisingly, Germany, France, and Great Britain were the least likely to demand restrictions for the newcomers' access to the ERDF.

5.5 The demand for compensation: conclusion

In this chapter, I assessed the empirical support for my first theoretical hypothesis. I examined the conditions that make EU members more likely to expect serious distributional conflicts from the unconditional accession of candidates in each of three policy areas. I then analyzed the probability that these members will demand differentiated membership rights for the newcomers in these policy areas.

The general conclusion is that the empirical tests provide strong support for the theoretical claims. Gains and losses from enlargement are distributed unevenly among EU member states. When outsider states seek to join the Union, existing members assess the likely impact this widening would have on their expected benefits. If this assessment projects relative losses, members are very likely to oppose the unconditional accession of the applicants. They will seek to protect their labor markets when they are afraid that massive migration will require costly social adaptations. They will seek to limit the candidate's ability to obtain agricultural subsidies when they expect it to threaten their own access to direct payments through Common Agricultural Policies. Similarly, they will tend to restrict the candidate's eligibility for structural transfers if they are among the main recipients of the ERDF/ESF.

The theoretical causal relationship is corroborated by the analysis of three separate policy areas. This provides three independent tests of the theory. Furthermore, as expected by the theory, some variables have different effects depending on the policy area under scrutiny.[26] Hence, we can be relatively confident that the strategy choices of EU members during enlargement negotiations are highly dependent on their expectations about resulting conflicts with social and distributional consequences.

---

[26] I also conducted several tests for the specificity of factors for the different policy areas. Results are available upon request.

This empirical evidence stands in stark contrast to the claims one finds in the scholarly literature on EU enlargement negotiations. In particular, the results do *not* support the contention that EU members deliberately maximize their gains from expansion. Instead, it appears that EU members seek to avoid the worst forms of distributional conflict by demanding phase-ins of membership rights for some candidates or asking for some other form of compensation *only* when they fear that such conflicts may arise and leave them worse off. Ultimately, this means that there is a very good chance that cooperation among members will deepen with the widening of the Union.

Although this analysis substantiates the first component of my theory, it cannot by itself be taken as conclusive evidence that the theory is useful. The reason is that at least one theory also anticipates the relationship between expected distributional conflicts and the demands for discrimination but makes different ultimate claims. Schimmelfennig's "rhetorical action" theory acknowledges such conflicts but claims that they were *not* resolved through side-payments. Instead, the supporters of enlargement rhetorically trapped the relative losers into accepting the accession of candidates in spite of the large costs. This is contrary to my theory which focuses on the redistribution of enlargement costs and benefits. In my view, either discriminatory membership or intra-Union redistribution can be used to compensate the enlargement losers. Accession negotiations help achieve Pareto-efficiency whenever possible. Enlargement outcomes are then explained by the ability of all involved actors to locate these deals and coordinate on their specifics. Because this needs to be demonstrated empirically, in the next chapter I present a study of the second component of my theory.

5.6 Appendix

Table A-1. *Multivariate probit model for the likelihood of the demand for differentiated membership.*

	Model 1	Model 2	Model 3
Free Movement of Labor			
Candidate GDP	−0.037*	−0.039*	−0.033**
	−(0.013)	−(0.015)	−(0.009)
Distance between capitals	−0.601	−0.815†	−0.529
	(0.403)	(0.456)	(0.356)
EU member share of foreigners	0.280**	0.994*	0.258**
	(0.072)	(0.417)	(0.061)
EU member industry employment	0.118**	0.191**	0.197*
	(0.035)	(0.060)	(0.081)
Candidate industry employment	0.075*	0.093*	0.073*
	(0.026)	(0.038)	(0.027)
EU member unemployment	0.073	−0.047	0.016
	(0.102)	(0.119)	(0.098)
Candidate unemployment	0.062*	0.065	0.047
	(0.033)	(0.041)	(0.035)
EU member exports to candidate		−0.005	
		(0.004)	
Candidate democracy		−0.120†	
		(0.073)	
EU member budget contributions		−0.360†	
		(0.196)	
EU member population over 65		1.527	
		(0.991)	
Expected size of the EU			0.114
			(0.092)
Constant	−6.020*	−6.678*	−10.550*
	(2.045)	(2.864)	(4.426)

Appendix

Table A-1. *(Cont.)*

	Model 1	Model 2	Model 3
Common Agricultural Policies			
Candidate agriculture GVA	0.076*	0.052	0.075†
	(0.038)	(0.038)	(0.042)
EU member agriculture GVA	0.047*	0.066*	0.058*
	(0.019)	(0.025)	(0.022)
Expected size of EU	0.160**	0.153**	
	(0.039)	(0.044)	
EU member budget contributions	0.042*	0.034	0.040†
	(0.022)	(0.023)	(0.021)
Candidate agriculture employment		0.034*	
		(0.014)	
EU member exports to candidate		−0.007	
		(0.014)	
Candidate democracy		−0.014	
		(0.026)	
Candidate GDP		−0.013*	
		(0.005)	
EAGGF budget ceiling			2.227**
			(0.547)
Common Structural Policies			
Constant	−4.300**	−3.658**	−2.519**
	(0.939)	(1.079)	(0.598)
Candidate GDP	−0.009†	−0.013*	−0.005*
	(0.005)	(0.005)	(0.002)
EU member share of ERDF/ESF	0.839**	0.779**	0.777**
	(0.210)	(0.226)	(0.216)
Candidate industry employment	0.029†	0.041*	0.042*
	(0.017)	(0.017)	(0.017)
Candidate agriculture employment	0.024*	0.026*	0.036*
	(0.011)	(0.011)	(0.017)
EU member budget contributions	−0.140*	−0.134*	−0.133*
	(0.054)	(0.057)	(0.058)
Expected size of the EU	0.079	0.048	
	(0.065)	(0.058)	

Table A-1. *(Cont.)*

	Model 1	Model 2	Model 3
EU member exports to candidate		−0.122*	−0.122†
		(0.062)	(0.064)
Candidate democracy		0.065	0.027
		(0.049)	(0.043)
ERDF/ESF budget ceiling			0.938
			(0.626)
Constant	−3.123*	−2.935*	−2.807**
	(1.052)	(1.065)	(0.612)
N (within models)	214	214	214
LR test of correlation	10.437*	2.872	7.331†

† $p < 0.1$, * $p < 0.05$, ** $p < 0.001$. Robust standard errors in parentheses.

Table A-2. *Free Movement of Workers: descriptive statistics.*

Variable	N	Mean	SD	Min	Max
Demand for discrimination	214	0.15	0.36	0	1
Candidate GDP	214	62.35	24.94	31.10	129.70
Distance between capitals	214	1.48	0.78	0.07	3.77
EU member share of foreigners	214	1.30	1.79	0.06	7.34
EU member industry employment	214	29.45	6.39	20.80	49.30
Candidate industry employment	214	31.95	5.26	24.10	45.70
EU member unemployment	214	6.74	3.65	0	18.60
Candidate unemployment	214	10.15	5.25	0.90	18.70
EU member exports to candidate	214	7.65	34.18	0.02	422.00
Candidate democracy	214	9.27	1.12	6	10
EU member budget contributions	214	7.81	8.25	0.12	31.14
EU member population over 65	214	1.21	1.23	0.02	3.89

N = number of observations; SD = standard deviation; Min = minimum; Max = maximum.

Appendix

Table A-3. *Common Agricultural Policies: descriptive statistics.*

Variable	N	Mean	SD	Min	Max
Demand for discrimination	214	0.47	0.50	0	1
EU member agriculture GVA	214	9.04	9.31	0.04	31.66
Candidate agriculture GVA	214	1.85	2.30	0.16	10.20
Expected size of EU	214	20.42	6.18	9	25
EU member budget contributions	214	7.81	8.25	0.12	31.14
Candidate agriculture employment	214	11.74	7.72	1.20	32.00
Candidate GDP	214	62.35	24.94	31.10	129.70
EU member exports to candidate	214	7.65	34.18	0.02	422.00
Candidate democracy	214	9.27	1.12	6	10
EAGGF budget ceiling	214	0.63	0.48	0	1

N = number of observations; SD = standard deviation; Min = minimum; Max = maximum.

Table A-4. *Common Structural Policies: descriptive statistics.*

Variable	N	Mean	SD	Min	Max
Demand for discrimination	214	0.31	0.46	0	1
Candidate GDP	214	62.35	24.94	31.10	129.70
EU member ERDF/ESF amount	214	1.25	1.66	0.00	6.16
Candidate industry employment	214	31.95	5.26	24.10	45.70
Candidate agriculture employment	214	11.74	7.72	1.20	32.00
EU member budget contributions	214	7.81	8.25	0.12	31.14
EU member exports to candidate	214	7.65	34.18	0.02	422.00
Candidate democracy	214	9.27	1.12	6	10
ERDF/ESF budget ceiling	214	0.63	0.48	0	1
Expected size of EU	214	20.42	6.18	9	25

N = number of observations; SD = standard deviation; Min = minimum; Max = maximum.

6 EU accession negotiations and the allocation of discriminatory membership rights

The enlargement of the European Union often causes conflict about the distribution of costs and benefits among members. States that receive significant agricultural subsidies oppose the unconditional accession of applicants with large and inefficient agricultural sectors. States that are eligible for structural subsidies expect competition for these funds from relatively large and poor newcomers with inadequately developed infrastructure. States that project high unemployment fear the liberalization of the labor market for relatively poor neighbors. EU member states that expect net losses from these distributional conflicts can stall negotiations and threaten to sabotage enlargement unless the relative winners within or without the Union agree to defray some of these costs. However, there have been many instances of candidates acceding unconditionally despite such opposition. In fact, some candidates did not have to accept any limitations on their membership even though some members had threatened to veto enlargement if these applicants were to accede without transitional differentiation.

In this chapter I evaluate the second set of hypotheses: When do EU members and candidates agree to implement transitional qualifications of membership rights for the acceding states? My theory of differentiated membership predicts that this stage of the accession negotiations will be crucial for explaining the outcomes of the enlargement process because this is where the distributional conflict can be resolved. When one or more EU members expect net losses and ask for discriminatory measures against newcomers, enlargement cannot succeed without additional conditions. Either the relative winners in the Union or the candidates will have to accept some sort of redistribution that satisfies the "brakemen." If they do not, enlargement will likely fail. This suggests a straightforward testable implication: If distributional conflict arises during the accession negotiations and EU members demand discriminatory measures, it should be more likely for membership rights to be phased-in.

Although the logic of this implication is clear, the relationship between distributional conflict and enlargement outcomes is not trivial. Some scholars claim that EU members and candidates could not resolve the distributional conflicts by compensating the relative losers (e.g. Schimmelfennig 2001, 2003). Others argue that enlargement outcomes are contingent upon the states' bargaining power and less so on the presence of distributional conflict (e.g. Moravcsik and Vachudova 2003). This suggests that my theory will be supported only if this conflict is resolved by redistribution of enlargement gains from relative winners to relative losers.

To test this hypothesis, I estimate the probability that acceding states obtain restricted access to EU club goods (common policies). In turn, these restrictions help explain how distributional conflict affects the outcome of enlargement talks. The empirical findings provide strong support for the theoretical argument. Enlargement is not necessarily doomed to failure when distributional conflict occurs. Instead, members and candidates negotiate the reallocation of enlargement gains to ensure that widening succeeds. The qualification of membership rights for newcomers then serves as an instrument for redistribution, with one caveat. The more important the accession of a candidate is to existing EU members, the less likely they are to force discriminatory measures. In these cases, members resort to the alternative strategy of intra-Union redistribution, and this decreases the likelihood of membership restrictions for the newcomer.

The analysis shows how governments choose among different strategies to sustain the cooperation of states during the accession process. In doing so, it underscores the importance of diverging preferences *inside* the Union as well as the opportunities to negotiate the reallocation of enlargement gains among states. This approach explains why EU widening succeeds even when it might be expected to fail.

6.1 Research design

As in Chapter 5, I focus on the first five EU enlargements to analyze the conditions under which EU members grant restricted membership rights to acceding states. I will look at three common EU policy areas: the Free Movement of Workers (FMW), the Common Agricultural Policies (CAP), and the Common Structural Policies (CSP).[1] I measure the extent of distributional conflict in the accession negotiations and use this information to estimate the probabilities of discrimination against newcomers and of unconditional accession. As in Chapter 5, the unit of analysis is the *member-applicant policy dyad*. Descriptive statistics for all variables can be found in the appendix to this chapter.

6.1.1 *Dependent variable*

The theory predicts that members and applicants will agree to restrictions of membership rights for newcomers when they must resolve distributional conflicts. I code such qualifications with an indicator variable, which takes the value of 1 if the applicant formally accepts differentiated membership in the policy area under consideration, or the value of 0 if the applicant is not discriminated against.

The EU accession treaties for each enlargement round specify all temporary derogations from the common *acquis*. The discriminatory measures over the transitional period across policy areas are as follows: (a) for the FMW, restricted access to the EU labor market for newcomers; (b) for the CAP, asymmetric allocation of subsidies to farmers among existing members and newcomers; and (c) for the CSP, asymmetric allocation of direct payments among existing members and newcomers.

Approximately 65% of the cases over the five enlargement rounds involved some qualification of membership rights. Perhaps not surprisingly, the two Mediterranean and Eastern expansions were the most discriminatory, especially for the CAP. Nonetheless, there is considerable variation across all enlargement rounds. For example, the UK, Ireland, and Denmark had to accept some restrictions – mostly for labor market integration – in the 1972 widening.

6.1.2 *Explanatory variables*

To test my main hypothesis – that membership rights are phased-in when distributional conflict occurs – I code the existence and extent

---

[1] See Chapter 5 for a detailed discussion of the overall research design.

of such conflict in the enlargement process. (In Chapter 7 I also assess this hypothesis qualitatively in a comparative case study of the negotiations about the CSP in the second Mediterranean and the Eastern enlargement rounds.)

One way to measure the extent of distributional conflict is to use the probability that members demand discrimination as a proxy. (Recall that I estimated the probabilities for these demands in Chapter 5.) The higher the predicted probability that members demand the limitation of membership rights for a candidate in a given policy area, the more intense the distributional conflict.[2]

There are several important advantages to using predicted probabilities. First, they control for random or strategic requests for differentiated membership not accounted for by the structural factors in the theory. This cannot be done with a simple dichotomous variable. Second, they provide more information about the probable existence of conflict and help avoid omitted variable bias that could happen if I did not account for all factors that influence EU members' decision to ask for discrimination. Third, they account simultaneously for conflict propensity and discrimination demands, the two driving factors identified by the theory.

The main disadvantage of using these probabilities is that it complicates the estimation of the model. Because these probabilities are estimated statistically, we have to account for the confidence intervals around the point estimates for the predictions. This introduces additional uncertainty in the model and weakens the statistical significance of the findings. (Because this makes for a more difficult hurdle, however, if the findings are statistically significant, then we can be quite confident of the results.) I bootstrap the estimation of the present model to account for the uncertainty introduced by the use of predicted probabilities.[3]

---

[2] I use the predicted probabilities from the baseline models (Model 1) in Tables 5.1, 5.6, and 5.10. Using any of the other models does not change the results.

[3] I also estimate the models with the dichotomous dependent variable from Chapter 5. Recall that *Distributional Conflict* is an indicator variable that takes a value of 1 if distributional conflict arose during the accession negotiations and a value of 0 otherwise. This variable perfectly predicts the outcome in the FMW and CAP areas, so it cannot be used for the regressions. For the CSP, its coefficient is positive and highly significant. I did not use an instrument variable approach in the model with the dichotomous operationalization of distributional conflict

In addition to the main explanatory variable, I control for several other factors that may affect the distribution of gains and losses from EU expansion.[4] As I noted above, the dependent variable measures only redistribution at the expense of the candidate. However, the theory also predicts that enlargement can succeed when some members agree to bear some of the distributional costs themselves. To test whether differentiated membership is less likely when some EU members value highly the candidate's accession, I look at whether enlargement supporters agree to raise the budget in an attempt to convince the opposers that accession would not be exceedingly costly to them. The variable *Budget Ceiling* measures the budget cap as percentage of the Union's Gross National Product (GNP). An increase in the budget ceiling should make differentiated membership less likely. Historically, the EU increased this ceiling incrementally until the second Mediterranean expansion with the exception of the Northern enlargement when it was temporarily reduced.

I use two variables to measure the expected costs of enlargement for EU members. *EU Member Council Power* is the change in each member's voting power as a percentage of total votes in the Council of Ministers. EU members that expect their voting influence to decline should object to the accession of new states.

Recall that candidates with valuable alternatives to Union membership have more bargaining leverage. The more attractive its outside options are, the less likely the candidate is to have to accept limitations on its membership. The more EU members care about enlargement, the more likely are they to engage in intra-Union redistribution to ensure that this candidate does not forsake accession altogether. Measuring the value of outside options is notoriously difficult. There are several plausible measures but none of them is fully satisfying because it is not really possible to estimate completely the utility from non-membership. I consider several factors that at least indirectly capture the candidate's dependence on the Union.

> because we do not have a decent instrument for the emergence of such conflict. Using weak instruments may cause more problems than it solves because point estimates, hypothesis tests, and confidence intervals are all unreliable. These problems only get worse in non-linear models and persist even in large samples (Bartels 1991, Stock et al., 2002).
>
> [4] The variables from the first stage cannot be incorporated into the second stage because this would cause collinearity problems. However, the predicted probabilities account for these variables indirectly. For instance, I cannot use either the size of the EU or the enlargement round count because two of the specifications used to estimate the predicted probabilities in Chapter 5 already account for EU size.

Research design   143

The higher the volume of imports from the EU in the candidate country, the more established the trading relationship is, which means that the candidate policies are probably already in line with the EU. This should make discrimination against such candidates much less likely. *Candidate Imports from EU* expresses the amount of imports from the EU as a percentage of the candidate's GDP. The bargaining power of accession countries also depends on their outside options as a group. The higher the volume of trade of the applicants with the EU relative to trade among themselves, the more likely are they to extract concessions from the EU and join without restrictions. *Candidate Export Ratio* measures the strength of trading relations between the EU and the candidates as a ratio of the candidates' trade with the EU and their trade among themselves. The data source for both variables is the *Direction of Trade Statistics* of the International Monetary Fund (IMF various years).

6.1.3 Model specification

The dependent variable is limited and can take only two values, so *probit* is an appropriate statistical model.[5] I begin by testing whether the demand for a phase-in of membership rights for a particular policy area exerts a systematic impact on the likelihood that candidates will have to accept restrictions on their rights in that area. As before, let $z \in \{CAP, CSP, FMW\}$ index the policy area. I estimate the following area-specific model:[6]

$$\Pr(\text{Discrimination in } z) = \Phi(\alpha + \beta_1 \text{Budget Ceiling}$$
$$+ \beta_2 \Pr(\text{Demand for Discrimination in } z)$$
$$+ \beta_3 \text{Candidate Imports from EU}$$
$$+ \beta_4 \text{Candidate Export Ratio}$$
$$+ \beta_5 \text{EU Member Council Power}). \quad (6.1)$$

---

[5] Using a selection model would be inappropriate because the data are not censored. Some candidates accepted limited membership rights when they acceded to the Union even though EU members had not demanded qualifications. This happened when restrictions demanded for one of them were extended to the entire group. The model implicitly acknowledges that the two stages are related when it uses probabilities predicted at the first stage.

[6] The empirical results are robust when all three policy areas are analyzed together (Plümper and Schneider 2007).

Recall that the predicted probabilities of discrimination demand in area z are not data and have their own uncertainty. To account for this, I bootstrap the estimation of the models given by (6.1) as follows. I draw (with replacement) $M = 1,000$ random samples of size N from the data set. For each draw, I estimate the original *probit* equations from Chapter 5 and generate predicted values for the dependent variables. This yields M samples of size N with predicted probabilities of discrimination demand, which I then use to estimate the model in (6.1). This generates M predicted probabilities of discrimination for each observation in these samples, from which I take the mean and 95% confidence intervals.

6.2 Estimation results

Table 6.1 presents the estimation results from the three area-specific *probit* models using bootstrapped bias-corrected 95% confidence intervals for the estimates.

To get a sense of the fit with the data, I generate contingency tables of predicted and observed values of the dependent variable.

Table 6.1. *Discriminatory membership in the EU: area models with bootstrapped 95% bias-corrected confidence intervals.*

	FMW model	CAP model	CSP model
Discrimination demand (FMW, predicted)	6.37* (3.37, 14.32)		
Discrimination demand (CAP, predicted)		5.09* (1.81, 15.10)	
Discrimination demand (CSP, predicted)			28.54* (5.61, 2153.32)
Budget ceiling	14.59* (10.69, 20.10)	8.07* (5.10, 13.09)	3.61 (−13.98, 1718.06)
Candidate imports from EU	−0.03 (−0.05, 0.01)	−0.11* (−0.17, −0.06)	−0.17 (−2.50, 0.14)
Candidate export ratio	−3.38* (−4.75, −1.85)	0.93 (−7.14, 7.65)	21.62 (−37.43, 98.06)
EU member council power	0.70* (0.26, 1.66)	1.29* (0.27, 2.90)	−2.22* (−193.74, −0.38)
Constant	−13.75* (−20.75, −9.54)	−7.82* (−12.08, −1.18)	−24.26* (−2089.37, −5.62)

* significant at the 95% level. Bias-corrected confidence intervals in parentheses.

Estimation results 145

Bootstrapping introduces some complications here as well. To get the expected number of correct predictions, I estimate the first stage model to generate predicted probabilities of demand, and then estimate the second stage model to obtain predicted probabilities of discrimination using the unbiased coefficients. With the usual 50% threshold, I then generate predicted values for the dependent variable and tabulate these against the observed values. Table 6.2 shows the expected percent correctly predicted observations for each policy area. I also report the expected percent of correct predictions of discrimination (how often the model gets it right when it predicts discrimination) and non-discrimination (how often the model gets it right when it predicts non-discrimination). Finally, I generate 95% confidence intervals for these expected values from the bootstrapping by taking the appropriate percentiles of the predictions at the end of all estimations.

Overall, the models fit the data very well. Even the least successful of them, the CSP model, predicts about 83% of the observations correctly, although most of this success is driven by its nearly perfect record in getting discrimination right (almost 99%) which masks its relative weakness in getting non-discrimination right (about 56%). The other two models present slightly more balanced fits, with 88% (FMW) and 91% (CAP) success rates overall and pretty narrow confidence intervals. These two models also perform much better when it comes to predicting discrimination: the FMW model gets 94% and the CAP model gets 95% right. As we shall see, this should not come as

Table 6.2. *Discriminatory membership in the EU: models fit with 95% confidence intervals.*

	Correctly Predicted	Correct Discrimination	Correct Non-Discrimination
Free Movement of Workers	87.76% (79.67%, 95.79%)	94.46% (90.27%, 98.62%)	68.82% (48.30%, 89.74%)
Common Agricultural Policies	90.85% (85.75%, 95.79%)	94.71% (91.02%, 98.71%)	77.22% (64.10%, 89.36%)
Common Structural Policies	82.99% (76.64%, 88.79%)	98.85% (95.80%, 100.00%)	55.89% (43.21%, 68.49%)

95% confidence intervals in parentheses.

a surprise because the probability of discrimination demand turns out to be a fairly strong predictor of actual discrimination. Unlike the CSP model, however, they also deliver fairly good results when predicting non-discrimination: 69% correct for FMW, and 77% for CAP. Given the parsimoniousness of these models, the fit with the data is indeed remarkable.

Turning now to the statistical significance of the estimated coefficients as reported in Table 6.1, the first thing to note is that the principal explanatory variable, the predicted demand for discrimination, is significant at the 95% level in each of the three models. The coefficient also has the expected sign, meaning that the higher the probability of such demand, the higher the probability that actual discrimination will occur. The confidence intervals for the estimates in the FMW and CAP models are tight, which should make us fairly sure about the results. The CSP model is a bit more problematic in the sense that even though we can be quite certain that the variable does have a statistically discernible effect in the expected direction, we cannot be very confident about its strength (note the large upper bound of the interval). Still, the results are quite unequivocal: the more extensive the distributional conflict – as reflected in higher probabilities that EU members demand discrimination – the more likely are candidates to have to accept limited membership rights. This is true regardless of the policy area, and the effect persists with the inclusion of control variables. Recalling that bootstrapping essentially inflates the standard errors (because it accounts for the uncertainty of the first-stage estimates), these results are indeed impressive.

Among the control variables, only *EU Member Council Power* attains statistical significance in all three policy area models although its effect is inconsistent. The coefficient is positive in the CSP model but negative (and contrary to the theoretical expectations) in the FMW and CAP models. I generated predicted probabilities for all values of this variable in each of the policy areas holding all other variables at their median values. Figure 6.1 presents the results with 95% confidence intervals around the point estimates.[7]

---

[7] The predicted probabilities were generated with Clarify Version 2.1 (Tomz et al., 2003). The simulations use "fundamental" and "estimation" uncertainty. Adding this fundamental uncertainty (through a random draw from the posterior distribution of the unknown parameters) to the already very high estimation uncertainty generated by the bootstrapping of the first stage will generally make

Estimation results

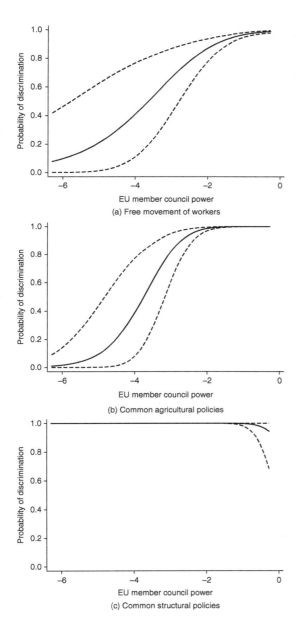

Fig. 6.1 Discriminatory membership in the EU: effect of EU member council power on discrimination. Solid line shows predicted probabilities; dashed lines show 95% confidence intervals.

Figure 6.1(c) supports the hypothesized relationship: the larger the expected decline in voting power, the more likely discrimination becomes. However, even here one can clearly see that the effect is negligible because the probability of discrimination starts out at extremely high levels (over 90%) and quickly climbs to certainty as the expected decline in voting power worsens. After that, further deterioration has no effect because opposition is already at its highest. The finding is generally in line with previous results that support the hypothesis that members value their political power and are generally averse to the accession of states that would dilute it, especially when these newcomers have divergent policy preferences (Plümper et al., 2006).

It is not obvious to me what one should make of the discrepant results exhibited by Figures 6.1(a) and (b). Despite the relatively wide confidence intervals, the effect is unmistakable: the larger the decline in voting power the EU member expects, the *less likely* is the candidate to be forced to accept limited rights. One possible explanation for this anomaly may be that very large candidates whose accession would have the largest effect on the bargaining influence of the medium to small current members are precisely the ones that these members may find it exceedingly hard to oppose. If countries with more clout are less likely to have to accept transitional limitations in general, then this could account for this relationship. Note, for example, Figure 6.1(b) and consider the potential accession of a relatively large candidate: the larger EU members (who would expect the smallest relative decline in bargaining power) are still able to impose differentiated rights on that candidate. On the other hand, the small members (who would expect the largest relative decline in bargaining power) may have to cope with the loss of influence unless supported by others. All of this, of course, remains speculative at this point and is an interesting venue for future research.

The results about the effect of *Budget Ceiling* also confound theoretical expectations. Recall that the hypothesis goes as follows: the higher the budget ceiling the less likely discrimination should be because the increase in the ceiling is supposed to reflect EU members' willingness to

---

the predictions exceedingly uncertain (in this case, in the CAP and CSP models). Because of this, I use the standard errors without bootstrapping as the estimation uncertainty and then simulate predicted probabilities with fundamental uncertainty.

Estimation results

redistribute the costs internally to secure the accession of a particularly desirable candidate. The estimated coefficient on the variable, however, is positive, indicating the exact opposite effect. Figure 6.2 shows the predicted probabilities of discrimination for FMW and CAP, the

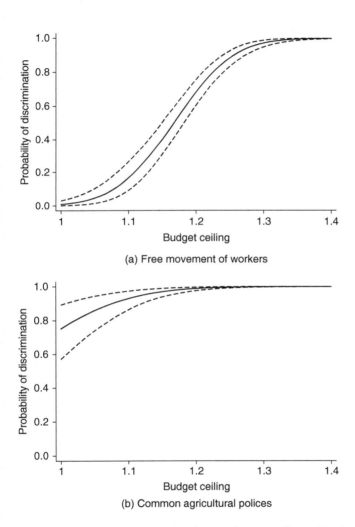

Fig. 6.2 Discriminatory membership in the EU: effect of budget ceiling on discrimination. Solid line shows predicted probabilities; dashed lines show 95% confidence intervals.

two areas for which the coefficient is also statistically significant (all other variables at their sample medians).

As already implied by the positive sign on the coefficient, increasing the budget ceiling seems to make discrimination more likely. In the CAP, Figure 6.2(b), the effect appears negligible in the sense that it seems to contribute very little at the median values of the other variables. In the FMW, Figure 6.2(a), however, it is strong and highly significant statistically, as readily seen in the very narrow confidence intervals. There are at least two potential explanations of this phenomenon. First, the ceiling itself may not adequately reflect "strategic budgeteering" – that is, there may be other ways to effect intra-Union redistribution without necessarily going to an overall budget cap. For example, during the second Mediterranean enlargement round, Germany agreed to increase its budget contributions to finance the accession of Spain and Portugal. Second, even when EU members decide to cap the budget, the ceiling may still be relatively high, implying a somewhat loose constraint on spending. For example, the cap imposed right before the Eastern enlargement was still higher than the ceiling that existed at the time of the second Northern enlargement. It is not possible to resolve these issues at such a high level of aggregation as I am forced to use for the statistical analysis. Consequently, I address some of these issues in the comparative case study in Chapter 7 where I discuss in greater detail the trade-off between the allocation of discriminatory membership rights and intra-Union redistribution of enlargement gains and losses among EU members.

The other two control variables have very weak effects that cannot even be statistically discerned in more than one model. *Candidate Imports from EU* is only significant in the CAP model, where it has the expected effect: the more the candidate imports from the EU prior to accession, the less likely it is to be forced to accept transitional limitations. Similarly, the more the applicants trade with the EU than among themselves, the more likely are they to acceded without discrimination, at least when it comes to FMW (the coefficient is not significant in the other two models). These findings, albeit weak, support the theoretical expectations: differentiated membership becomes more likely when candidates do not have valuable outside options. In general, the stronger the trading relationship between a candidate and the EU, the less likely are members to demand differentiated rights upon the accession of that candidate.

Overall, the empirical findings provide solid support for my main theoretical hypothesis: the allocation of restricted membership rights is determined by three-way negotiations between members that oppose unconditional accession, members that stand to gain substantially from it, and the candidates themselves. Each of these actors has different preferences about enlargement. Because the institutional environment may preclude unconditional enlargement, the "drivers" may support redistribution at the expense of the candidate. But even then, the outcome is not necessarily discrimination. The outside options of the candidates and the potential for intra-Union redistribution also affect the likelihood that the EU would restrict the rights of the new member states.

6.3 Predicted probabilities

I now turn to a more systematic analysis of the effects of the principal explanatory variable. We already know that the predicted demand for discrimination is highly significant statistically in each of the three policy areas, and it has the hypothesized sign. To gain some more insight into the strength of its substantive impact as well, I conduct simulations analogous to those I did in Chapter 5. I create hypothetical baseline scenarios that vary in their proneness to the imposition of discriminatory rights, and then examine the effect of changes in the main explanatory variable given the contexts created by these scenarios. To determine discrimination-proneness, I separate the control variables into two groups, depending on whether they contribute positively or negatively to discrimination. For example, *Budget Ceiling* has a positive coefficient in all three area models, so it will be in the first group regardless of policy area. *EU Member Council Power* will be in the same group for the FMW and CAP models but in the other group in the CSP model. With these two groups of controls, I then create three contexts for each of the policy areas by setting the variables for the hypothetical dyads as follows: (a) for dyads whose discrimination proneness is low, I set the variables with positive coefficients at their 25th percentile values, and the variables with negative coefficients at their 75th percentile values; (b) for dyads whose discrimination proneness is moderate, I set all variables at their median values; and (c) for dyads whose discrimination proneness is high, I set the variables with positive coefficients at their 75th percentile values, and the variables with negative coefficients at their 25th percentile values. For each of these hypothetical dyads, I then vary the predicted demand for discrimination within the relevant policy area from its 25th percentile value, to the median, and then to the 75th percentile value. Table 6.3 presents the results with 95% confidence intervals around the predictions.

The table reveals two general patterns. First, the degree of distributional conflict has a strong effect on the probability of differentiated

Table 6.3. *Discriminatory membership in the EU: predicted probabilities (%).*

	Scenario proneness to discrimination		
	Low	Moderate	High
Discrimination demand (FMW, predicted)			
25th percentile: 0.001	5.24	88.58	97.91
	(2.41, 9.80)	(81.55, 94.03)	(95.65, 99.24)
Sample median: 0.05	8.90	93.19	99.00
	(4.85, 14.81)	(89.38, 96.27)	(97.94, 99.60)
75th percentile: 0.19	33.34	99.17	99.94
	(20.45, 48.78)	(98.30, 99.71)	(99.83, 99.99)
Discrimination demand (CAP, predicted)			
75th percentile: 0.17	1.31	89.61	98.10
	(0.16, 4.49)	(77.81, 96.80)	(94.96, 99.59)
Sample median: 0.48	23.60	99.78	99.99
	(10.06, 41.96)	(99.50, 99.94)	(99.96, 100.00)
25th percentile: 0.66	56.12	99.99	100.00
	(25.19, 83.25)	(99.93, 100.00)	(100.00, 100.00)
Discrimination demand (CSP, predicted)			
25th percentile: 0.04	0.00	20.80	71.86
	(0.00, 0.00)	(0.01, 91.32)	(6.08, 99.97)
Sample median: 0.26	3.34	99.98	100.00
	(0.02, 19.28)	(99.89, 100.00)	(100.00, 100.00)
75th percentile: 0.39	90.17	100.00	100.00
	(53.74, 99.92)	(100.00, 100.00)	(100.00, 100.00)

95% confidence intervals in parentheses.

membership in all policy areas. Looking down within each column shows that as the predicted probability of discrimination demand increases, the likelihood of discrimination being imposed goes up as well, sometimes dramatically so. For instance, even in scenarios that are not discrimination-prone, going up from the median to the 75th percentile value nearly quadruples the probability of discrimination in FMW, more than doubles it in CAP, and multiplies it almost by a factor of 30 in CSP. This leads to the second observation. The CSP area is the one where the effect is also strong in the moderately and highly discrimination prone contexts, where it occurs at even lower values of the explanatory variable. At the 25th percentile value of the predicted degree of conflict, the probability of discrimination is about 21% in the moderate scenario and 72% in the highly discrimination prone one. Going up to the median value essentially makes discrimination certain in both cases. The effect in the other two areas is analogous but because discrimination is very likely already in the moderately and highly discrimination-prone scenarios, the independent contribution of the principal explanatory variable is correspondingly smaller. In other words, the impact of distributional conflict is highly context-dependent, both in terms of policy area and in the discrimination-proneness of the hypothetical dyad.

To get a better sense of the dynamic across the entire range of the main explanatory variable, Figure 6.3 presents the predicted probability of discrimination in each policy area for the dyads that are not prone to discrimination (I chose these rather than the moderately discrimination-prone dyads because this is where the effect varies the most).

The graphs illustrate the strong effect of the intensity of distributional conflict on the outcomes of accession negotiations even when all other factors tend to ameliorate the likelihood of discrimination. The most drastic and decisive impact seems to occur in the CSP area: whenever the probability of a demand for discrimination exceeds 50% (which means that the first-stage model would predict that such a demand will, in fact, occur), the expected probability of actual discrimination leaps from negligible to 100%. The effect is also very strong albeit a bit more gradual in the FMW area: the model begins predicting discrimination even at lower demand probabilities (around 20%) but the outcome is not expected to become certain until relatively higher ones (around 70%). The impact is most gradual in

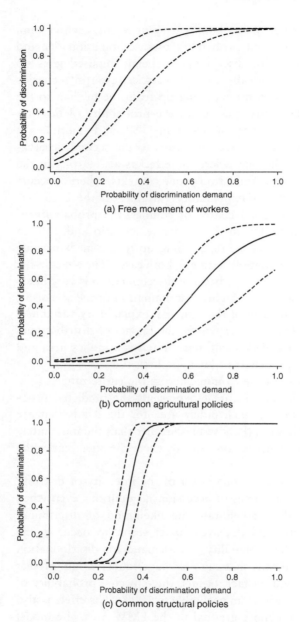

Fig. 6.3 Discriminatory membership in the EU: effect of (predicted) demand for discrimination on discrimination. Solid line shows predicted probabilities; dashed lines show 95% confidence intervals.

CAP: the model predict that discrimination will be likely once demand probability exceeds 60%, and the predicted probability never reaches 100% even when demand is at its highest. It is worth emphasizing that these strong effects occur in scenarios that are not prone to discrimination themselves. As Table 6.3 suggests, when the dyad is already highly conflictual, the small marginal effect of the demand for discrimination is generally decisive in ensuring that actual discrimination occurs. Another way of saying this would be to note that even fairly intense distributional conflict would not necessarily lead to discrimination by itself. Whenever other economic and political contextual factors ameliorate the situation – that is, there are enough benefits to go around – then countries may be admitted to the Union without being forced to accept differentiated membership rights, especially in the CAP and FMW areas and somewhat less so in CSP area. Hence, it would be incorrect to state that EU enlargement is driven solely by members seeking to maximize their own benefits at the expense of newcomers. Accession negotiations are embedded in a larger and much more complex framework of costs and benefits, and we can understand their outcomes only if we account for this complexity.

6.4 Conclusion

In this chapter I assessed the empirical support for my second theoretical hypothesis. I examined the conditions that make new members more likely to have to accept differentiated membership rights upon their accession to the Union. This analysis built upon the findings in Chapter 5 and incorporated the degree of distributional conflict expressed by the predicted probability of discrimination demands within policy dyads. In accordance with the theoretical hypothesis, I evaluated the effect of distributional conflict on the outcomes of the EU enlargement process controlling for the bargaining power of the dyad members and the possibility of intra-Union redistribution.

In general, the empirical tests provide fairly strong support for the theoretical claims. Clearly, the probability that a newcomer will have to accept transitional limitations on its membership rights within certain EU policy areas depends on whether its accession is expected to cause serious distributional conflict among the EU member states. Given the potential for such a conflict, EU members seem to restrict candidate's rights and because of the institutional framework of enlargement, they often succeed in securing some sort of compensation for their losses. It appears that whenever these members decide to ask for transitional qualifications, they very often manage to obtain them. The findings in this chapter demonstrate that differentiated membership is an instrument that may be used to resolve distributional conflicts. Although unconditional accession to the EU is highly unlikely when such conflicts exist, enlargement is not necessarily doomed to fail. Granting limited membership rights, even if for a transitional period only, is a viable alternative especially when some important members expect to benefit from enlargement.

The theoretical causal relationship is corroborated by the analysis of three separate policy areas. This provides three independent tests of the theory. Interestingly, some of the control variables had different effects across the policy areas. However, the principal explanatory variable which captured the extent of distributional conflict remains statistically robust across areas and always has the predicted direction. Despite the context-dependence of the precise strength of the effect, we can be fairly confident that serious distributional conflict is very likely to cause EU members to demand discrimination and candidates to have to accept some transitional limitations to their rights.

Despite its overall success in fitting predictions with observable outcomes, the model does predict discrimination in the second Mediterranean enlargement for some dyads. Hence, the unconditional accession of Spain and Portugal, at least in the CSP area, remains somewhat of a puzzle. I have already hinted at one possible explanation – the trade-off between the imposition of discriminatory membership and intra-Union redistribution of enlargement gains. I explore this question in greater detail in the following chapter.

6.5 Appendix

Table A-5. *Differentiated membership in the EU: descriptive statistics.*

Variable	N	Mean	SD	Min	Max
Budget ceiling	214	1.23	0.10	1.00	1.40
Candidate imports from EU	214	11.76	11.10	0.25	35.88
Candidate export ratio	214	7.65	34.12	0.02	422.00
EU member council power	214	−1.67	1.01	−6.29	−0.27
Discrimination demand FMW	214	0.15	0.23	0.00	0.98
Discrimination demand CAP	214	0.47	0.30	0.00	0.98
Discrimination demand CSP	214	0.32	0.31	0.00	1.00

N = number of observations; SD = standard deviation; Min = minimum; Max = maximum.

7 Discriminatory membership and intra-union redistribution

Spain and Portugal joined the European Union (EU) in January 1986. To the surprise of many, neither one had to accept a phase-in of structural transfers even though their accession considerably increased the number of regions eligible for structural aid under the formal rules. This threatened to reduce seriously the amount of European Reconstruction and Development Funds (ERDF) and European Social Funds (ESF) going to existing members. Yet, neither Spain nor Portugal were forced to agree to a discriminatory allocation of structural aid.

Contrast this with the last enlargement round when all acceding countries were given only limited access to the ERDF/ESF until 2006.[1] Even though the EU did not announce a transitional period, the members created a separate fund for the newcomers. Unlike Spain, Greece, and Portugal, which received about €231 of structural aid per capita in 2006, the new members merely got €137 per capita (EU Commission 2002). Figure 7.1 shows the average amount of structural aid going to existing and new members until 2006.[2] As the plot makes clear, new members consistently were allocated a smaller amount of the ERDF/ESF than existing members that were most eligible for structural aid under the Common Structural Policies (CSP).

---

[1] The budget for 2007–13 was still being revised when accession negotiations began. In 2005, EU members decided to raise the budget for 2007–13 to €862.3 billion (1.045% of the EU Gross National Income). With the full participation of the candidates in the negotiations, the EU members also agreed on two measures to ameliorate distributional conflict over structural aid. In particular, they altered the Objectives of the EU Cohesion Policy such that (a) structural aid would be phased-out for regions that exceed the magic 75%-threshold after enlargement; and (b) three new objectives would shift the focus from redistributing wealth to sustaining competitiveness, employment, and territorial cooperation (Regulation No 1080/2006–1085/2006 of the European Parliament and of the Council).

[2] Statistical data from Eurostat.

Discriminatory and intra-union redistribution 159

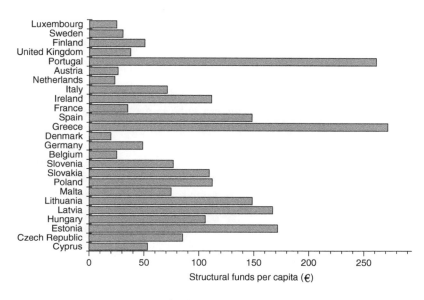

Fig. 7.1 Average structural funds per capita in euros until 2006 (Source: Eurostat).

I now study why Spain and Portugal did not have to accept a smaller share of the ERDF when they joined the EU but the Eastern European countries did when they joined in 2004. The comparative study reveals the trade-off between discriminatory membership and intra-Union redistribution. Recall that in Chapter 4 I argued that EU members can dispose of two instruments to resolve distributional conflicts. First, they can discriminate against acceding states. Second, the relative winners can compensate the relative losers by defraying some of the enlargement costs. This can be accomplished by increasing one's contributions to the common EU budget, for example. Both strategies serve the same goal and can be substitutes for each other. All else equal, increasing intra-Union redistribution should decrease the degree of discrimination against newcomers and could even lead to their accession without a transitional phase-in period for their membership rights. The statistical analysis in the last two chapters could not demonstrate clearly the role of compensation at the expense of relative winners inside the Union. The main reason for this is the lack of quantifiable information about these strategies. This case study, therefore, provides the missing link and exhibits the trade-off between intra-Union redistribution and differentiation of membership rights. Because I focus on the CSP, it is worth noting that Spain and Portugal are not outliers in general but only with respect to the phasing-in of membership rights in this area.

The conclusions of the comparative study support the argument for both the Mediterranean and Eastern enlargements. Budgetary issues, sequencing of moves, and issue-linkages are all crucial determinants of strategy choice in the enlargement process. During the Mediterranean round, enlargement succeeded only because the net contributors to the EU budget who expected to gain economically and politically from the accession of Spain and Portugal agreed to raise the budget. Greece, and several other countries, had made it clear that they would not approve the widening without a concomitant increase in the funds available to the main ERDF beneficiaries. Raising the budget satisfied their demands and paved the way for expansion. This strategy, however, was not available in the Eastern round because of the provisions in *Agenda 2000*. The Berlin agreement put a ceiling on the budget, and as a result the main beneficiaries of structural transfers could not demand more funds.

These budgetary considerations, however, only provide the context for negotiations and constrain the possible outcomes. The actual bargaining outcomes appear to depend on the precise sequencing of moves. The common EU position varies in the identity of the first proposer because the first proposal sets the course of the negotiations. Thus, it matters if the initiative comes from enlargement skeptics or enlargement supporters. In the debates on the ERDF/ESF, the net beneficiaries were the first to move. Their request for expanding the ERDF set the tone for the entire accession negotiations.

In the next section, I explain why it is quite puzzling that discrimination happened only to countries in the Eastern enlargement round. In the sections that follow I describe the debates about the CSP and the allocation of ERDF during the two enlargement rounds under consideration. I then compare and contrast the two cases to explicate the factors that determined the outcomes.

7.1 The puzzle

From a theoretical standpoint, it appears odd that the EU did *not* discriminate against Spain and Portugal. This is especially so when we consider the apparent resemblance between the Mediterranean and Eastern enlargement waves; resemblance that has consistently caused researchers to draw comparisons between the two cases. The most obvious shared characteristics are population sizes and the recent transitions from some type of authoritarian regime to democracy. In addition to the substantial similarities in socio-economic conditions in the accession countries, the two enlargement waves also increased the economic disparities within the EU. Two years prior to accession, the per capita Gross Domestic Product (GDP) of Greece was 51.4% of the EU average, that of Portugal was 56%, and that of Spain was 73%. These numbers are very similar to their analogues in the last enlargement wave. In 2001, the per capita GDP of the candidates ranged from 31.1% of the EU average for Latvia to 76.2% for Cyprus.[3]

The regional disparities between candidates and members are also quite similar between the two rounds. The main criterion for eligibility to receive regional funds from the EU is whether the region's GDP is below 75% of the EU average. The country with the highest number of regions qualifying for aid in the Northern enlargement of 1995 was Finland, with 16.7% of its regions being under-developed. In contrast, most regions in the Mediterranean as well as Central and Eastern Europe fell below the threshold. For example, among the eight Central and Eastern European (CEE) applicants, the percentage of regions qualifying for aid varied between 75 and 100.

In addition, the agricultural sectors in the accession countries in both rounds were quite large compared to those in EU member states. The portion of the workforce still employed in agriculture was about 32% in Greece, 26% in Portugal, and about 18.8% in Spain. Considering that at the time the numbers for the EU ranged from the low 2.7% in the UK to the high 17.3% in Ireland, the candidates had comparatively huge agricultural sectors. A similar pattern can be observed in the last enlargement round. In 2001, the share of the workforce still employed in agriculture in candidate states was between 5.2% (Czech Republic) and 18.7% (Poland). In contrast, the share in EU members ranged from 0.1% (Luxembourg) to 17% (Greece).

All these similarities suggest that the EU should have discriminated against Spain and Portugal for the access to structural funds just like

---

[3] Statistical data from Eurostat.

it did against the CEE countries. The fact that it did not seems to go against the expectations of the theory.

One possible explanation turns on the common EU budget. In the 1980s, when the three Mediterranean countries joined the Union, the budget was well-funded and relatively free of problems. This was not the case in the 1990s, prompting the members to restrict newcomer access to structural aid in the Eastern enlargement round. This argument works if all EU members opposed differentiated membership in the Mediterranean round but supported it in the Eastern round. This was not the case because member government did not share the same preference about discrimination. Whereas some wanted to put restrictions, others wanted the full unconditional admission of the applicants. Even worse for the argument, the Mediterranean candidates were forced to accept restricted access to the agricultural funds over a transitional period. This strains the healthy budget explanation because it cannot account for these exceptions. There should have been no need to qualify membership rights in any area if all that mattered was to have a large enough budget.

Given the substantial similarities between the two enlargement rounds, it is indeed puzzling that whereas candidate rights to agricultural funds were limited in both cases, candidate rights in the Common Structural Policies were limited only in the Eastern enlargement.

7.2 ERDF/ESF and the second Mediterranean enlargement

Portugal applied for European Community (EC) membership in March 1977. The EC opened accession negotiations in October 1978, and it took nearly 80 months for Portugal to join the Union. Similarly, Spain applied in July 1977, entered negotiations in February 1979, and took 76 months. Both countries became members in January 1986. In comparison, accession negotiations lasted for 19 months in the first enlargement round, 34 months with Greece, 13 months in the Northern enlargement round, and 47 months with the first wave of CEE countries.

The unusual length of negotiations in the Mediterranean round was primarily caused by the many controversial issues that had to be resolved with bargaining between the candidates and EU members. For both countries, textiles, agriculture, and the free movement of workers proved to be serious sticking points.[4] The Spanish case was even more complicated by additional conflicts over fisheries and the ERDF. In the CAP, Spain and Portugal not only threatened net recipients of agricultural subsidies but also competed with member states (like France and Italy) in the production of olive oil and Mediterranean fruits and vegetables. Luxembourg and Germany worried about a large influx of cheap Spanish and Portuguese labor. Some members also doubted that it would be possible to integrate Spain's large fishing fleet (*Financial Times*, December 10, 1984).

Faced with these problems, the French President Francois Mitterand, openly considered vetoing the admission of Spain at the very least, causing the *de facto* delay of the enlargement process.[5] Spain had hoped to complete negotiations by 1983, but now it had to postpone this to 1984, at which point all governments admitted that 1985 would be the earliest realistic accession year.

Another obstacle to admission surfaced at the Council of Ministers summit in Stuttgart in 1983, when the heads of EU governments formulated some general conditions for the Iberian enlargement. In particular, they agreed that the admission of the two candidates can only occur after the Common Agricultural Policies (CAP) were reformed and the EC budgetary problems solved. Germany even insisted on an increase in the long-term budget contributions but finally agreed not to block enlargement for budgetary reasons.[6] In return, the other EC members raised their individual contributions to the common budget and acknowledged the validity of Germany's demand to reduce the resources allocated to the Integrated Mediterranean Programs (IMP). The Council of Ministers eventually struck mutually acceptable deals in 1984: at Dublin on agriculture, and at Fountainbleau on the budget. With the last controversies over the accession of Spain and Portugal seemingly resolved, the way to accession in 1985 appeared clear.

These hopes proved premature. Soon after the Dublin summit the Greek government – in power since 1981 and dominated by the euroskeptic socialist PASOK – made public its fundamental reservations about the accession of the two Iberian states. It was particularly

---

[4] Textiles constituted over 40% of Portugal's industrial output and 33% of its exports.
[5] *Financial Times*, June 26, June 30, and July 1, 1982.
[6] *Financial Times*, January 17 and January 28, 1985; *Business Week*, December 5, 1993; and *New York Times*, June 13, 1980.

resentful about the wine deal the Council formulated at Dublin.[7] The Greek Prime Minister Andreas Papandreou made it clear that the continuation and successful conclusion of the enlargement talks would only be possible provided the EU members created an acceptable package of programs for the Mediterranean regions.[8] The Greeks were not alone: the Italian government announced its displeasure with the terms of the Dublin deal and the French supported the Greek demand for revisions.[9] France requested a substantial increase in ERDF spending and the establishment of the IMP (from which it would gain tremendously as well).[10]

The most important objection of the Greek government concerned the proposed reduction of financial resources available for the IMP to a mere ECU 4.5–5.5 billion.[11] Papandreou expressed strong reservations about the vagueness of the formal procedure and the uncertainty of the distribution of available funds among the Mediterranean countries (France, Italy, and Greece). He was quite fearful that Greece would receive a disproportionately small share of the funds. On the other hand, the major net contributors regarded the proposed upper bound of ECU 5.5 billion for the IMP as far too generous and reiterated their call for an increase in contributions to the EU budget. This created a major policy roadblock.[12] The Greek request was also opposed by some other net recipients who worried that they would not receive any of the extra funds. Margaret Thatcher, the United Kingdom (UK) Prime Minister at the time, claimed that the requested funds are "so far out of sight that they should never have been mentioned" (Nicholson and East 1987, 227). Ireland was concerned that instead of drawing on additional funds for the IMP, the EU would redistribute the existing funds.[13]

These conflicts were eventually resolved at the Council summit in Brussels in the spring of 1985. The EC member states agreed to fund

---

[7] *Financial Times*, December 8, 1984; *The Guardian*, December 3, 1984.
[8] *Financial Times*, December 8, 1984; *Facts on File World News Digest*, April 5, 1985.
[9] *The Guardian*, March 14, 1985.
[10] *Financial Times*, March 19, 1984.
[11] *Financial Times*, March 11, 1985. At the Dublin summit, Germany and the UK had blocked EC Commission's plan to spend ECU 6.6 billion (*Financial Times*, January 29, 1985).
[12] *Financial Times*, February 28, and April 1, 1985.
[13] *Financial Times*, April 1, 1985.

the IMP to the tune of ECU 6.6 billion. The money would come from the larger national budget contributions that increased from a 1% Value-Added Tax (VAT) ceiling to 1.5%. This satisfied the net contributors, like Germany and Denmark, and appeased the Greeks who lifted their veto threat. Indeed, Greece did a complete about-face and stated enthusiastically that the accession of Spain and Portugal would "reinforce the front of Mediterranean countries in the Community."[14] In practice, the package would boost the Mediterranean regions' ability to compete with Spanish and Portuguese agricultural production. The spending scheme provided for equal funds for France, Italy, and Greece. In addition, Ireland's Prime Minister, Dr. Garret FitzGerald, managed to secure a requirement that the IMP would not affect adversely the transfers to the less prosperous and lower priority regions of the Community. In the end, neither Spain nor Portugal had to accept transitional periods for access to structural aid; the conflicts arising from their accession were resolved entirely through intra-Union redistribution. The outcome in the Eastern enlargement was very different.

7.3 ERDF/ESF and EU Eastern enlargement

Whereas Spain and Portugal avoided even temporary restrictions on their rights to structural funds, the CEE newcomers have yet to gain full access to the Common Structural Policies (Treaty of Accession 2002). The difference is puzzling: the Mediterranean countries were quite similar to the CEE candidates and EU members fiercely opposed unconditional accession in both cases. To understand why the last enlargement round ended with discrimination in the Common Structural Policies but the Iberian expansion did not, we must compare the two enlargement waves more carefully.

The key to the divergent outcome in the CEE round is in the constraints created by *Agenda 2000*, the agreement reached among EU members at the 1999 Berlin Summit.[15] After protracted debates, the members finally decided to reverse the high-growth trend in the common EU budget despite the upcoming enlargement. They set a ceiling on resources to 1.27% of EU Gross National Product (GNP), and

---

[14] *Financial Times*, April 1, 1985.
[15] EU Commission (1997a, 1997b, 1997c, 1999).

limited real expenditure to 1.13%. To meet these restrictions, some fundamental reforms of the CAP and the CSP were necessary. For the CAP, the budget was limited to €40.5 billion annually for 2000–06. This was accompanied by measures that improved competitiveness – such as the 15–20% reduction of the subsidies for diary products, cereals, and beef – enhanced environmental protection, introduced a stronger orientation toward world market prices, and created new instruments for rural development. The reforms of the CSP were similarly extensive. First, structural transfers would target for assistance areas with the greatest needs. This reduced the share of the EU population supported by such aid from 52% to 42%. Second, the ERDF Objectives went down from six to three, and the Community initiatives from thirteen to three. Third, total expenditures were not to exceed €213 billion between 2000 and 2006. Fourth, the cohesion funds for countries with GNP below 90% of the EU average – Greece, Ireland, Spain, and Portugal – would continue to be available.

It was in the context of these binding constraints that the EU members had to negotiate the enlargement of the Union by as many as 12 new states. The members gravitated toward one of two camps. One of them comprised countries that had, until this point, benefitted most from the allocated funds. Spain, Greece, Portugal, and Italy were among them. These countries would be most affected by the expansion because they stood to lose most of their structural benefits. For instance, with 53 new regions expected to become eligible for the ERDF/ESF funds after enlargement, eight out of thirteen Spanish regions receiving structural aid would no longer be able to get it.[16]

The other camp mostly consisted of net contributors to the common budget. These strongly opposed any attempt to increase the budget – and thus their own contributions – above the ceiling set by *Agenda 2000*. Instead, they favored redistribution of available reconstruction and development funds from current net recipients to the newcomers. The German Foreign Minister at the time, Joschka Fischer, articulated this position as follows: "It is a question of solidarity. After helping the poorer regions of western Europe to catch up, it is time to extend solidarity to the poorer regions of the East." The German stance was shared by Austria, Belgium, Finland, the Netherlands, Sweden, and

---

[16] *Financial Times*, May 7, May 15, November 14, 2001; *European Report*, May 3, 2001.

the UK. Even France, which traditionally supported the continuation of costly European Agricultural Guidance and Guarantee Funds (EAGGF) subsidies, demurred and admitted that the ERDF allocation for the acceding countries would be prohibitively expensive.[17]

The conflict between the two camps prolonged the negotiations and delayed accession. Many possible solutions were proposed but they proved unacceptable to one group or another. The net beneficiaries insisted on an increase in individual monetary contributions to the budget. Alternatively, the EU Economic and Social Committee recommended to raise the eligibility threshold. This would allow current members to continue to receive structural aid after enlargement.[18] The net contributors vehemently resisted these suggestions and countered with a proposal to cap the cohesion funds, which itself was blocked by the net recipients.[19] The situation was aggravated by the applicants who generally opposed the creation of one criterion for eligibility for existing members and another for new members because they did not want to be second-class citizens of the Union.[20]

As neither an increase of budget contributions nor a reduction in current member access to the cohesion funds appeared likely to garner sufficient support in the Union, the governments looked for alternative strategies. In 2001, Spain suddenly threatened to hold up the resolution on the free movement of labor until the EU reached a decision over the allocation of the ERDF/ESF. The Spanish Minister of Foreign Affairs, Josep Piqué, put a diplomatic twist on the ultimatum by attempting to link Spanish demands with concerns others had in different issue areas: "Spain," he stated, "is ready to show solidarity with countries that recognize its own difficulties." The reality was that the success of enlargement was now hostage to Spanish demands. Germany, the country with the strongest interest in resolving the free movement of labor conflict, reacted immediately and unequivocally. The German Minister of Foreign Affairs, Joschka Fischer, rejected the linkage of the two issue areas and even wondered "whether the word

---

[17] *Financial Times*, February 11, 2002.
[18] *European Report*, May 3, and June 30, 2001.
[19] *European Report*, November 7, 2001.
[20] *European Report*, June 30, 2001; *EU Observer*, May 22, 2001.

'solidarity' was entirely appropriate since free movement costs nothing whereas structural policy is very costly." The minister also flatly refused any financial commitment to the costs of enlargement.[21]

Spain's attempt to gain some reassurances for the continuation of structural aid for its regions by blackmailing Germany foundered on the general opposition of other members. Initially, other net recipients of the ERDF supported Spain. At an informal meeting at Nyköping in early May, Portugal and Italy asked for a declaration that would recognize the distinctiveness of countries partaking in the cohesion funds. The Italian public and politicians were particularly concerned with the fate of the economically and structurally underdeveloped region of Mezzogiorno. The Finance Minister Designate, Giulio Tremonti, explicitly stated that the enlargement process had to take place over a reasonable period of time, and only if it was compatible with the interests of the South. The Portuguese Foreign Minister Jaime Gama also threatened to veto the accession of more countries.[22]

This support evaporated when the Spaniards tried to link the two issue areas. The EU Commission led the opposition, with its President Romano Prodi articulating the objection very clearly:

The EU is not an intergovernmental Internal Market where member states fight for their interests, but a community of shared values and solidarity.[23]

Many EU governments were also outraged at the Spanish maneuver and openly insisted that Spain withdraw its demand.[24]

The solution to the intra-Union controversy was a bit of a compromise. Spain abandoned the linkage between the two issue areas and agreed not to make its approval of transitional periods for the free movement of labor conditional on a solution to its problems with the allocation of structural funds. In return, EU members and the EU Commission undertook to address Spain's concerns in the near future. The delaying tactics had paid off.[25]

---

[21] *Financial Times*, May 7, 2001; *European Report*, May 3, 2001.
[22] *European Report*, May 3, 2001; *Financial Times*, May 15, 2001; *London Edition*, May 18, 2001.
[23] *EU Observer*, May 16, and May 22, 2001.
[24] *European Report*, May 12, 2001; *Financial Times*, May 15, 2001; *EU Observer*, May 16, 2001.
[25] *Financial Times*, June 8, 2001.

The deal itself, however, did not offer an immediate solution to the inherent differences between the net recipients of structural aid and the net contributors. The latter still sought to freeze the amount of funds allocated to structural policies. In their search for a mutually acceptable solution, the member states consistently tended to the imposition of transitional periods. One proposal was to phase out structural aid for those regions that would become ineligible to receive it after enlargement. This would avoid the "hard landing" for the affected regions and sweeten the pill for the respective governments.[26] Alternatively, structural aid for newcomers could be phased in over a transitional period. In July 2001, the EU Commission proposed an action plan for 23 border regions in Finland, Germany, Austria, Italy, and Greece. It further recommended to limit structural aid for future members to a maximum of 4% of the EU GNP.[27] In January 2002, the Commission followed with another proposal designed to deal with the outstanding issue of the allocation of ERDF after enlargement. Summarizing the Commission's goals, the EU Commissioner on Enlargement, Günther Verheugen, said that

> this offer strikes the right balance between the expectations of the candidate countries, who will become full members of the EU, and the budgetary limits of the EU. In other words: this represents the best possible deal, and not an invitation for haggling. For the candidates, it means that they can substantially benefit from the solidarity of the EU. There will be transitional phases as agreed for a number of other issues, but no new Member State will be treated as second class member. For the current Member States, it means that they don't need to fear further financial burdens because of enlargement (EU Commission 2002).

According to the Commission's plan, new EU member states would receive €27.7 billion between 2004 and 2006, of which €5.3 billion would be granted in 2004, €10.4 billion in 2005, and €12 billion in 2006. The ERDF would be phased in, starting from just 55% of the EU level in 2004. New members would receive €126 per capita, which would increase to €137 per capita in 2006 (2.5% of the GDP of the new members). Compared to the €231 per capita reserved for Spain, Portugal, Ireland, and Greece, this implied *de facto* discrimination against the newcomers until 2006 at the very least. It was the

---

[26] *European Report*, May 3, 2001.
[27] *European Report*, July 28, and September 22, 2001.

Commission's opinion that the candidates would not be able to absorb structural aid during the first few years of membership anyway. As a bonus, the scheme was also compatible with the rule that limited regional aid for new members to 4% of the GNP.[28]

Six of the smaller EU member states welcomed the proposal as fair and enforceable. However, despite the consensus that some of the conventional ERDF should be redistributed toward the Cohesion Funds, the net contributors did not think the proposal went far enough. They were afraid that without a thorough reform, especially in the CAP, the budget would increase dramatically.[29] A German diplomat described his country's problem with the Commission's proposal very succinctly: "What we need is some perspective that spending will decrease. The German Public is tired of paying when other member states expect to keep receiving even when enlargement happens."[30] The Netherlands, Austria, Denmark, the UK, France, and Sweden all summarily rejected the plan citing various reasons.[31] And yet, the net beneficiaries clung to their positions. Neither Spain, nor Ireland, neither Greece, nor Portugal softened or withdrew their demands. As an Irish diplomat aptly put it, "Do you really think we would go against our interest by agreeing to phase out direct payments?"[32]

The candidates tried to find formulas that would make the solutions more favorable to themselves. They offered several suggestions about finding extra money in the common budget to finance the enlargement. Initially, they thought it would be possible to expand the funds by about €8.5 billion because that would correspond to the 20% increase in European population. Then, they proposed a redistribution of the €15.5 billion planned for them in 2002–03 under the original assumption that they would accede in one of these two years. Finally, they recommended the application of €6 billion that had remained unused in the Structural Funds section over the same period.[33]

---

[28] EU Commission, 2002.
[29] *Financial Times*, February 11, 2002; *European Report*, February 16, 2002.
[30] *Financial Times*, February 11, 2002.
[31] *European Report*, February 16, 2002. Denmark, for instance, opposed direct aid to farmers in candidate countries. Austria wanted the recommended allocation of funds not to exceed €31 billion between 2004 and 2006.
[32] *Financial Times*, February 11, 2002.
[33] *European Report*, March 23, 2002.

The EU governments, however, gravitated toward measures that would be even more restrictive than those in the Commission's proposal. In April 2002, they announced that new members would be expected to contribute fully to the common EU budget upon enlargement. Still, they did admit that some temporary budget compensations would be necessary in several cases for 2004–06.[34] In October, the Danish Presidency of the European Council partially responded to these concerns and released a detailed draft proposal. Under the new plan for the ERDF/ESF, a third of the overall financial resources would be committed to the cohesion funds, and the total available to new members would be cut from €27.7 billion to €25.6 billion.

This did not settle the distributional conflicts and the debates over the details of an acceptable compromise raged unabated. Once again, Portugal insisted on an increase in contributions to the budget, arguing that an adjustment of the Nice Treaty would be the best solution for all members.[35] In the meantime, the Commission was looking for creative ways to expand the budget without making the burden on contributors more onerous. It even tried to squeeze out more money from non-member partner countries in the European Economic Area (EEA).[36] While this was going on, France and Germany worked out a deal in Brussels that would freeze the budget for the CAP, thereby clearing the way for a decision on the ERDF (Avery 2004). The other members guaranteed Germany that it would not have to contribute more in the future, and promised France that CAP would stay in place as is and reform would be delayed. In exchange, the two countries agreed to leave the cohesion funds alone, and to grant transition periods to regions that would no longer be eligible for structural aid after enlargement. Over the first years of membership, the new members would receive the same amount of financial aid they had received in 2003. This deal provided for a mere €23 billion of structural aid for the first three years of membership, €2.5 billion less than the budget proposed by the Danish Presidency, and €5.7 billion less than the one proposed by the Commission.[37]

---

[34] *Euro-East*, October 26, 2002.
[35] *BBC Monitoring Europe*, June 30, 2002.
[36] It proposed a 3000% increase of EEA member contributions to the EU budget (*European Report*, December 7, 2002).
[37] *European Report*, October 30, 2002; *Hungary Business Post*, October 28, 2002.

Despite lingering opposition from some member states (e.g., the UK), the EU governments agreed to make this deal their common position in the enlargement negotiations.[38] The EU made it clear to the candidates that its decision on agricultural subsidies and structural funds was non-negotiable. After a burst of outrage over the uncompromising, but united, front presented by the EU, the candidates acquiesced to the terms of the deal as given, and this was finalized in the accession treaties.

7.4 Comparison of the two cases

Comparing the EU enlargement negotiations for the 1986 Iberian round and the 2004 CEE round reveals why the Eastern European countries were forced to accept limited access to the ERDF while neither Spain nor Portugal had to. Issue-linkages and budgetary concerns emerge as crucial elements in determining the outcomes of accession negotiations. EU members afraid of losing their benefits from structural transfers reacted very strongly in both rounds by (a) requesting an increase in the total amount of funds, (b) demanding discrimination of candidate states, or (c) opposing the admission of new members *per se*. Greece was the primary obstacle to enlargement in the Iberian round, with Italy, Ireland, and to some extent France providing support for its position. In the CEE round, it was Spain that fought most intensely for its share of the structural aid. Both countries tried to achieve their goals by linking the fate of enlargement to the successful solution of the structural aid issue. Greece openly threatened to veto the admission of candidates unless a compromise on the allocation of structural funds was worked out. Its government flatly stated that any decrease in the amount of aid going to Greece would constitute an unsurmountable obstacle to expansion. Spain attempted a subtler tactic by linking its demands to an issue of great importance to Germany and Austria. The German government was very anxious to please its voters by securing transitional restrictions on the free movement of labor. Because Germany was also a net contributor and among the members most ardently insistent on freezing the common budget, this made it a tempting target for blackmail. Spanish officials hoped that Germany would be forced to abandon its opposition on

---

[38] *European Report*, February 30, 2002.

the financial issue in order to obtain the necessary limitations of the free movement of workers. Germany's strong aversion to any such deal and the unexpected vehement opposition from other members ensured that Spain's request would become a precondition for successful enlargement that would have to be resolved in some way other than intra-Union redistribution.

The accession negotiations about the CSP had a great deal in common. In both enlargement rounds, some EU members – the net contributors to the common EU budget in particular – initially resisted any attempts to expand the financial resources for the ERDF beyond a certain limit. As a result, the admission of the applicants would have greatly reduced the amount of funds going to the net recipients. Even though all members receive some structural aid, it was the main beneficiaries who stood to lose most, and consequently it was they that demanded the discrimination against the newcomers. In the Iberian round, the expected sharp decline was offset by the dramatic expansion of the ERDF.

Figure 7.2 shows the trends in the access to structural funds for the main beneficiaries between 1975 and 2003. On the average, the amount of ERDF aid allocated to them gradually increased until 1999. Because the EU had not planned to freeze or reduce the common budget until the accession of Spain and Portugal, member states were not particularly concerned about diminished access to the ERDF. On the contrary, even after the admission of the two Iberian countries – and partially as a result of the development of the internal market – the budget doubled between 1987 and 1993 (Bollen 2003, Van der Beek and Neal 2004). The accession of Finland, Sweden, and Austria was even less problematic because these countries would not have been eligible for significant structural transfers. Current members had no reason to make any special demands. In fact, the EU and the candidates even established an additional ERDF Objective that granted the new members a share of these funds anyway.[39]

The crucial difference between the Iberian and CEE enlargements on one hand and the other expansion rounds on the other hand appears to be in the net contributors' request to either increase individual contributions or, more advantageously to them, freeze the budget altogether.

---

[39] Objective 6 supports regions with a population density below eight people per square kilometer.

174 *Discriminatory and intra-union redistribution*

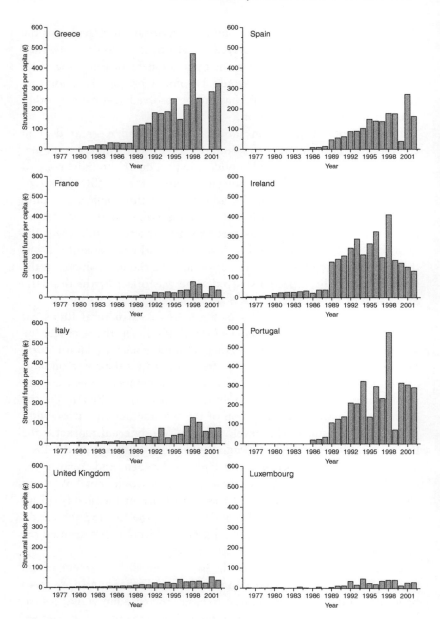

Fig. 7.2 Structural funds, euros/ECU per capita, constant 1975 prices (Source: Eurostat).

Both strategies redistributed the costs of enlargement among all members but the latter came primarily at the expense of countries that receive most of the EAGGF subsidies and ERDF/ESF transfers.

To explain why the new member countries from Central and Eastern Europe obtained only limited access to the cohesion funds, however, requires an examination of the negotiations about the specific financial provisions. In the Iberian enlargement round, the governments could locate a deal that was acceptable to net contributors and net recipients alike. This could not happen in the CEE round because of constraints created by existing intra-Union agreements.

Germany was among the countries that expected to gain most from the accession of Spain and Portugal. In political terms, joining the EC would increase stability and foster the development and consolidation of parliamentary democracy in the two countries. In economic terms, the liberalization of markets was particularly attractive because Germany was the largest net exporter to Spain and Portugal at the time, and a net importer of Mediterranean agricultural products. The integration of the two countries could only lead to even better prices for these products. At the same time, Germany had no concerns about competition in low-priced labor-intensive goods because it specialized in advanced technology and capital equipment. German investors even expected to gain from a more stable economic and political environment (Tsoukalis 1981, 146f.).

As a result, Germany was one of the most consistent supporters of Mediterranean enlargement and, as one of the main net contributors to the budget, could do the most to appease the Greeks and forestall their veto. Germany, along with Denmark, established the Integrated Mediterranean Programs, and the other members agreed to increase their long-term contributions from a 1% VAT ceiling to 1.5%. This neatly precluded a decline in the amount of ERDF available to Greece and Italy, and at the same time spread the costs more evenly among all member states.

There was no such room for manoeuvre in the accession negotiations with the CEE governments. Several obstacles prevented the formulation of a deal that would satisfy all parties. At the Berlin summit in 1999, members had agreed to reform substantially the EU. *Agenda 2000* not only capped the budget but also froze structural expenditures at their 1999 levels. Figure 7.3 illustrates the implications of these decisions for the budget and the ERDF allocations.

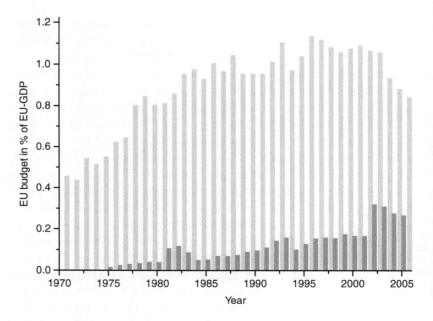

Fig. 7.3 Development of the common EU budget (light gray bars) and ERDF/ESF (dark gray bars) from 1970 to 2005 (Source: Commission 2003).

The EU expanded the budget more or less continuously until 2000. Since then, the budget has been frozen and declining. An analogous trend can be seen for the structural funds, which implied decrease in funding in a larger Union with more poor members. Any attempt to renegotiate this agreement was doomed to failure because it met with the implacable opposition of net contributors to the budget. Even blackmailing did not work. When Spain tried to link issues – a tactic the Greeks had used successfully – Germany simply refused to budge on the budget.[40]

With the options of increasing the entire budget or redistributing resources from other items to the ERDF closed, the governments sought alternative solutions that would enable a successful expansion to the East. The final compromise that opened the way for this expansion combined a gradual phase-out of structural funds for regions that

---

[40] This defiance may have been at least partially due to the coming parliamentary elections in the following year.

would become ineligible after enlargement with temporary restrictions of newcomer access to ERDF/ESF at least until 2006. The EU also refused to negotiate provisions for 2007–2013 before enlargement is completed but guaranteed cohesion funds for their main beneficiaries.

In sum, in the 1980s Greece successfully linked the fate of enlargement to the maintenance of ERDF amount it received, eventually forcing the other members to comply with its wishes. The EU created a special Mediterranean program for France, Greece, and Italy, and increased individual contributions to the budget. In the last enlargement round, the net contributors flatly rejected any attempt to weaken the constraints agreed upon at the Berlin summit in 1999. Still, net recipients of structural aid were quite reluctant to support the unconditional accession of new members. Some of them were prepared to go to great lengths to secure their benefits, as illustrated by the Spanish threats during the negotiations. Enlargement failure seemed imminent and quite likely unless some compensation was forthcoming. The final deal split the burden by discriminating against new members and phasing out of structural transfers for several regions in existing member states.

These findings show the paramount importance of budgetary considerations and issue-linkages in the EU accession negotiations. The restrictions on CEE member access to the ERDF could have been avoided had EU members agreed to raise their budget contributions. However, these members could not have simply refused to increase the budget: enlargement itself would have been jeopardized had they not taken seriously Spain's concerns in their quest for a solution that would make expansion possible.

7.5 Conclusion: structural transfers and discriminatory membership

At the time, many observers were puzzled why Spain and Portugal were not asked to agree to a phase-in of structural transfers upon joining the Union in 1986. After all, their accession dramatically increased the number of regions eligible for structural aid. And yet, neither country was forced to accept limited membership rights. In this chapter, I explored the accession negotiations in the Iberian round and analyzed why these two countries were admitted without qualification of their rights in the Common Structural Policies. I compared this enlargement with the Eastern expansion to fill the gap between the demand for differentiated membership and the probability that discriminatory measures get imposed on the newcomers.

The comparative case study reveals that new members are less likely to be discriminated against when it comes to structural funds when EU governments agree to offset expected losses of individual states by increasing the common budget. In the 1980s, for example, EU members increased their contributions to buy off Greece and prevent its veto of enlargement. Differentiated membership, on the other hand, becomes much more likely when it is impossible to use budget expansion to compensate the beneficiaries for losses occasioned by the increase in the number of ERDF recipients. In the Eastern enlargement, the net contributors to the budget blocked any attempt to renegotiate the provisions of *Agenda 2000*. Given this hard fiscal constraint, the admission of new members was only made feasible by the introduction of transitional periods that would guarantee the net recipients of structural aid continued access to these funds.

These empirical findings lend further support to my theory that predicates a trade-off between discriminatory membership and intra-Union redistribution of enlargement costs and benefits. When some members expect losses that cannot be compensated by enlargement gains, the members that expect a net benefit from expansion have several options. They can let enlargement fail, they can propose differentiated membership for newcomers, or they can resolve the distributive conflict by agreeing to increasing the common funds. The latter involves either boosting their individual contributions or redirecting resources from other funds. Unfortunately, it was not possible to get access to enough information for all expansion rounds to determine whether EU members agreed to increase the budget to ensure enlargement. The present case study can at least substantiate the mechanism for the ERDF in the third and fifth enlargement waves.

The comparison also points to three factors that play a crucially important role in explaining why differentiated membership is imposed in some cases but not in others. First, the adoption of the budget provides one part of the explanation. Until 1988, the budget was adopted annually. Since 1989, however, the EU works in budget periods. The budget relevant to the Eastern expansion covered the years from 1999 to 2006. Because the EU had adopted the budget for the period before enlargement, new members had no say in its formulation and would not influence the budget until negotiations for the 2007–13 period began. As a result, the ERDF allocation for new members was *not* made part of the overall budget but had to remain separate until the next budgetary period. In other words, all applicants knew that whatever deal the EU worked out for the 2007–13 period, as full-fledged participants in the ensuing negotiations they would not be forced to accept involuntarily further restrictions. There was no such loophole in the Iberian round when the budget was still decided annually. Consequently, discriminating against Spain and Portugal over several years would have been much more difficult, simply because of existing procedure.

Second, and more important, is the sequence in which EU members made their proposals in the intra-Union bargaining process. In the Iberian enlargement round it was Greece that reacted first and set the agenda for the subsequent negotiations by requesting an increase in the budget. Most discussions then focused on the creation of the Integrated Mediterranean Programs to satisfy Greek demands. In the Eastern enlargement negotiations, the net recipients of structural transfers at first demanded an increase of ERDF expenditures that would compensate them for their expected losses. Only after the EU explicitly excluded an increase in the budget as an option did discussions turn to the transitional discrimination of new member states.

Third, and just as important, is the use of issue-linkage as an instrument to buttress member claims. Both Greece and Spain made it clear that they were prepared to block expansion without some compensation from the other parties at the bargaining table. Even though Spain did not obtain the concessions Greece got in the 1980s, its resistance did result in a compromise according to which new members would receive limited access to the ERDF over a transitional period while previously eligible regions would have their funds phased out gently.

Appendix 7-A: Discriminatory membership and intra-union redistribution: newspaper sources

BBC Monitoring Europe, June 30, 2002: Portuguese president wants EU funds continue after enlargement.

Business Week, December 5, 1983: Farm subsidies could plow the EC under, p. 93.

EU Commission, 1999: Europe's Agenda 2000. Office for Official Publications of the European Community: Luxembourg.

EU Commission, 2002: Press Release: Commission offers a fair and solid approach for financing EU enlargement, January 30, 2002.
EUObserver.com, May 16, 2001: Sweden reacts critically to Spain over enlargement, www.euobserver.com.
EUObserver.com, May 22, 2001: Top EU leaders reject enlargement subsidies link, www.euobserver.com.
European Report, December 6, 2000: Regional Policy: Committee of the Regions looks at the challenge of enlargement, Section 2550.
Euro-East, October 26, 2002: Enlargement: Another round of talks, another small step towards accession.
European Report, May 3, 2001: ESC says poor regions should keep cohesion grants after enlargement, Section 2589.
European Report, May 12, 2001: EU enlargement: EU ministers face tough talks, Section 2592.
European Report, June 30, 2001: EU enlargement: Candidates reject post enlargement plans for two-tier structural funding, Section 2605.
European Report, July 28, 2001: Regional Policy: Limited plan to ease impact of enlargement on Eastern border regions, Section 2613.
European Report, September 22, 2001: Budget: Commission split over enlargement funding, Section 2620.
European Report, November 7, 2001: Regional Policy: Committee of the Regions conference on the impact of enlargement, Section 2633.
European Report, November 7, 2001: Regional Policy: Committee of the Regions conference on the impact of enlargement, Section 2633.
European Report, February 16, 2002: Enlargement: Finance Ministers split over funding plan, Section 2660.
European Report, March 23, 2002: Enlargement: All for one and Euro 24 billion for all, Section 2670.
European Report, October 30, 2002: Enlargement: Negotiations 'end game' begins", Section 2723.
European Report, December 7, 2002: Enlargement: Will EEA help to pay for Central European candidates?, Section 2734.
Facts on File World News Digest, April 5, 1985: Spain, Portugal OK EC Terms; Greece lifts veto threat, p. 535.
Financial Times, June 24, 1982: France may block entry by Portugal and Spain to EEC, p. 1.
Financial Times, June 30, 1982: Mitterand reveals his Gaullist streak, p. 3.
Financial Times, July 1, 1982: Madrid dismay at delay in membership, p. 2.
Financial Times, March 19, 1984: France outlines basis for global agreement, p. 3.
Financial Times, December 8, 1984: Greece clarifies stand on wine deal, p. 2.

Conclusion: structural transfers and discriminatory membership 181

Financial Times, December 10, 1984: Demonstration of the art of compromise, p. 6.

Financial Times, January 17, 1985: EEC budget linked to entry talks, p. 24.

Financial Times, January 29, 1985: EEC in new bid to dispel Greek concern on expansion, p. 16.

Financial Times, February 28, 1985: EEC enlargement deadline threatened, p. 1.

The Financial Times, March 11, 1985: EEC farm ministers prepare for fight over price proposals, p. 2.

Financial Times, April 1, 1985: Enlargement pact clears way for Community reform, p. 1.

Financial Times, May 7, 2001: EU ministers at odds over funding for enlargement, p. 6.

Financial Times, May 15, 2001: Spain blocks EU agreement on labour, p. 11.

Financial Times, June 8, 2001: The lure of enlargement, p. 25.

Financial Times, November 14, 2001: Enlargement at a stretch: Admitting 10 countries in one go would impose huge demands on existing EU states and would-be entrants, p. 23.

Financial Times, February 11, 2002: Paying for a bigger Europe: EU members are united over enlargement but divided over how it should be financed, p. 23

Hungary Business Post, October 28, 2002: EU summit in Brussels reaches agreement on financing enlargement.

New York Times, June 13, 1980: Schmidt bids trade bloc cut farm aid, p. 20.

The Guardian; December 3, 1984: Economy overshadows Dublin summit, p. 3.

The Guardian, March 15, 1985: EEC farm ministers vote for conservation grants, p. 2.

London Edition 1, May 15, 2001: Italy warns against speedy enlargement of EU to the east, p. 11.

8 Conclusion

The collapse of communism, symbolized by the fall of the Berlin Wall in 1989, made it possible to expand the EU to the East. This expansion was immediately perceived as a great opportunity to extend European integration to Central and Eastern Europe. As the European Union (EU) Commission aptly put it,

> The economic impact of enlargement will be significant, as a bigger and more integrated market boosts economic growth for new and old members alike. The newcomers stand to benefit from investments from firms based in western Europe and from access to EU funding for their regional and social development. Integration of their economies with the rest of the EU is already under way, as trade agreements, negotiated and applied in advance of membership, have already removed virtually all tariff and quota barriers on their exports to current member states.[1]

Policy harmonization deepens the cooperation within the Union but the widening of the EU is the second pillar of EU integration. Consequently, explaining the conditions under which enlargement succeeds contributes not only to our understanding of the enlargement process itself but to our understanding of EU integration in general. Given how important such understanding is and how beneficial EU members and candidates alike have perceived integration to be, it is indeed astonishing how little we still know about the enlargement process itself.

Few notable exceptions aside, scholars have typically either underestimated or ignored altogether the distributional conflicts that occur during EU enlargement. Frank Schimmelfennig was among the first to point out that explaining EU enlargement from a strictly rationalist perspective creates a serious puzzle if such conflicts are taken into account. His solution to the puzzle requires one to abandon

---

[1] EU web site: www.europa.eu.int, last accessed 20.07.2005.

the cost-benefit analysis implicit in the rational choice framework in favor of what he terms "rhetorical action." My book is grounded in Schimmelfennig's important insight about how problematic existing explanations are but I provide an alternative way of thinking about enlargement that resolves the puzzle while preserving the rationalist perspective. I do so by explicitly taking into account the possibility that EU members and candidates negotiate the distribution of enlargement gains and losses among themselves. In my view, the EU expands in the face of fairly serious distribution conflict when some members – who normally could veto unpalatable accession of new states – get compensated for their expected losses, not when they are "entrapped" by the rhetoric of enlargement supporters. France was reluctant to admit the Central and Eastern European (CEE) states out of fear of losing its significant agricultural subsidies. When the EU invited these countries to join the Union in 2004, it was not because France was helpless to block enlargement but because it was induced to agree to it when the newcomers were forced to accept transitional limitations on their access to Common Agricultural Policies (CAP) funds thereby preserving undiminished French access to these subsidies for the near term.

I explicitly analyze all steps in the EU enlargement process, starting with the formal application for membership and the accession negotiations, to identify the conditions under which EU members will favor enlargement sufficiently to ensure its success. My central, and straightforward, theoretical claim is that when the accession of a new state causes conflict over the distribution of membership benefits, the danger to successful enlargement can be greatly reduced if states redistribute the enlargement gains either from enlargement supporters within the EU or from the candidates to the relative losers to compensate them for the costs they have to suffer.

More to the point, EU member states that expect to be on the losing side after enlargement with respect to the distribution of benefits in some policy area have incentives to delay the accession talks indefinitely. Because widening can only succeed when it is unanimous, each relative loser can use its veto power, either explicitly or implicitly, to compel the relative winners to offer some additional inducements that would defray its expected costs. For example, both France and Italy were generally supportive of Spanish and Portuguese accession in the early 1980s. However, both were also gravely concerned that the newcomers' participation in the CAP would seriously harm their farming interests. Clearly, these concerns were well-founded: Spain alone would increase the agricultural area of the EU by 30%, and the workforce in the primary sector by 25%. It is not surprising, then, that the French government insisted that substantive talks would not even open until both sides could agree on a common basis for negotiations. Obviously, without some resolution to the French and Italian problems with the accession of the two countries, enlargement could not succeed.

As it turned out, the relative winners of EU widening still managed to get the process going. Despite fundamental reservations against enlargement among some important EU members, it was possible to admit both Spain and Portugal and avoid French (or Italian) veto. In general, this can happen when the net gains from enlargement are positive and when relative winners within the EU and/or the candidates themselves prove willing to redistribute some of these gains in favor of members that threaten the expansion. One strategy for such redistribution saddles the newcomers with most of the enlargement costs, at least for a transitional period during which they receive limited membership rights designed to preserve the benefits for existing members. In other words, the newcomers agree not to make full use of their rights so that current members can continue to enjoy their customary benefit. In the second Mediterranean expansion, Spain and Portugal agreed to a gradual phase-in of their agricultural subsidies, which appeased French fears and eliminated the danger of a French veto to their accession.

The allocation of differentiated membership rights is not the only means through which members and candidates can resolve their distributional conflicts: The compensation of the losers need not be shouldered entirely by the candidates. A comparison between the Iberian and Eastern enlargement rounds reveals that one important alternative strategy is for relative winners of enlargement to defray themselves some of the costs of the relative losers. In both rounds, EU members who were also principal beneficiaries of the structural aid policies moved first and requested an increase in the budget. This was an attempt at intra-Union redistribution because at this time, they did not discuss the possible asymmetric allocation of these funds. The net contributors agreed to this in the Iberian round but not in the Eastern one. When it became clear that intra-Union redistribution would not be possible, the enlargement debate shifted toward discriminatory membership for the CEE newcomers.

More generally, this work contributes to our understanding of EU integration in several ways. First, I argue that the EU members and the candidates should not be treated as two homogenous groups that negotiate the conditions of enlargement as if they were two monoliths. Examining members and candidates as individual entities with possibly divergent preferences made it possible to understand the emergence of distributional tensions that could threaten to derail the widening of the Community.

Second, I open up the black box of accession negotiations and explicitly analyze the three-way bargaining between the relative losers of EU widening, the relative winners, and the candidates. Specifically, I looked at how these three groups negotiated over the terms of enlargement and resolved their distributional conflicts through some sort of redistribution of benefits among themselves. In doing so, the book innovates in two additional ways: it shows how the allocation of enlargement gains is endogenous to the accession negotiations, and why different members have divergent attitudes toward enlargement. Such an approach can resolve the puzzle of enlargement because it reveals the importance of alternative strategies for appeasing veto players who feel threatened enough to contemplate blocking the widening. The comparative historical overview of the accession negotiations during the five EU enlargement waves was indispensable for detecting these processes.

Third, by offering an explanation of the politics of EU enlargement, the book yields new insights into the mechanics of EU integration in general. The analysis of the conditions that allow the resolution of distributional conflict by altering the balance of costs and benefits in a way that makes enlargement a universally acceptable policy has important implications for the further integration into the European framework. In my view, the differentiation of membership rights for acceding states is not an instrument used by current members to maximize their gains at the expense of the candidates that are usually in weak bargaining positions. Instead, discriminatory membership serves as a means to maximize the aggregate gains of integration and make enlargement Pareto-optimal.

These results suggest several directions for future research that would improve our understanding of the processes of enlargement and integration. Three of these appear especially promising.

First, it would be desirable to expand the theoretical analysis to a wider variety of possible enlargement outcomes. There are at least two alternatives to discriminatory membership and intra-Union redistribution that have been widely debated in the EU but not discussed here (because they have never been used in practice). One of them, the so-called *á-la-carte* approach, would permit the permanent separation of the Union into a hard core of members that adopt nearly all of the common policies and a group of less integrated states that pick and choose which policies to adhere to. Another possibility would be to create the so-called *multi-speed* or *variable-speed* tracks to integration according to which the core group proceeds with deep integration and the remaining states follow them at apposite times, eventually converging at the same deep level of integration. Theoretically, each of these strategies should enhance the chances of EU widening because interested governments could deepen their cooperation without waiting for the approval of all other members. However, EU members have proved quite reluctant to attempt any of these alternatives. The transitional differentiation of membership rights and the intra-Union redistribution remain the principal instruments of distributional conflict resolution.

Second, it would be useful to analyze in depth the relationship between enlargement outcomes and the precise extent of discrimination against newcomers. This would increase the explanatory power of the theoretical framework and simplify the comparison across different policy areas. For instance, when Greece entered the European Community in the 1980s, it had to accept restrictions for the free movement of workers, just like the CEE candidates in the Eastern enlargement. However, in the first case the Community explicitly gave priority to Greek workers whenever it was necessary to recruit labor outside the Community (Nicholson and East 1987, 190). There was no such exception in the second case. My theoretical analysis implicitly suggests that the extent of discrimination against new members should be an important factor in deciding the outcome of enlargement. Consequently, it would be fruitful to analyze not simply *whether* candidates accept some form of transitional membership or *whether* members agree on some intra-Union redistribution, but also *how much* discrimination or redistribution is necessary to ensure the success of expansion.

One of the major contributions of this project is to provide the general framework that would permit such an extension without making the analysis intractable. At least when it comes to the EU, this framework allows one to analyze different accession phenomena without losing track of the overall distribution of costs and benefits and its influence on the EU members' valuations of enlargement. Future research should examine the possible application of this model to other international organizations and future EU enlargement rounds.

When it comes to future enlargement rounds, the potential accession of Turkey is most rife with conflict. Some EU members have already declared their opposition to unconditional membership for Turkey and have made their support of enlargement conditional on *permanent* derogations in several policy areas, including the Free Movement of Workers, the Common Agricultural Policies, and the Common Structural Policies. It would be instructive to see whether these positions can be reconciled enough for Turkey to join the Union. Although its accession has some supporters, many governments appear to favor postponement of any further expansion after the accession of Bulgaria and Romania (which accepted a wide range of discriminatory measures), and Croatia (a small country not expected to cause significant distributional conflicts within the Union).

Several other factors suggest a greater emphasis on discriminatory membership in the future. For example, current debates in the EU focus on the possible strengthening of the influence of national interests in the enlargement process. Domestic parliaments are typically much less enthusiastic about enlargement than heads of government. Candidates will be more likely to face discrimination if France manages to push through the introduction of a national veto to the closure of individual *acquis* chapters. The EU has already specified a break clause that allows the suspension of negotiations in cases of serious and persistent breaches of the principles of liberty, democracy, and respect for human rights and fundamental freedoms. Even if the EU governments agree on Turkey's accession in principle, it appears most likely that Turkey would have to accept serious (and possibly permanent) limitations on its membership rights.

Still, looking at the broader picture presented by my analysis offers a positive normative conclusion. Discriminatory membership is not simply a strategy that EU governments pursue to maximize their own gains. Quite often EU members were willing to bear a significant share of enlargement costs as long as doing so was conducive to successful widening and did not leave them worse off after the fact. Thus, discriminatory membership should not be viewed as a worse alternative to unconditional admission. Instead, it should be viewed as a means to ensure the admission of states under conditions that would have doomed enlargement to failure otherwise.

Bibliography

Abott, Kenneth and Duncan Snidal. 1998. "Why States Act Through Formal International Organizations." *Journal of Conflict Resolution* 42(1):3–32.

Alesina, Alberto, Iganzi Angelino and Frederico Etro. 2001. "The Political Economy of International Unions." *NBER Working Paper 8645.*

Alter, Karen J. 1996. "The European Court's Political Power." *West European Politics* 19(3):458–487.

Alter, Karen J. 1998. "Who Are the "Masters of the Treaty"?: European Governments and the European Court of Justice." *International Organization* 52(1):121–147.

Austrian Government. 2000a. "The Free Movement of Persons in the Context of Enlargement. Additional Facts on the Austrian Situation Relating to the Commission's Information Note of 17th April 2000." *Information Note.*

Austrian Government. 2000b. "Österreich Neu Regieren." *FPÖ-ÖVP Regierungsprogramm.*

Avery, Graham. 1994. "The European Union's Enlargement Negotiations." *The International Oxford Review* 5(3):27–32.

Avery, Graham. 1995. "The Commission's Perspective on the EFTA Accession Negotiations." *Sussex European Institute Working Paper 12.*

Avery, Graham. 2004. The Enlargement Negotiations. In *The Future of Europe. Integration and Enlargement*, ed. Fraser Cameron. Oxford: Routledge pp. 35–62.

Axelrod, Robert. 1984. *The Evolution of Cooperation.* New York: Basic Books.

Baldwin, Richard E. 1994. *Towards an Integrated Europe.* London: CEPR.

Baldwin, Richard E., Joseph F. Francois and Richard Portes. 1997. "The Costs and Benefits of Eastern Enlargement: The Impact on the EU and Central Europe." *Economic Policy* 12(24):126–176.

Baldwin, Richard E. and Mika Widgrén. 2005. "The Impact of Turkey's Membership on EU Voting." *NBER Working Paper 4954.*

Bartels, Larry M. 1991. "Instrumental and "Quasi-Instrumental" Variables." *American Journal of Political Science* 35(3):777–800.

Batory, Agnes. 2001. "*Opposing Europe I: The Comparative Party Politics of Euroscepticism. Hungarian Party Identities and the Question of European Integration.*" Political Studies Association Conference, Manchester, UK.

Bauer, Thomas and Klaus F. Zimmermann. 1999. "Assessment of Possible Migration Pressure and its Labour Market Impact Following EU Enlargement to Central and Eastern Europe." *Study for the UK Department for Education and Employment, IZA* Bonn, CEPR London.

Becker, Ulrich. 1999. *EU-Erweiterung und differenzierte Integration. Zu beitrittsbedingten Übergangsregelungen am Beispiel der Arbeitnehmerfreizügigkeit*. Baden-Baden: Nomos.

Benz, Arthur. 1998. "Politikverflechtung ohne Politikverflechtungsfalle – Koordination und Strukturdynamik im europäischen Mehrebenensystem." *Politische Vierteljahresschrift* 39(3):558–589.

Bliss, Chestner I. 1935. "The Calculation of the Dosage–Mortality Curve." *Annals of Applied Biology* 22:134–167.

Bollen, Frank. 2003. "Cohesion Policy in an Ever Larger Union." *European Institute of Public Administration Working Paper*.

Bolton, Patrick and Gérard Roland. 1997. "The Breakup of Nations: A Political Economy Analysis." *Quarterly Journal of Economics* 112(4):1057–1090.

Böri, Tito and Herbert Brücker. 2000. *The Impact of Eastern Enlargement on Employment and Labor Markets in the EU Member States*. Berlin: European Integration Consortium.

Böri, Tito and Herbert Brücker. 2001. *Eastern Enlargement and EU-Labour Markets: Perceptions, Challenges and Opportunities*. Bonn: Forschungsinstitut zur Zukunft der Arbeit.

Böri, Tito and Herbert Brückner. 2000. *The Impact of Eastern Enlargement on Employment and Labor Markets in the EU Member States*. Berlin and Milano: European Integration Consortium.

Böri, Tito and Katherine Terell. 2002. "Institutional Determinants of Labor Reallocation in Transition." *Journal of Economic Perspectives* 16(1):51–76.

Bornschier, Volker, Mark Herkenrath and Patrich Ziltener. 2003. Politische Klubs als Tauschgemeinschaft: Eine Untersuchung der Konvergenz der Mitglieder der Europäischen Union im Vergleich zu Nichtmitgliedern. In *Politische Integration*, ed. Thomas Plümper. Obladen: Westdeutscher Verlag pp. 134–170.

Brams, Steven J. 1975. *Game Theory and Politics*. New York: Free Press.

Brams, Steven J. and Paul Affuso. 1985. "New Paradoxes of Voting Power on the EC Council of Ministers." *Electoral Studies* 4(2):135–139.

Brancati, Dawn. 1999. "The Wisdom of Widening: The Enlargement of the EU to Central and Eastern Europe." Unpublished Working Paper.

Braun, Dietmar. 2001. "Intergovernmentale Beziehungen und Fiskalpolitik in Bundesstaaten." *Politische Vierteljahresschrift* 42(4):624–654.

Brenton, P. 2002. "The Economic Impact of Enlargement on the European Economy: Problems and Perspectives." *CEPS Working Document 188*.

Breuss, Fritz. 2002. "Benefits and Dangers of EU Enlargement." *Empirica* 29(3):245–274.

Brou, Daniel and Michele Ruta. 2004. "A Positive Explanation of EU Enlargement." *EUI Working Paper 30*.

Brücker, Herbert, Parvati Trübswetter and Christian Weise. 2000. "EU-Osterweiterung: Keine massive Zuwanderung zu erwarten." *DIW Wochenbericht 21*.

Buchanan, James M. 1965. "An Economic Theory of Clubs." *Economics* 32(125):1–14.

Buchanan, James M. and Craig Stubblebine. 1962. "Externality." *Economica* 29(116):371–384.

Bueno de Mesquita, Bruce and Frans N. Stokman. 1994. *Twelve into One: Models of Decision-Making in the European Community*. New Haven: Yale University Press.

Bulmer, Simon J. 1983. "Domestic Politics and European Community Policy-Making." *Journal of Common Market Studies* 21(4):349–363.

Burda, Michael. 1998. "The Consequences of EU Enlargement for Central and East European Labour Markets." *CPER Working Paper 1881*.

Burda, Michael. 1999. "Mehr Arbeitslose – Der Preis für die Osterweiterung? Zur Auswirkung der EU-Erweiterung auf die europäischen Arbeitsmärkte im Osten und Westen." *Schriften des Vereins für Sozialpolitik: Die Erweiterung der EU* 274(9):79–101.

Burley, Anne-Marie and Walter Mattli. 1993. "Europe before the Court: A Political Theory of Legal Integration." *International Organization* 47(1):41–76.

Caporaso, James. 1998. Regional Integration Theory: Understanding Our Past and Anticipating Our Future. In *Supranational Governance: The Institutionalization of the European Union*, ed. Wayne Sandholtz and Alex Stone Sweet. Oxford: Oxford University Press pp. 334–352.

Cappellari, Lorenzo and Stephen P. Jenkins. 2003. "Multivariate Probit Regression Using Simulated Maximum Likelihood." *Stata Journal* 3(3):278–294.

Casella, Alessandra. 1994. "On Markets and Clubs: Economic and Political Integrations of Regions with Unequal Productivity." *American Economic Review Papers and Proceedings* 115: 268.

Casella, Alessandra and Bruno Frey. 1992. "Federalism and Clubs: Towards an Economic Theory of Overlapping Political Jurisdictions." *European Economic Review* 36(2-3):639–649.

Caves, Richard. 1996. *Multinational Enterprise and Economic Analysis*. Cambridge: Cambridge University Press.

Chatzopoulou, Sevasti. 2006. "The Implications of Europeanisation on Domestic Institutional Structures. CAP and Greek Agriculture." *Unpublished Working Paper*.

Christiansen, Thomas. 1997. "Tensions of European Governance: Politicized Bureaucracy and Multiple Accountability in the European Union." *Journal of European Public Policy* 4(1):73–90.

Christiansen, Thomas. 2002. "The Role of Supranational Actors in EU Treaty Reform." *Journal of European Public Policy* 9(1):33–53.

Cornes, Richard and Todd Sandler. 1996. *The Theory of Externalities, Public Goods, and Club Goods*. Cambridge: Cambridge University Press.

Coudenhove-Kalergi, Richard N. 1926. *Pan-Europe*. New York: Knopf.

Courchene, Tom, Friedrich Schneider, Charles Goodhart, Alberto Mjocchi, Remy Prud'homme, Stephen Smith, Bernd Spahn and Cliff Walsh. 1993. *European Economy Stable Money - Sound Finances*. Brussels: EU Commission.

Deubner, Christian. 1997. *Frankreich in der Osterweiterung der EU, 1989 bis 1997*. Berlin: Heinz Nixdorf Stiftung.

Deutsch, Karl W. 1966. *Nationalism and Social Communication*. Cambridge, MA: MIT Press.

Donges, Jürgen B. 1982. *The Second Enlargement of the European Community: Adjustment Requirements and Challenges for Policy Reforms*. Tübingen: Mohr.

Donges, Jürgen B. 1983. "From Six to Ten and Beyond: the European Community at the Crossroad." *Kieler Arbeitspapiere*.

Downs, George W., David M. Rocke and Peter N. Barsoom. 1998. "Managing the Evolution of Multilateralism." *International Organization* 52(2):397–419.

Drazen, Allan. 2000. *Political Economy in Macroeconomics*. Princeton, NJ: Princeton University Press.

Dunning, John. 1989. *Explaining International Production*. London: Unwin Hyman.

EU Commission. 1997a. *Communication: For a Stronger and Wider Union*. Vol. I. Luxembourg: Office for Official Publications of the European Communities.

EU Commission. 1997b. *Communication: The Effects on the Union's Policies of Enlargement to the Applicant Countries of Central and Eastern Europe*. Vol. II. Luxembourg: Office for Official Publications of the European Communities.

EU Commission. 1997c. *Summary and Conclusions of the Opinions of Commission Concerning the Application for Membership to the European Union Presented by the Candidate Countries*. Luxembourg: Office for Official Publications of the European Communities.

EU Commission. 1999. *Europe's Agenda 2000*. Luxembourg: Office for Official Publications of the European Community.

EU Commission. 2000a. *Strukturpolitische Massnahmen. Kommentare und Verordnungen; Strukturfonds, Kohäsionsfonds, strukturpolitisches Instrument zur Vorbereitung auf den Beitritt*. Luxembourg: Office for Official Publications of the European Community.

EU Commission. 2001. *Information Note. The Free Movement of Workers in the Context of Enlargement*. Luxembourg: Office for Official Publications of the European Communities.

EU Commission. 2003. *Haushaltsvademekum*. Luxembourg: Office for Official Publications of the European Communities.

EU Commission. 2006a. *Enlargement Strategy and Main Challenges 2006-2007 Including Annexed Special Report on the EU's Capacity to Integrate New Members*. Brussels: Communication from the Commission to the European Parliament and the Council.

EU Commission. 2006b. "Enlargement, Two Years After: an Economic Evaluation." *European Economy Occasional Papers 24*.

EU Commission. January 30, 2002. "Commission offers a fair and solid approach for financing EU enlargement." Press Release, January 30.

EU Council. 2003. *Conclusions of the Presidency – Copenhagen, June 21-22 1993*. Copenhagen: Office for Official Publications of the European Communities.

European Parliament. 1999. *Livre Blanc Sur L'Élargissement De L'Union Europénne. Volume II. Rapport Sur Les Positions Des États Membres Et Des états Candidats Sur L'Élargissement De L'Union Européenne*. Luxembourg: European Parliament.

Eurostat. 2003. *50 years of figures on Europe—Data 1950-2001*. Luxembourg: Office for Official Publications of the European Communities.

Eurostat. 2005. "Statistical Indicators for EU Member States and Acceding States." www.eu-datashop.de/.

Fearon, James D. 1993. "Cooperation and Bargaining Under Anarchy." *Unpublished Manuscript*.

Fierke, Michele and Antje Wiener. 1999. "Constructing Institutional Interests: EU and NATO Enlargement." *European Public Policy* 6(5):721–42.

Fink Hafner, Danica. 1999. "Dilemmas in Managing the Expanding EU: The EU and Applicant States' Point of View." *Journal of European Public Policy* 6(5):783–801.

Fischer, J. 1998. Interview. "Wir Wollen Keine Soli tanzen." *Der Spiegel* November 23.
Francisco, Granell. 1995. "The European Union's Enlargement Negotiations with Austria, Finland, Norway, and Sweden." *Journal of Common Market Studies* 33(1):117–141.
Fratianni, Michele. 1998. "Variable Integration into the European Union." *Tijdschrift voor Economic in Management* XLIII(3):315–336.
Fratianni, Michele and John Pattison. 1982. "The Economics of International Organizations." *Kyklos* 35(2):244–62.
Fratianni, Michele and John Pattison. 2001. "International Organizations in a World of Regional Trade Agreements: Lessons from Club Theory." *Journal of World Economy* 24(3):333–57.
Frey, Bruno. 1997. "The Public Choice of International Organizations." In *Perspectives on Public Choice*, ed. Dennis C. Müller. Cambridge: Cambridge University Press.
Friis, Lyke and Anna Murphy. 1999. "The European Union and Central and Eastern Europe: Governance and Boundaries." *Journal of Common Market Studies* 37(2):211–232.
Froot, Kenneth A. 1989. "Consistent Covariance Matrix Estimation with Cross-Sectional Dependence and Heteroskedasticity in Financial Data." *Journal of Financial and Quantitative Analysis* 24(3):333–355.
Garrett, Geoffrey. 1992. "International Cooperation and Institutional Choice: the European Communities Internal Market." *International Organization* 46(2):533–560.
Garrett, Geoffrey, Daniel R. Kelemen and Heiner Schulz. 1998. "The European Court of Justice, National Governments, and Legal Integration in the European Union." *International Organization* 52(1):149–176.
Garrett, Geoffrey and George Tsebelis. 1996. "An Institutional Critique of Intergovernmentalism." *International Organization* 50(2):269–299.
Gehring, Thomas. 1995. "Regieren im Internationalen System. Verhandlungen, Normen und Internationale Regime." *Politische Vierteljahresschrift* 36(2):197–219.
Gilligan, Michael J. 2004. "Is there a Broader–Deeper Trade-off in International Multilateral Agreements?" *International Organization* 58(3): 459–484.
Grabbe, Heather and Kirsty S. Hughes. 1998. *Enlarging the EU Eastwards*. Chatham House Papers London: The Royal Institute of International Affairs.
Grosse Hüttmann, Martin. 2004. "Die Osterweiterung der Europäischen Union." *Der Bürger im Staat* 54(1):4–10.
Gstöhl, Siglinde. 2002. "Scandinavia and Switzerland: Small, Successful and Stubborn towards the EU." *Journal of European Public Policy* 9(4):529–549.

Guerot, Ulrike. 2002. *The European Paradox: Widening versus Deepening in the European Union.* The Brookings Institution.
Haas, Ernst. 1958. *The Uniting of Europe.* Stanford: Stanford University Press.
Haas, Ernst. 1961. "International Integration: The European and the Universal Process." *International Organization* 15(3):366–392.
Haas, Ernst. 1975. *The Obsolescence of Regional Integration Theory.* Berkeley: University of California Press.
Haas, Ernst. 1976. "Turbulent Fields and the Study of Regional Integration." *International Organization* 30(2):173–212.
Hampton, Jean. 1987. "Free-Rider Problems in the Production of Collective Goods." *Economics and Philosophy* 3:245–273.
Hasenpflug, Hajo. 1977. *Die Süd-Erweiterung der Europäischen Gemeinschaft: Wende oder Ende der Integration.* Hamburg: Verlag Weltarchiv.
Hausken, Kjell, Walter Mattli and Thomas Plümper. 2006. "Widening Versus Deepening of International Unions." *Social Science Research Network Working Paper.*
Heckathorn, Douglas. 1996. "The Dynamics and Dilemmas of Collective Action." *American Sociological Review* 61(2):250–277.
Heijdra, Ben J. and Christian Keuschnigg. 2000. "Integration and Search Unemployment: An Analysis of Eastern EU Enlargement." *CESifo Working Paper 341.*
Heijdra, Ben J., Christan Keuschnigg and Wilhelm Kohler. 2002. "Eastern Enlargement of the EU: Jobs, Investment and Welfare in Present Member Countries." *CESifo Working Paper 18.*
Heijman, W. 2001. "European Structural Policy: Bend or Break?" *European Journal of Law and Economics* 11(2):165–75.
Henrekson, Magnus, Johan Torstensson and Rasha Torstensson. 1997. "Growth Effects of European Integration." *European Economic Review* 41(8):1537–1557.
Herzog, Judith. 2003. "Das Migrationspotenzial der EU-Osterweiterung und dessen Folgen für den deutschen Arbeitsmarkt." *WIP Occasional Papers 21.*
Hiemenz, Ulrich and Klaus Werner Schatz. 1979. *Trade in Place of Migration.* Geneva: International Labor Office.
Hille, Hartmut and Thomas Straubhaar. 2000. "The Impact of the EU Enlargement on Migration Movements and Economic Integration: Results of Recent Studies." *OECD Discussion Paper.*
Hinteregger, Gerald. 1998. "Österreich und die Osterweiterung der Europäischen Union. Argumente und Fakten." *Unpublished Manuscript.*
Hoffmann, Stanley. 1964. "The European Process at Atlantic Crosspurposes." *Journal of Common Market Studies* 3(2):85–101.

Hoffmann, Stanley. 1966. "Obstinate or Obsolete? The Fate of the Nation-State and the Case of Western Europe." *Daedalus* 95(Summer):862–915.

Hollifield, James. 1992a. *Immigration, Markets and States: The Political Economy of Postwar Europe*. Cambridge: Harvard University Press.

Hollifield, James. 1992b. "Migration and International Relations: Cooperation and Control in the European Community." *International Migration Review* 26(2):568–595.

Holzinger, Katharina. 2001. Optimal Regulatory Units. A Concept of Regional Differentiation of Environmental Standards in the European Union. In *Environmental Policy in a European Union of Variable Geometry*, ed. Katharina Holzinger and Peter Knöpfel. Basel: Helbig and Lichtenhahn pp. 65–107.

Hönekopp, Elmar. 2000. "Überblick über die Ergebnisse bisher vorliegender Schätzungen zum Migrationspotential im Falle einer Arbeitskräftefreizügigkeit im Rahmen der Osterweiterung der EU." *Unpublished Manuscript*.

Hönekopp, Elmar. 2004. "Arbeitsmarktperspektiven in der erweiterten Europäischen Union." *Der Bürger im Staat* 54(1):34–40.

Hosli, Madeleine O. 1993. "Admission of European Free Trade Association States to the European Community: Effects on Voting Power in the European Community Council of Ministers." *International Organization* 47(4):629–643.

Hosli, Madeleine O. 1996. "Coalitions and Power: Effects of Qualified Majority Voting in the Council of the European Union." *Journal of Common Market Studies* 34(2):255–273.

Huber, Peter J. 1967. The Behavior of Maximum Likelihood Estimates Unter Non-Standard Conditions. In *Proceedings of the Fith Berkeley Symposium on Mathematical Statistics and Probability*. Berkeley: University of California Press pp. 221–233.

Huber, Peter J. 1981. *Robust Statistics*. Wiley-Interscience.

IMF. various years. *Direction of Trade Statistics*. Washington, DC: International Monetary Fund.

Johnston, Ronald J. 1995. "The Conflict over Qualified Majority Voting in the European Union Council of Ministers: An Analysis of the UK Negotiating Stance Using Power Indices." *British Journal of Political Science* 25(2):245–288.

Kant, Immanuel. [1975] 1991. *Kant. Political Writings*. Cambridge: Cambridge University Press. Ed. Hans Reiss.

Karp, Jeffrey A. and Shaun Bowler. 2006. "Broadening and Deepening or Broadening versus Deepening: The Question of Enlargement and

Europe's Hesitant Europeans." *European Journal of Political Research* 45(3):369–390.
Kennedy, Peter. 2003. *A Guide to Econometrics.* Cambridge: MIT Press.
Keohane, Robert O. 1984. *After Hegemony: Cooperation and Discord in the World Political Economy.* Princeton, NJ: Princeton University Press.
Keohane, Robert O. and Helen V. Milner. 1996. *Internationalization and Domestic Politics.* Cambridge: Cambridge University Press.
Kim, Anderson and Rodney Tyers. 1993. "Implications of EC Expansion for European Agricultural Policies, Trade and Welfare." *NBER Working Paper 829.*
King, Gary and Langche Zeng. 2001. "Explaining Rare Events in International Relations." *International Organization* 55(3):693–715.
Kivikari, Urpo. 2001. "Die erweiterte EU und Russland. Ein uneingeschränkter Gewinn für beide Seiten." *Internationale Politik* 56(5):49–52.
Kok, W. 2001. Interview. "Die Slowakei stimmt für EU–Übergangsfristen. Dänemark und Niederlande gewähren volle Freizügigkeit," *Der Standard* June 28.
König, Thomas and Mirja Päter. 2001. "Examining the EU Legislative Process: The Relative Importance of Agenda and Veto Power." *European Union Politics* 2(3):329–351.
König, Thomas and Thomas Bräuninger. 2000. "Governing the Enlarged European Union: Accession Scenarios and Institutional Reform." *Central European Political Science Review* 1(1):42–64.
König, Thomas and Thomas Bräuninger. 2002. From an Ever-growing Towards an Ever-slower Union? In *Institutional Challenges in the European Union*, ed. Madeleine O. Hosli, Adrian Van Deemen and Mika Widgrén. London/New York: Routledge pp. 155–172.
König, Thomas and Thomas Bräuninger. 2004. "Accession and Reform of the European Union." *European Union Politics* 5(4):419–439.
Koremenos, Barbara, Charles Lipson and Duncan Snidal. 2001. "The Rational Design of International Institutions." *International Organization* 55(4):761–799.
Kraus, Margit and Robert Schwager. 2004. "EU Enlargement and Immigration." *Journal of Common Market Studies* 42(1):165–181.
Kydd, Andrew. 2001. "Trust Building, Trust Breaking: The Dilemma of NATO Enlargement." *International Organization* 55(4):801–828.
Laurent, Pierre-Henri and Marc Maresceau. 1998. *The State of the European Union: Deepening and Widening.* Boulder, CO: Lynne Rienner.

Lejour, Arjan M., Ruud A. Mooij and Richard Nahuis. 2001. "EU Enlargement: Economic Implications for Countries and Industries." *CESifo Working Paper 585*.

Lindberg, Leon N. 1963. *The Political Dynamics of European Economic Integration*. Stanford: Stanford University Press.

Long, Scott J. 1997. *Regression Models for Categorical and Limited Dependent Variables*. Advanced Quantitative Techniques in the Social Science Series London: Sage Publications.

Long, Scott J. and Jeremy Freese. 2001. *Regression Models for Categorical Dependent Variables Using Stata*. College Station, Texas: Stata Press.

Lopian, Arthur. 1993. *Übergangsregime für Mitgliedstaaten der Europäischen Gemeinschaften*. Baden-Baden: Nomos.

Ludlow, Piers N. 1997. *Dealing with Britain. The Six and the First UK Application to the EEC*. Cambridge: Campridge University Press.

Marks, Gary, Liesbet Hooghe and Kermit Blank. 1996. "European Integration from the 1980s: State-Centric Versus Multi-level Governance." *Journal of Common Market Studies* 34(3):341–378.

Marshall, Monty G. and Keith Jaggers. 2003. *Polity IV Dataset Version p4v2002e [Computer File]*. College Park, MD: Center for International Development and Conflict Management, University of Maryland.

Martin, Lisa L. and Beth A. Simmons. 1998. "Theories and Empirical Studies of International Institutions." *International Organization* 52(4):729–757.

Mattli, Walter. 1999. *The Logic of Regional Integration. Europe and Beyond*. Cambridge: Cambridge University Press.

Mattli, Walter and Anne-Marie Slaughter. 1998. "Revisiting the European Court of Justice." *International Organization* 52(1):177–209.

Mattli, Walter and Thomas Plümper. 2002. "The Demand-Side Politics of EU Enlargement: Democracy and the Application for EU Membership." *Journal of European Public Policy* 9(4):550–574.

Mattli, Walter and Thomas Plümper. 2004. "The Internal Value of External Options: How the EU shapes the Scope of Regulatory Reforms in Transition Countries." *European Union Politics* 5(3):307–330.

Mayhew, Alan. 2000. "Enlargement of the European Union: An Analysis of the Negotiations with the Central and Eastern European Candidate Countries." *SEI Working Paper 39*.

Mayhew, Alan. 2002. "The Negotiating Position of the European Union on Agriculture, the Structural Funds and the EU Budget." *SEI Working Paper 52*.

Mayhew, Alan. 2003. *Recreating Europe: The European Union's Policy Towards Central and Eastern Europe*. Cambridge: Cambridge University Press.

Meyer, Thomas. 2002. "The Shaping of Capital Markets." *Ezoneplus Working Paper 5*.
Milbrandt, Beate. 2001. *Die Finanzierung der Europäischen Union*. Baden-Baden: Nomos.
Milner, Helen V. 1997. *Interests, Institutions, and Information*. Princeton, NJ: Princeton University Press.
Mitrany, David. 1933. *The Progress of International Government*. London: George Allen and Unwin.
Mitrany, David. 1965. "The Prospect of Integration: Federal or Functional?" *Journal of Common Market Studies* 4(2):119–149.
Mitrany, David. 1966. *A Working Peace*. Chicago: Quadrangle Books.
Monnet, Jean. 1976. *Memoirs (translated by R. Mayne)*. London: William Collins.
Moravcsik, Andrew. 1991. "Negotiating the Single European Act: National Interests and Conventional Statecraft in the European Community." *International Organization* 45(1):19–57.
Moravcsik, Andrew. 1993. "Preferences and Power in the European Community: A Liberal Intergovernmentalist Approach." *Journal of Common Market Studies* 31(4):473–534.
Moravcsik, Andrew. 1997. "Taking Preferences Seriously: A Liberal Theory of International Politics." *International Organization* 51(4): 513–553.
Moravcsik, Andrew. 1998a. *The Choice for Europe: Social Purposes and State Power from Messina to Maastricht*. Ithaca: Cornell University Press.
Moravcsik, Andrew. 1998b. "A New Statecraft? Supranational Entrepreneurs and International Cooperation." *International Organization* 53(2):267–306.
Moravcsik, Andrew and Anna Vachudova. 2003. "National Interests, State Power, and EU Enlargement." *East European Politics and Societies* 17(1):42–57.
Moravcsik, Andrew and Kalypso Nicolaidis. 1999. "Explaining the Treaty of Amsterdam: Interests, Influence, Institutions." *Journal of Common Market Studies* 37(1):59–86.
Moser, Peter. 1997. "A Theory of the Conditional Influence of the European Parliament in the Cooperation Procedure." *Public Choice* 91(3-4):333–350.
Navracsics, Tibor. 1997. "A Missing Debate? Hungary and the European Union." *SEI Working Paper 21*.
Nicholson, Frances and Roger East. 1987. *From the Six to the Twelve: The Enlargement of the European Communities*. Keesing's International Studies. Harlow: Longman.

North, Douglas. 1993. "Institutions and Credible Commitments." *Journal of Institutional and Theoretical Economics* 149(1):11–23.
Nye, Joseph. 1965. "Patterns and Catalysts in Regional Integration." *International Organization* 95(4):870–884.
OECD. 2004. "Organisation for Economic Co-operation and Development. International Migration Data." www.oecd.org.
Olson, Mancur. 1965. *The Logic of Collective Action. Public Goods and the Theory of Groups*. Cambridge, MA: Harvard University Press.
Organa, Malgorzata. 2002. "Presentation of EU Member States' Positions on the Freedom of Movement of Polish Workers – Prevailing Opinions of Governments, Trade Unions and the Public. Special Emphasis on Germany and Austria." *Unpublished Working Paper*.
Oye, Kenneth. 1985. "Explaining Cooperation under Anarchy." *World Politics* 38(1):1–24.
Padoan, Pier Carlo. 1997. Regional Agreements as Clubs: The European Case. In *The Political Economy of Regionalism*, ed. Edward Mansfield and Helen Milner. Columbia: Columbia University Press pp. 106–133.
Persson, Göran. March 10, 1999. From the Discussion of the Swedish Premier Minister at the Swedish Institute for International Relations/Central Defense and Societal Integration. In *Livre Blanc Sur L'Élargissement De L'Union Européenne. Volume II. Rapport Sur Les Positions Des États Membres Et Des États Candidats Sur L'Élargissement De L'Union Européenne*. Luxembourg: Office for Official Publications of the European Communities.
Persson, Torsten and Guido Tabellini. 2002. *Political Economics. Explaining Economic Policy*. Cambridge: MIT Press.
Peterson, John. 2001. "The Choice for EU Theorists: Establishing a Common Framework for Analysis." *European Journal of Political Research* 39(3):289–318.
Pezaros, Pavlos D. 2004. The CAP in the Greek Context. In *Greece in the European Union*, ed. Dionyssis G. Dimitrakopoulos and Argyris G. Passas. New York: Routledge pp. 19–34.
Phare, Robert. 2001. "Most-Favored-Nation Clauses and Clustered Negotiations." *International Organization* 55(4):859–890.
Pierson, Paul. 1995. "The Path of European Integration: A Historical Institutionalist Analysis." *Comparative Political Studies* 29(2):123–166.
Pierson, Paul. 1998. The Path to European Integration: A Historical Institutionalist Analysis. In *European Integration and Supranational Governance*, ed. Wayne Sandholtz and Alex Stone Sweet. Oxford: Oxford University Press pp. 27–58.
Pigou, Arthur. C. 1925. *The Economics of Welfare*. London: McMillan.

Plümper, Thomas and Christina J. Schneider. 2007. "Discriminatory EU Membership and the Redistribution of Enlargement Gains." *Journal of Conflict Resolution* 51(4):568–87.

Plümper, Thomas, Christina J. Schneider and Vera E. Troeger. 2006. "The Politics of EU Eastern Enlargement: Evidence from a Heckman Selection Model." *British Journal of Political Science* 36(1):17–38.

Pollack, Mark A. 1996. "The New Institutionalism and EC Governance: the Promise and Limits of Institutional Analysis." *Governance* 9(4):429–458.

Pollack, Mark A. 1997. "Delegation, Agency, and Agenda Setting in the European Community." *International Organization* 51(1):99–134.

Preston, Christopher. 1997. *Enlargement & Integration in the European Union*. London: Routledge.

Price, Victoria Curzon. 1999. *The Enlargement of the European Union: Issues and Strategies*. London: Routledge.

Putnam, Robert D. 1988. "Diplomacy and Domestic Politics." *International Organization* 42(3):427–460.

Raunio, Tapio and Matti Wiberg. 1998. "Winners and Losers in the Council: Voting Power Consequences of EU Enlargements." *Journal of Common Market Studies* 36(4):549–562.

Redmond, John. 2000. *The 1995 Enlargement of the European Union*. Aldershot: Ashgate.

Roland, Gérard and Thierry Verdier. 2000. "Law Enforcement and Transition." *Unpublished Working Paper*.

Rosamond, Ben. 2000. *Theories of European Integration*. Basingstoke: Palgrave MacMillan.

Ross, George. 1995. *Jacques Delors and European Integration*. New York: Oxford University Press.

Ruano, Lorena. 2002. "Origin and Implications of the European Union's Enlargement Negotiations Procedure." *European University Institute Working Paper 62*.

Rudolph, Christopher. 2003. "Security and the Political Economy of International Migration." *American Political Science Review* 97(4):603–20.

Russett, Bruce and John R. Oneal. 2001. *Triangulating Peace: Democracy, Interdependence, and International Organizations*. London, New York: W.W. Norton.

Russett, Bruce, John R. Oneal and David R. Davis. 1998. "The Third Leg of the Kantian Tripd for Peace: International Organizations and Militarized Disputes, 1950-85." *International Organization* 52(3):441–467.

Ruta, Michele. 2005. "Economic Theories of Political (Dis)Integration." *Journal of Economic Surveys* 19(1):1–21.

Sandholtz, Wayne. 1984. *High-tech Europe: The Politics of International Cooperation*. Berkley: University of California Press.
Sbragia, Alberta M. 1993. "The European Community: A Balancing Act." *Publius* 23(3):23–38.
Schelling, Thomas. 1996. *Micromotives and Macrobehavior*. New York: Norton.
Schimmelfennig, Frank. 1999. "The Double Puzzle of EU Enlargement. Liberal Norms, Rhetorical Action, and the Decision to Expand to the East." *Arena Working Paper 15*.
Schimmelfennig, Frank. 2000. NATO's Enlargement to the East: An Analysis of Collective Decision-Making. *Technical Report 1998–2000 EAPC-NATO Individual Fellowship Report*.
Schimmelfennig, Frank. 2001. "The Community Trap: Liberal Norms, Rhetorical Action, and the Eastern Enlargement of the European Union." *International Organization* 55(1):47–80.
Schimmelfennig, Frank. 2002. "Liberal Community and Enlargement: An Event History Analysis." *Journal of European Public Policy* 9(4):598–626.
Schimmelfennig, Frank. 2003. *The EU, NATO and the Integration of Europe: Rules and Rhetoric*. Cambridge: Campridge University Press.
Schimmelfennig, Frank and Ulrich Sedelmeier. 2002. "Theorizing EU Enlargement: Research Focus, Hypotheses, and the State of Research." *Journal of European Public Policy* 9(4):500–528.
Schneider, Christina J. 2003. The Political Economy of Organizational Enlargement. Finding the Link Between Insider and Outsider. *Master's Thesis, University of North Texas*.
Schneider, Christina J. 2006. "Differenzierte Mitgliedschaft und die EU-Osterweiterung: Das Beispiel der Arbeitnehmerfreizügigkeit." *Swiss Political Science Review* 12(2):67–99.
Schneider, Christina J. 2007. "Enlargement Processes and Distributional Conflicts: The Politics of Discriminatory Membership in the European Union." *Public Choice* 132(1-2):85–102.
Schneider, Gerald and Mark Aspinwall. 2001. *The Rules of Integration. Institutionalist Approaches to the Study of Europe*. Manchester: Manchester University Press.
Schröder, Gerhard. 2000. "Speech of the German Chancelor, Gerhard Schröder, at the Oberpfalz Regional Conference, December 18, 2000, Weiden." www.bundesregierung.de/bulletin-,413.27251/Rede-von – Bundeskanzler -Gerhard.htm, last accessed 10.10.2004.
Sedelmeier, Ulrich. 1998. The European's Association Policy Towards the Countries of Central and Eastern Europe: Collective EU Identity and

Policy Paradigms in a Composite Policy. *PhD Thesis. University of Sussex.*

Sedelmeier, Ulrich. 2002. "Sectoral Dynamics of EU Enlargement: Advocacy, Access and Alliances in a Composite Policy." *Journal of European Public Policy* 9(4):627–649.

Shevtsova, Lilia. 1992. "Post-Soviet Emigration Today and Tomorrow." *International Migration Review* 26(2):241–257.

Sinn, Hans-Werner, Gebhard Flaig, Martin Werding, Sonja Munz, Nicola Duell and Herbert Hofmann. 2001. "EU-Erweiterung und Arbeitskräftemigration: Wege zu einer schrittweisen Annäherung der Arbeitsmärkte." *Ifo Beiträge zur Wirtschaftsforschung 2.*

Sjurson, Helene. 2002. "Why Expand? The Question of Legitimacy and Justification in the EU's Enlargement Policy." *Journal of Common Market Studies* 40(3):491–513.

Smyrl, Mark E. 1998. "When (and How) Do the Commission's Preferences Matter?" *Journal of Common Market Studies* 36(1):79–100.

Spiesberger, Manfred. 1998. "Übergangsregime zur Abfederung von Differenzen bei EG/EU-Beitritten." *Österreichische Zeitschrift für Politikwissenschaften* 27(4):407–417.

Spinelli, Altiero. 1972. The Growth of the European Movement since the Second World War. In *European Integration*, ed. Michael Hodges. Harmondsworth: Penguin pp. 43–68.

Stein, Arthur. 1982. "Coordination and Collaboration: Regimes in an Anarchic World." *International Organization* 36(2):299–324.

Stock, James H., Jonathan H. Wright and Motohiro Yogo. 2002. "A Survey of Weak Instruments and Weak Identification in Generalized Methods of Moments." *Journal of Business & Economic Statistics* 20(4):518–529.

Stone Sweet, Alex and Wayne Sandholtz. 1997. "European Integration and Supranational Governance." *Journal of European Public Policy* 4(3):297–317.

Stubb, Alexander C.-G. 1996. "A Categorization of Differentiated Integration." *Journal of Common Market Studies* 34(2): 283–295.

Taylor, Paul. 1982. "Intergovernmentalism in the European Communities in the 1970s: Patterns and Perspectives." *International Organization* 36(4):741–66.

Thelen, Kathleen and Sven Steinmo. 1992. Historical Institutionalism in Comparative Politics. In *Structuring Politics: Historical Institutionalism in Comparative Analysis*, ed. Sven Steinmo, Kathleen Thelen and Frank Longstreth. Cambridge: Cambridge University Press pp. 1–33.

Tomz, Michael, Jason Wittenberg and Gary King. 2003. "CLARIFY: Software for Interpreting and Presenting Statistical Results, Version 2.1." Available at *http://gking.harvard.edu*; last accessed: December 20, 2007.

Torreblanca, José. 2001. *The Reuniting of Europe: Promises, Negotiations and Compromises*. Aldershot: Ashgate.

Tsebelis, George. 1994. "The Power of the European Parliament as Conditional Agenda Setter." *American Political Science Review* 88(1):128–142.

Tsebelis, George and Geoffrey Garrett. 2001. "The Institutional Foundations of Intergovernmentalism ans Supranationalism in the European Union." *International Organization* 55(2):357–390.

Tsoukalis, Loukas. 1981. *The European Community and its Mediterranean Enlargement*. London: Allen Unwin.

Van der Beek, Gregor and Larry Neal. 2004. "The Dilemma of Enlargement for the European Union's Regional Policy." *The World Economy* 27(4):587–607.

Viner, Jacob. 1950. *The Customs Union Issue*. New York: Carnegie Endowment for International Peace.

Wallace, William. 1978. *A Community of Twelve? The Impact of Further Enlargement on the European Communities*. College of Europe Bruges: Tempelhof.

Walterskirchen, Ewald and Raimund Dietz. 1998. "Auswirkungen der EU-Osterweiterung auf den Österreichischen Arbeitsmarkt." Österreichisches Institut für Wirtschaftsforschung.

Welfens, Paul J.J. 1995. "Die Europäische Union und die mitteleuropäischen Länder: Entwicklungen und wirtschaftspolitische Optionen." *Aus Politik und Zeitgeschichte* 39:22–31.

White, Halbert. 1980. "A Heteroskedastic-Consistent Covariance Matrix Estimator and a Direct Test of Heteroskedasticity." *Econometrica* 48(4):817–838.

Widgrén, Mika. 1994. "Voting Power in the EC Decision-Making and the Consequences of Two Different Enlargements." *European Economic Review* 38:1153–1170.

Williams, Rick L. 2000. "A Note on Robust Variance Estimation for Clustered-Correlated Data." *Biometrics* 56(2):645–646.

Yarbrough, Beth and Robert Yarbrough. 2001. *Cooperation and Governance in International Trade*. Princeton: Princeton University Press.

Zellner, Arnold. 1962. "An Efficient Method of Estimating Seemingly Unrelated Regressions and Tests for Aggregation Bias." *Journal of American Statistical Association* 57(298):348–368.

Index

absolute winners and losers, *see* enlargement
accession negotiations, 9, 19–20, 51, 53, 155, 183, 185
accession process, *see* enlargement
Accession Treaty, *see* Treaty of Accession
acquis chapters, *see* acquis communautaire
acquis communautaire, 7, 12, 14, 16, 18–19, 23, 39, 73, 81, 104, 187
   chapters, 18, 19, 52, 77
   implementation, 20–24, 46, 52, 71, 77
   permanent derogations, 7, 20, 23, 69, 73, 75, 187
   transitional periods, 20–23, 27
agenda 2000, 11, 48, 67, 107, 121, 160, 165–166, 175, 178
agricultural sector, 47, 48, 60, 66, 71, 72, 105, 108–110, 114, 122, 124, 130, 138, 161
agricultural subsidies, *see* European agriculture guidance funds
agriculture, *see* Common Agricultural Policies
Albania, 14
approaches
   constructivism, 3, 37, 43, 49–50, 182
   federalism, 35
   functionalism, 35–36
   institutional intergovernmentalism, 37
   institutionalism, 8, 37–38
   intergovernmentalism, 8, 36–39
   rational choice, 3, 47, 50–52, 57, 182
   transactionalism, 35
asymmetric interdependence, 37, 51, 81, 133

atlanticism, 1, 13
Austria, 2, 13, 21, 24–30, 48, 49, 68, 73, 80, 81, 83, 166, 169, 170, 172, 173
autonomy, *see* policy autonomy

bargaining, 3, 4, 7, 12, 36, 50, 51, 55, 56, 68, 81, 183, 185
Belgium, 49, 57, 67, 72, 166
benefits, *see* enlargement
Berlin summit, *see* Council of Ministers
black box, *see* enlargement
Bosnia and Herzegovina, 14
brakemen of enlargement, *see* enlargement
Britain, *see* United Kingdom
British accession, *see* enlargement
British rebate, 66
Brussels summit, *see* Council of Ministers
budget ceiling, 142
budget contributions, *see* EU budget contributions
budgetary ceiling, 48, 67, 122, 125, 148–150, 160
Bulgaria, 14, 18, 33, 69, 80, 90, 187

CAP, *see* Common Agricultural Policies
Central and Eastern EU member states, 2, 28, 46, 48, 50, 52, 64, 80, 122, 161, 162, 165, 172, 175, 177, 182, 183
Central and Eastern European states, 62, 70
club goods, 60–61, 139
   complementarity, 60
   neutrality, 60
   rivalry, 61

205

co-operation in the field of justice and home affairs, *see* justice and home affairs
cohesion funds, 166–168, 170, 171
Cold War, 49
collective action, 59
committee of permanent representatives, 19, 39
common acquis, *see* acquis communautaire
Common Agricultural Policies, 1, 22, 55, 60, 67–68, 72, 75, 104–108, 184
  predicted impact on EU members, 105–107
Common Environmental Policies, 60
common EU budget, 24, 48, 64, 65, 67, 120, 162, 166, 171, 172, 176, 178–179
  budget provisions 2007-13, 59, 158, 177, 179
common EU position, 4, 12, 18, 24, 27, 29, 39, 46, 160
Common Fisheries Policies, 7–8, 57, 68, 75, 81
  second Mediterranean enlargement, 6–7
Common Foreign and Security Policy, 18, 59
Common Organization of Agricultural Markets, 104
Common Structural Policies, 28, 67, 120–121, 158, 162–179
  puzzle, 160–162
  second Mediterranean enlargement, 8
Commonwealth, 1
company law, 21
compensation, *see* intra-Union redistribution
complementary, *see* club goods
concessions, *see* intra-Union redistribution
conditional effects, *see* predicted probabilities
conditional enlargement, *see* discriminatory membership
congestion, 61
constructivism, *see* approaches

contributions, *see* EU budget contributions
Copenhagen criteria, 16–18, 52
Copenhagen summit, *see* Council of Ministers
COREPER, *see* Committee of Permanent Representatives
costs, *see* enlargement
council, *see* Council of Ministers
Council of Ministers, 16, 39, 40, 59, 64, 82
  Berlin summit, 48, 67, 165, 166, 177
  Brussels summit, 164
  Copenhagen summit, 16, 52
  Dublin summit, 163, 164
  Fountainbleu summit, 163
  Göteburg summit, 29
  Stuttgart summit, 163
Council of the European Union, *see* Council of Ministers
Court of Justice, *see* European Court of Justice
Croatia, 3, 14
cultural approaches, *see* approaches
Cyprus, 14, 18, 21, 29, 64, 80, 87, 113, 161
Czech Republic, 14, 18, 22, 71, 88, 161

Danish Presidency, 171
De Gaulle, Charles, 2, 13
deepening, *see* EU integration
delaying strategies, 6, 19, 28, 52, 77, 163, 167–168, 172, 183
Delors, Jacques, 40
demand for discrimination, *see* discriminatory membership
democracy, 16, 43, 58, 89, 110, 122, 125, 161
Denmark, 13, 20, 23, 48, 72, 83, 95, 126, 140, 165, 170, 175
differentiated integration, 23, 186
  multi-speed, 186
  Union-à-la-carte, 186
  variable-speed, 186
differentiated membership, *see* discriminatory membership
direct payments, *see* European Agriculture Guidance Funds
discounting, 7, 57, 70, 73

Index

discriminatory membership, 7, 21–24, 51, 54, 55, 66, 68, 139, 140, 150–184
  definition, 23–24
  demand for, 81–83, 108, 144
  extent, 186–187
  outcome, 138, 140
  transitional nature, 69–73
distributional conflicts, *see* enlargement
Dublin summit, *see* Council of Ministers
duration of enlargement talks, *see* enlargement
Dyad, 80, 95, 140

EAGGF, *see* European Agriculture Guidance Funds
Eastern enlargement, *see* enlargement
EC, *see* European Union
EC Treaty, 85–86, 104, 121
Economic and Social Committee, 167
economic integration, *see* market integration
economic safeguard clause, 22
economic stability, *see* stability
ECSC, *see* European Coal and Steel Community
EEA, *see* European Economic Area
EFTA, *see* European Free Trade Association
EMU, *see* European Monetary Union
enlargement, 38
  absolute winners and losers, 5
  benefits and costs, 3, 41–47, 55, 57–60, 62, 183
    economic gains, 41–42
    political costs, 44–46
    political gains, 42–44
  black box, 4, 12, 34, 185
  distributional conflicts, 1, 5–6, 46–47, 55, 60–65, 141, 155, 162, 183
  duration, 14, 162
  Eastern enlargement, 14, 18, 21, 24, 33, 47, 61, 64, 68, 158, 165–172
  first Mediterranean enlargement, 13, 33, 40, 72, 75, 186
  first Northern enlargement, 1, 13, 33, 57
  formal enlargement process, 9, 16–19
  future enlargement rounds, 3, 14, 187
  history, 5, 13–14, 62–185
  impact on new members, 71–72
  ins, 18
  outcomes, 4, 6–8, 14, 33, 51, 53, 55, 68, 69, 138–139
  political conflicts, 59, 61, 63, 80
  pre-ins, 18
  puzzle of enlargement, 3, 33, 47–49, 53, 57, 182
  rational explanation, 5–8, 33–34, 50–52, 183, 185
  relative winners and losers, 5–7, 12, 24, 49, 52, 55, 62, 64, 74, 80, 173, 184, 185
  second Mediterranean enlargement, 6, 7, 13, 33, 55, 62, 158, 162–165
  second Northern enlargement, 13, 33, 68, 161, 173
enlargement benefits, *see* enlargement
enlargement costs, *see* enlargement
enlargement gains, *see* enlargement
enlargement losses, *see* enlargement
enlargement outcomes, *see* enlargement
enlargement process, *see* enlargement
enlargement puzzle, *see* enlargement
enlargement rounds, *see* enlargement
enlargement skeptics, *see* enlargement
enlargement talks, *see* accession negotiations
ERDF, *see* European Reconstruction and Development Funds
ERDF Objectives, 121–122, 166, 173
ESF, *see* European Social Funds
Estonia, 14, 18, 22, 126
EU, *see* European Union
EU Accession Process, *see* Enlargement
EU budget contributions, 89, 109, 110, 118, 122, 124, 130, 160, 163, 165, 170, 171, 173, 177, 185
EU budgetary ceiling, 165, 166, 175
EU budgetary Vade-Mekum, 89

EU Commission, *see* European Commission
EU Council, *see* Council of Ministers
EU Court of Justice, *see* European Court of Justice
EU deepening, *see* EU integration
EU enlargement, *see* enlargement
EU expansion, *see* enlargement
EU integration, 14, 34–38, 182, 185
EU net contributors, *see* EU budget contributions
EU Parliament, *see* European Parliament
EU social agenda, 71
EU widening, *see* enlargement
EUROCORPS, 23
EUROFOR, 23
European Agricultural Guidance and Guarantee Funds, 104
European Agriculture Guidance Funds, 5, 47, 63, 66, 68, 70, 104, 105, 107–110, 112, 125, 175
European Coal and Steel Community, 14
European Commission, 3, 16, 19–21, 24, 26, 29, 35, 71, 82, 86, 122, 168, 169, 171
European Community, *see* European Union, 75
European Court of Justice, 18, 35, 38, 40
European Defense Community, 59
European Economic Area, 171
European Free Trade Association, 1, 75
European integration, *see* EU integration
European Monetary Union, 23
European Parliament, 19, 38, 40, 81
European Reconstruction and Development Funds, 5, 47, 64, 122, 124, 158, 163, 164, 166, 169–171, 173, 175, 176, 178, 179
European social agenda, *see* EU Social Agenda
European Social Funds, 122
European Union, 1, 3, 14, 15, 19–21, 34, 43, 67, 138, 162, 183, 187
expansion, *see* enlargement

extent of discrimination, *see* discriminatory membership
externalities, 42, 43, 61

Federal Republic of Germany, *see* Germany
federalism, *see* approaches
Finland, 13, 14, 48, 68, 72, 161, 166, 169, 173
first Mediterranean enlargement, *see* enlargement
first Northern enlargement, *see* enlargement
Fischer, Joschka, 166, 167
FitzGerald, Garret, 165
formal accession process, *see* enlargement
Former Yugoslav Republic of Macedonia, 3, 14
Fountainbleu summit, *see* Council of Ministers
France, 1, 6–8, 20, 49, 55, 57, 60, 67, 70, 72, 75, 88, 91, 95, 107, 120, 125, 126, 132, 163–165, 167, 170–172, 177, 183, 187
Free Movement of Labor, 2, 24–30, 48, 64–65, 67–68, 72–73, 85–167
free movement of workers, *see* enlargement
free riding, 59
functionalism, *see* approaches
future enlargement rounds, *see* enlargement

Göteburg summit, *see* Council of Ministers
gains, *see* enlargement
Gama, Jaime, 168
geopolitics, 3
German-Spanish debate, 28
Germany, 2, 8, 11, 21, 24–30, 42, 48, 52, 64, 66–68, 73, 80, 83, 88, 89, 91, 107, 113, 128, 132, 150, 163–165, 167, 169–172, 175, 176
Grand Duchy of Luxembourg, *see* Luxembourg
Great Britain, *see* United Kingdom
Greece, 3, 8, 11, 13, 40, 49, 57, 60, 65, 67, 71, 72, 75, 83, 122, 126,

Index

128, 132, 158, 160–162, 164–166, 169, 170, 172, 175, 177–179, 186
Greenland, 13
gross domestic product, 48, 58, 67, 71, 87, 100, 110, 121, 124, 161, 167
gross national product, 67
gross value added, 105, 108, 109
GVA, *see* gross value added

harmonization, 58, 59, 63, 182
Hellenic Republic, *see* Greece
historical enlargement, *see* enlargement
horizontal institutionalization, 34
Hungary, 14, 18, 22, 71, 120
hypothesis, 74, 75

Iberian enlargement, *see* enlargement
IMF, *see* International Monetary Fund
impact of enlargement on new members, *see* enlargement
implementation, *see* acquis communautaire
IMPs, *see* Integrated Mediterranean Programs
industrial sector, 88, 93, 122, 124, 129
institutionalism, *see* approaches
institutionalist intergovernmentalism, *see* approaches
institutions, 5, 37, 38
  EU Commission, 38–40
integrated Mediterranean programs, 8, 40, 62, 163, 164, 175, 179
integration, *see* EU integration
interest groups, 1, 2, 24, 29, 43
intergovernmentalism, *see* approaches, 37
internal market, 173
international cooperation, 34, 57–59
International Monetary Fund, 143
international organization, 35, 41, 58
intra-Union redistribution, 7, 8, 50, 51, 56, 59, 65, 68, 73, 75, 142–143, 159, 184–185
Ireland, 6–8, 13, 27, 49, 57, 58, 75, 82, 105, 122, 132, 140, 161, 164–166, 169, 170, 172
issue-linkage, 160, 172, 176, 177, 179

Italy, 27, 49, 55, 57, 67, 72, 107, 120, 128, 163–166, 168, 169, 172, 175, 177, 183

justice and home affairs, 18, 22

Kant, Immanuel, 41, 58
Kingdom of Belgium, *see* Belgium
Kingdom of Denmark, *see* Denmark
Kingdom of Norway, *see* Norway
Kingdom of Spain, *see* Spain
Kingdom of Sweden, *see* Sweden
Kosovo, 14

labor migration, *see* migration
Latvia, 14, 18, 22, 126, 161
Lexis-Nexis, 82
limited membership rights, *see* discriminatory membership
Lithuania, 14, 18, 22
logrolling, 46
losses, *see* enlargement
Luxembourg, 49, 57, 62, 67, 72, 73, 83, 88, 91, 95, 105, 120, 161, 163

Macedonia, *see* Former Yugoslav Republic of Macedonia
Malta, 14, 21, 29, 64, 80
market integration, 3, 41, 62
membership conditions, *see* Copenhagen criteria
Mezzogiorno, 168
migration, 2, 25, 28, 42, 62, 67, 86
  forecasts, 87
Mitterand, Francois, 163
model specification, 83, 143
Monnet, Jean, 1
Morocco, 14
multi-speed integration, *see* differentiated integration
multilateral negotiations, 4, 9, 24, 30, 53, 151, 185
multivariate probit, *see* seemingly unrelated regression

NATO, *see* North Atlantic Treaty Organization
neo-functionalism, *see* approaches
Netherlands, 49, 57, 67, 72, 105, 166, 170
neutrality, *see* club goods

new institutionalism, *see* approaches
Nice Treaty, *see* Treaty of Nice
non-cooperative game theory, 57
normative approaches, *see* approaches
norms and values, 4, 43, 50
North Atlantic Treaty Organization, 49, 50
Norway, 69, 75, 80
Nyköping, 168

objectives, *see* ERDF objectives
OLS, *see* Ordinary Least Squares
Ordinary Least Squares, 105
outcomes of enlargement, *see* enlargement
outside options, 57, 68, 142, 150

Papandreou, Andreas, 164
Pareto-efficiency, 7, 33, 47, 50, 51, 53, 57, 65, 66, 68
Pareto-optimality, *see* Pareto-efficiency
PASOK, 163
permanent derogations, *see* acquis communautaire
Persson, Göran, 27
phase-in of membership rights, *see* discriminatory membership
Piqué, Josep, 167
Poland, 14, 18, 22, 71, 91, 95, 113, 120, 161
policy autonomy, 3, 35, 44, 45, 47, 148
political conflicts, *see* enlargement
political stability, *see* stability
Pompidou, Georges, 13
Portugal, 3, 8, 11, 13, 49, 57, 60, 62, 65–67, 72, 73, 83, 88, 105, 108, 121, 122, 126, 128, 132, 150, 156, 158–163, 165, 166, 168–173, 175, 177, 179, 184
pre-conditions, *see* Copenhagen criteria
predicted probabilities, 140–141, 144, 146, 151
    Common Agricultural Policies, 113–120
    Common Structural Policies, 126–131
    distributional conflicts, 152–155
    Free Movement of Labor, 94–103
prisoners' dilemma, 59
probit analysis, 83, 94, 110, 143

Prodi, Romano, 168
public goods, 60
public opinion, 2, 25, 27, 28, 56, 57, 69, 72, 93, 187
puzzle, *see* enlargement

ratification, 19
rational choice, *see* approaches
rational explanation, *see* enlargement
rationality, 56
redistribution, 6, 12, 53, 58, 65, 139
reform, 21, 24, 26, 45, 48, 67, 70, 72, 73, 166
regime type, *see* democracy
regional integration, 35
regional policy and coordination of structural instruments, 22
regional programs, *see* ERDF objectives
Republic of Austria, *see* Austria
Republic of Bulgaria, *see* Bulgaria
Republic of Cyprus, *see* Cyprus
Republic of Estonia, *see* Estonia
Republic of Finland, *see* Finland
Republic of Hungary, *see* Hungary
Republic of Ireland, *see* Ireland
Republic of Latvia, *see* Latvia
Republic of Lithuania, *see* Lithuania
Republic of Poland, *see* Poland
Republic of Slovenia, *see* Slovenia
rhetorical action, 4, 33, 49–50, 52, 133
rivalry, *see* club goods
Romania, 14, 18, 33, 44, 69, 80, 90, 187

sanctioning, 59
Sarkozy, Nicolas, 20
Schröder, Gerhard, 25, 27
second Mediterranean enlargement, *see* enlargement
second Northern enlargement, *see* enlargement
seemingly unrelated regression, 84, 93, 94, 113, 126, 134
Serbia and Montenegro, 14
side payments, *see* intra-Union redistribution
Sinn, Hans-Werner, 27
Slovak Republic, 14, 18, 22

Index

Slovenia, 14, 18, 65, 87, 95
social agenda, *see* EU social agenda
sociological approaches, *see* approaches
Spain, 3, 6–8, 11, 13, 14, 28, 29, 49, 50, 55, 57, 60, 62, 65–67, 72, 73, 80, 83, 87, 88, 108, 121, 122, 128, 132, 150, 156, 158–163, 165–170, 172, 173, 175–177, 179, 184
spillover effects, *see* externalities
stability, 3, 41, 42, 58, 62
state autonomy, *see* policy autonomy
state-centrism, 36
structural adjustments, *see* reform
structural transfers, *see* European Reconstruction and Development Funds
Stuttgart summit, *see* Council of Ministers
summit, *see* Council of Ministers
supranational institutions, *see* institutions
SURE, *see* Seemingly Unrelated Regression
Sweden, 13, 20, 28, 48, 68, 113, 166, 170, 173
Swiss Confederation, *see* Switzerland
Switzerland, 69, 80

Thatcher, Margaret, 164
The Netherlands, *see* Netherlands
transaction costs, 39, 41, 58, 61, 125
transactionalims, *see* approaches
transitional nature of discrimination, *see* discriminatory membership
transitional periods, *see* acquis communautaire,
transport policies, 22, 81
Treaty of Accession, 19, 20, 52, 67, 75, 140
Treaty of Nice, 171
Treaty on European Union, 16, 58, 59
Tremonti, Giulio, 168
triangulation, 9
tripartite negotiations, *see* multilateral negotiations
Tumpel, Herbert, 26
Turkey, 3, 14, 73, 187

unanimity, 5, 53, 55, 57, 64, 65
Union 'à la carte', *see* differentiated integration
United Kingdom, 1, 13, 23, 27, 36, 48, 50, 60, 66, 67, 80, 82, 87, 91, 128, 132, 140, 161, 164, 167, 170, 172
United Nations, 3
United Nations Security Council, 3

values, *see* norms and values
variable geometry, *see* differentiated integration
variable speed integration, *see* differentiated integration
Verheugen, Günther, 169
vertical institutionalization, 34, 38
veto power, *see* unanimity

Wald test, 91, 110, 123
Western European Union, 23
WEU, *see* Western European Union

For EU product safety concerns, contact us at Calle de José Abascal, 56–1°, 28003 Madrid, Spain or eugpsr@cambridge.org.

www.ingramcontent.com/pod-product-compliance
Ingram Content Group UK Ltd.
Pitfield, Milton Keynes, MK11 3LW, UK
UKHW011315060825
461487UK00005B/103